Some Clever Title

Other FoxTrot Books by Bill Amend

Anthologies

Some Clever Title

A FoxTrot Collection Blah Blah Blah

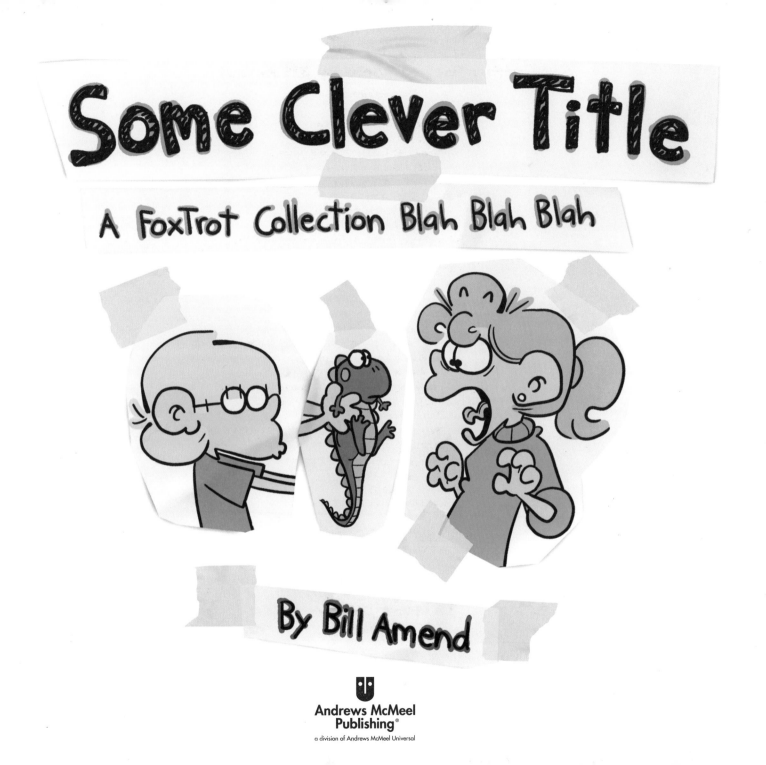

By Bill Amend

Andrews McMeel
Publishing®

a division of Andrews McMeel Universal

Food Coloring

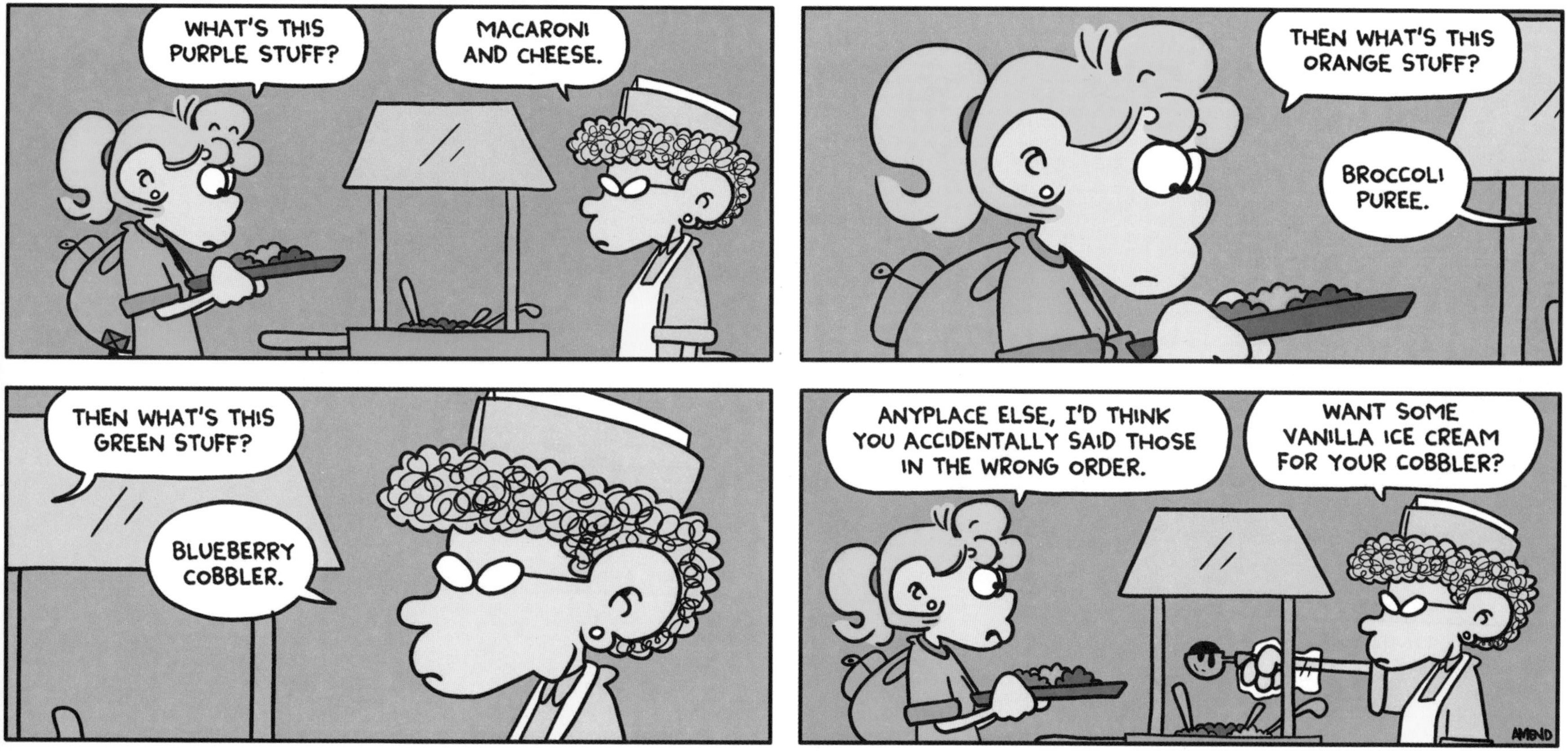
WHAT'S THIS PURPLE STUFF?
MACARONI AND CHEESE.
THEN WHAT'S THIS ORANGE STUFF?
BROCCOLI PUREE.
THEN WHAT'S THIS GREEN STUFF?
BLUEBERRY COBBLER.
ANYPLACE ELSE, I'D THINK YOU ACCIDENTALLY SAID THOSE IN THE WRONG ORDER.
WANT SOME VANILLA ICE CREAM FOR YOUR COBBLER?
AMEND

Avenger Fail

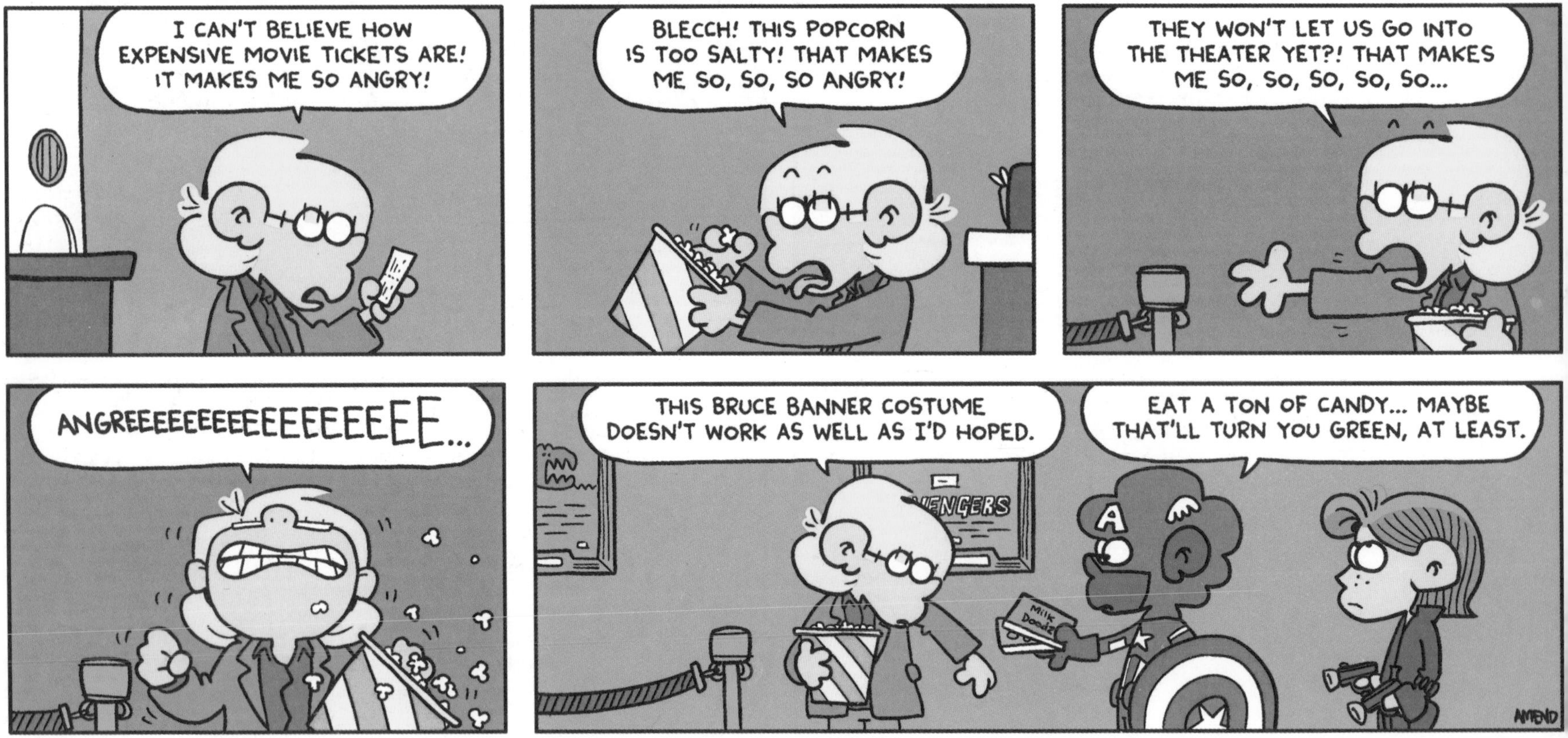

I CAN'T BELIEVE HOW EXPENSIVE MOVIE TICKETS ARE! IT MAKES ME SO ANGRY!
BLECCH! THIS POPCORN IS TOO SALTY! THAT MAKES ME SO, SO, SO ANGRY!
THEY WON'T LET US GO INTO THE THEATER YET?! THAT MAKES ME SO, SO, SO, SO, SO...
ANGREEEEEEEEEEEEEEEEEE...
THIS BRUCE BANNER COSTUME DOESN'T WORK AS WELL AS I'D HOPED.
EAT A TON OF CANDY... MAYBE THAT'LL TURN YOU GREEN, AT LEAST.
AMEND

You Snooze You Lose

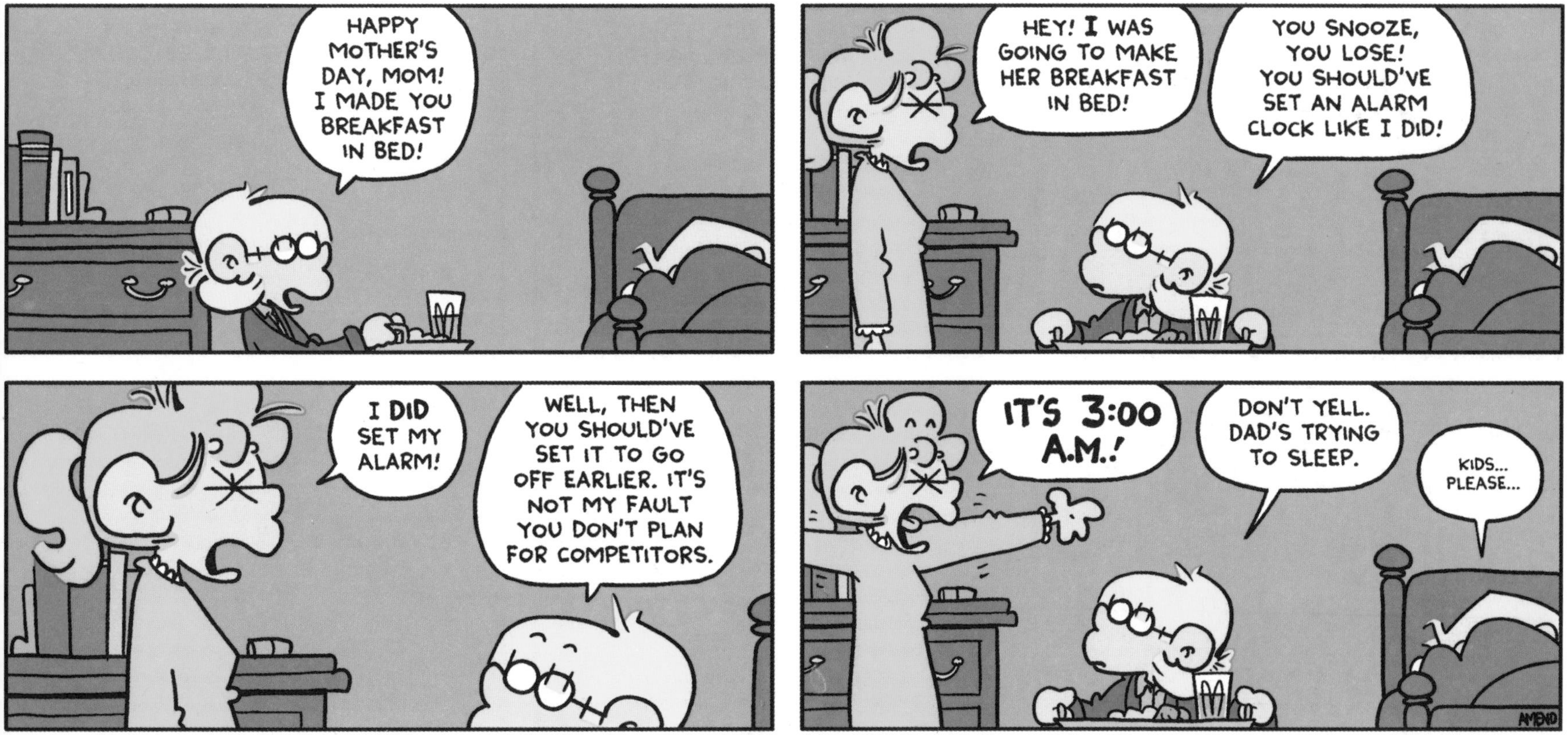
HAPPY MOTHER'S DAY, MOM! I MADE YOU BREAKFAST IN BED!
HEY! I WAS GOING TO MAKE HER BREAKFAST IN BED!
YOU SNOOZE, YOU LOSE! YOU SHOULD'VE SET AN ALARM CLOCK LIKE I DID!
I DID SET MY ALARM!
WELL, THEN YOU SHOULD'VE SET IT TO GO OFF EARLIER. IT'S NOT MY FAULT YOU DON'T PLAN FOR COMPETITORS.
IT'S 3:00 A.M.!
DON'T YELL. DAD'S TRYING TO SLEEP.
KIDS... PLEASE...
AMEND

But Just for Giggles

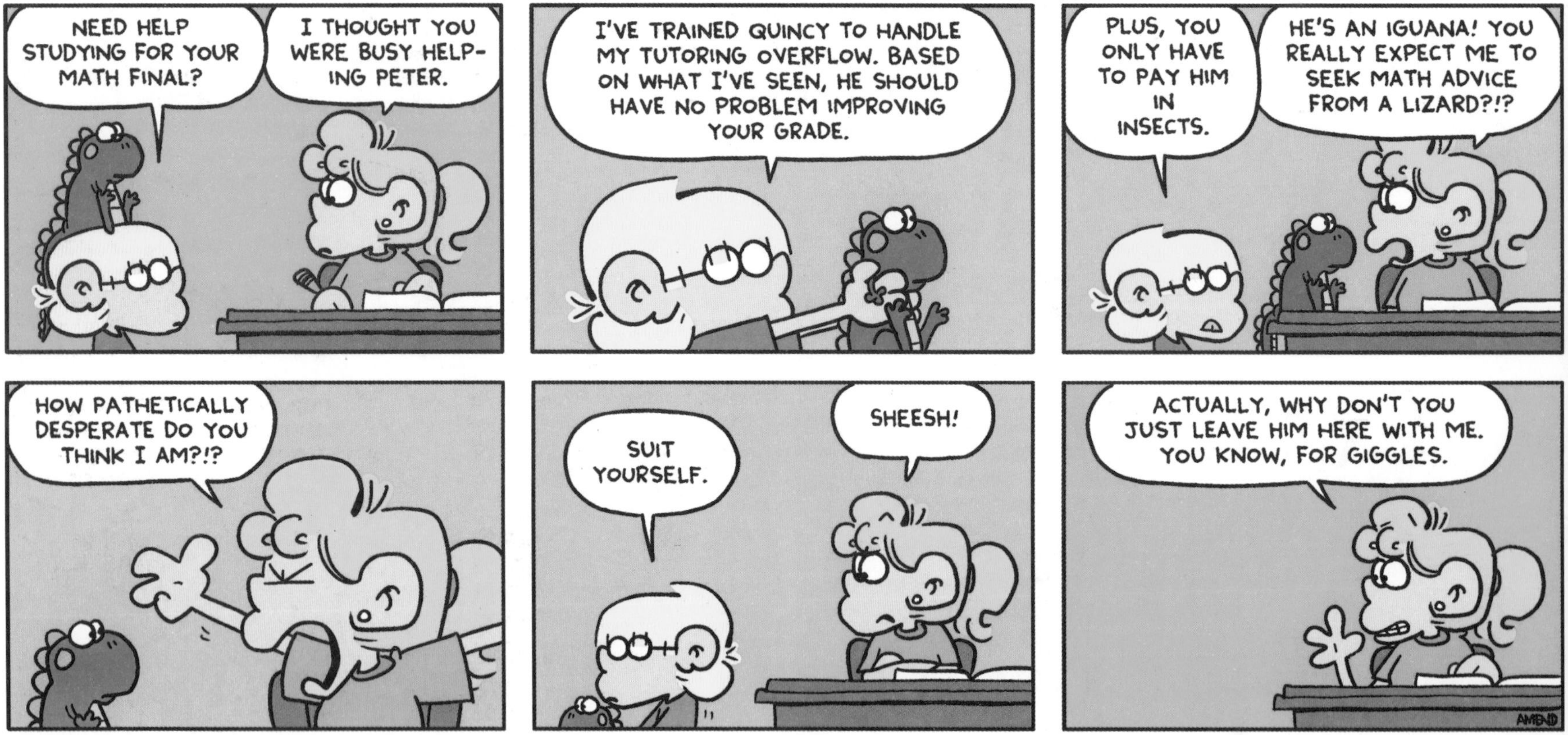
NEED HELP STUDYING FOR YOUR MATH FINAL?
I THOUGHT YOU WERE BUSY HELP-ING PETER.
I'VE TRAINED QUINCY TO HANDLE MY TUTORING OVERFLOW. BASED ON WHAT I'VE SEEN, HE SHOULD HAVE NO PROBLEM IMPROVING YOUR GRADE.
PLUS, YOU ONLY HAVE TO PAY HIM IN INSECTS.
HE'S AN IGUANA! YOU REALLY EXPECT ME TO SEEK MATH ADVICE FROM A LIZARD?!?
HOW PATHETICALLY DESPERATE DO YOU THINK I AM?!?
SUIT YOURSELF.
SHEESH!
ACTUALLY, WHY DON'T YOU JUST LEAVE HIM HERE WITH ME. YOU KNOW, FOR GIGGLES.
AMEND

The X-prise V

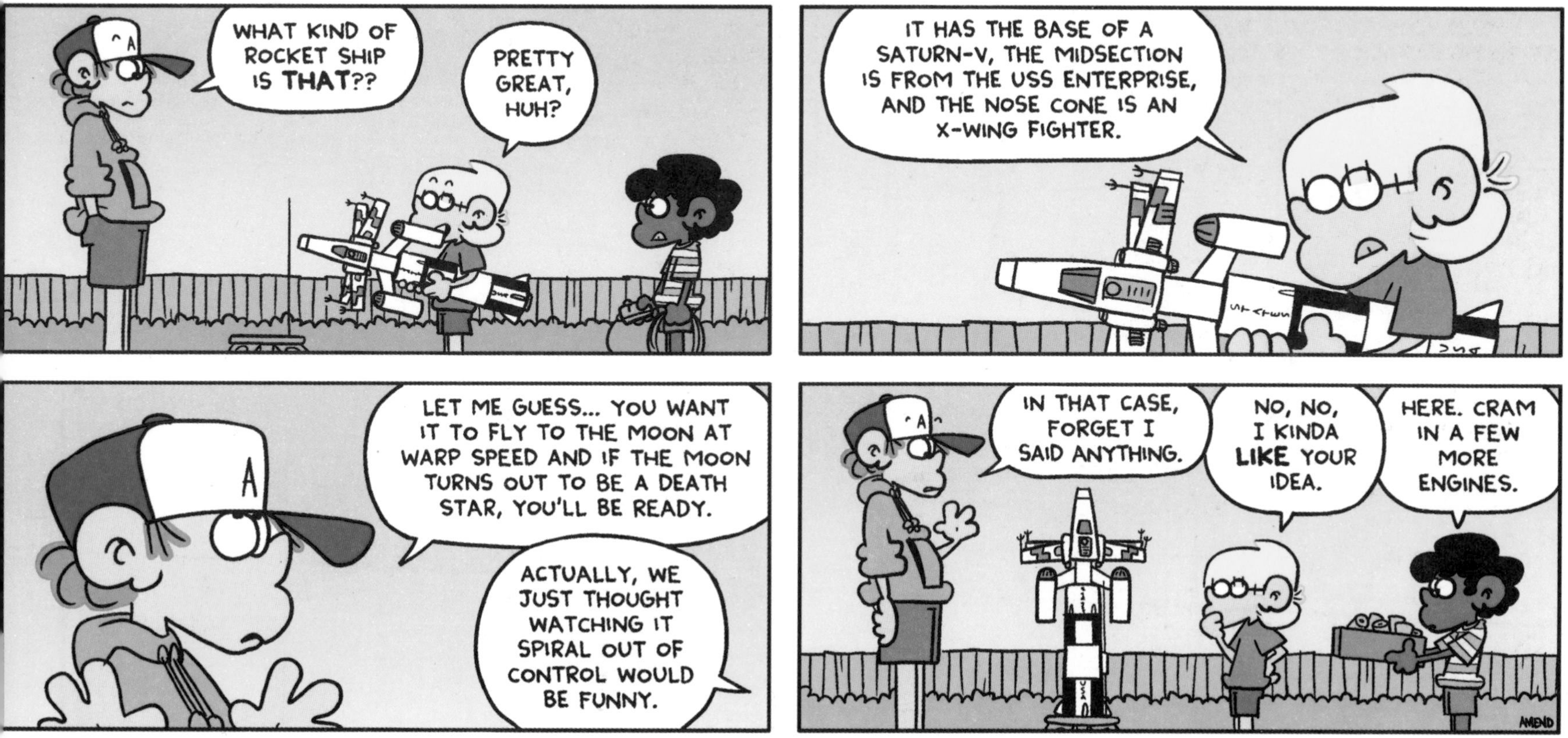
WHAT KIND OF ROCKET SHIP IS **THAT**??
PRETTY GREAT, HUH?
IT HAS THE BASE OF A SATURN-V, THE MIDSECTION IS FROM THE USS ENTERPRISE, AND THE NOSE CONE IS AN X-WING FIGHTER.
LET ME GUESS... YOU WANT IT TO FLY TO THE MOON AT WARP SPEED AND IF THE MOON TURNS OUT TO BE A DEATH STAR, YOU'LL BE READY.
ACTUALLY, WE JUST THOUGHT WATCHING IT SPIRAL OUT OF CONTROL WOULD BE FUNNY.
IN THAT CASE, FORGET I SAID ANYTHING.
NO, NO, I KINDA **LIKE** YOUR IDEA.
HERE. CRAM IN A FEW MORE ENGINES.
AMEND

Weight Weight

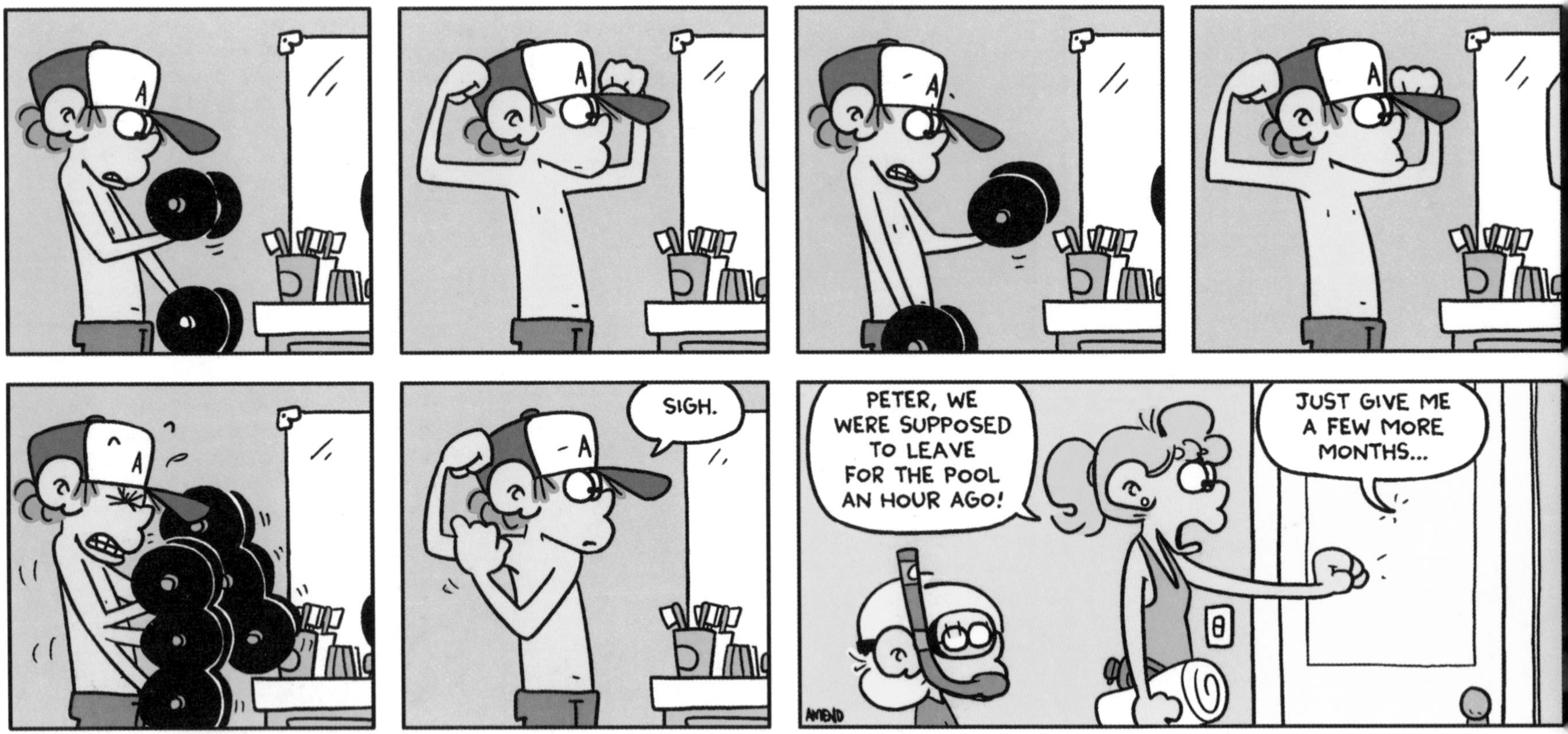
SIGH.
PETER, WE WERE SUPPOSED TO LEAVE FOR THE POOL AN HOUR AGO!
JUST GIVE ME A FEW MORE MONTHS...
AMEND

Permadeath

Panel 1:
MOM'S PRETTY ANGRY THAT YOU STILL HAVEN'T CLEANED UP YOUR MESS DOWNSTAIRS.

TELL HER IT'LL HAVE TO WAIT. I'M PLAYING DIABLO.

Panel 2:
CAN'T YOU JUST PAUSE OR SAVE IT?

UNFORTUNATELY, NO. I'M PLAYING IT IN HARDCORE-HARDCORE MODE.

Panel 3:
WHAT'S THAT?

IT'S LIKE NORMAL HARDCORE MODE, WHERE IF MY CHARACTER DIES IT'S GAME-ENDING PERMADEATH, BUT WITH A SELF-IMPOSED RULE THAT I HAVE TO PLAY IT NONSTOP WITHOUT ANY BREAKS. IT'S CRAZY DIFFICULT.

Panel 4:
I'VE ALREADY INVESTED FIVE HOURS IN THIS BARBARIAN. NO WAY AM I STOPPING.

Panel 5:
JASON FOX, I WANT THIS ROOM CLEANED NOW!!!

YOU KNOW, I'M PRETTY SURE IF MOM KILLS YOU, IT'S PERMADEATH, ALSO.

GOOD CALL. DO YOU KNOW IF WE HAVE ANY HEALTH POTIONS IN THE FRIDGE?

Preferred Customer

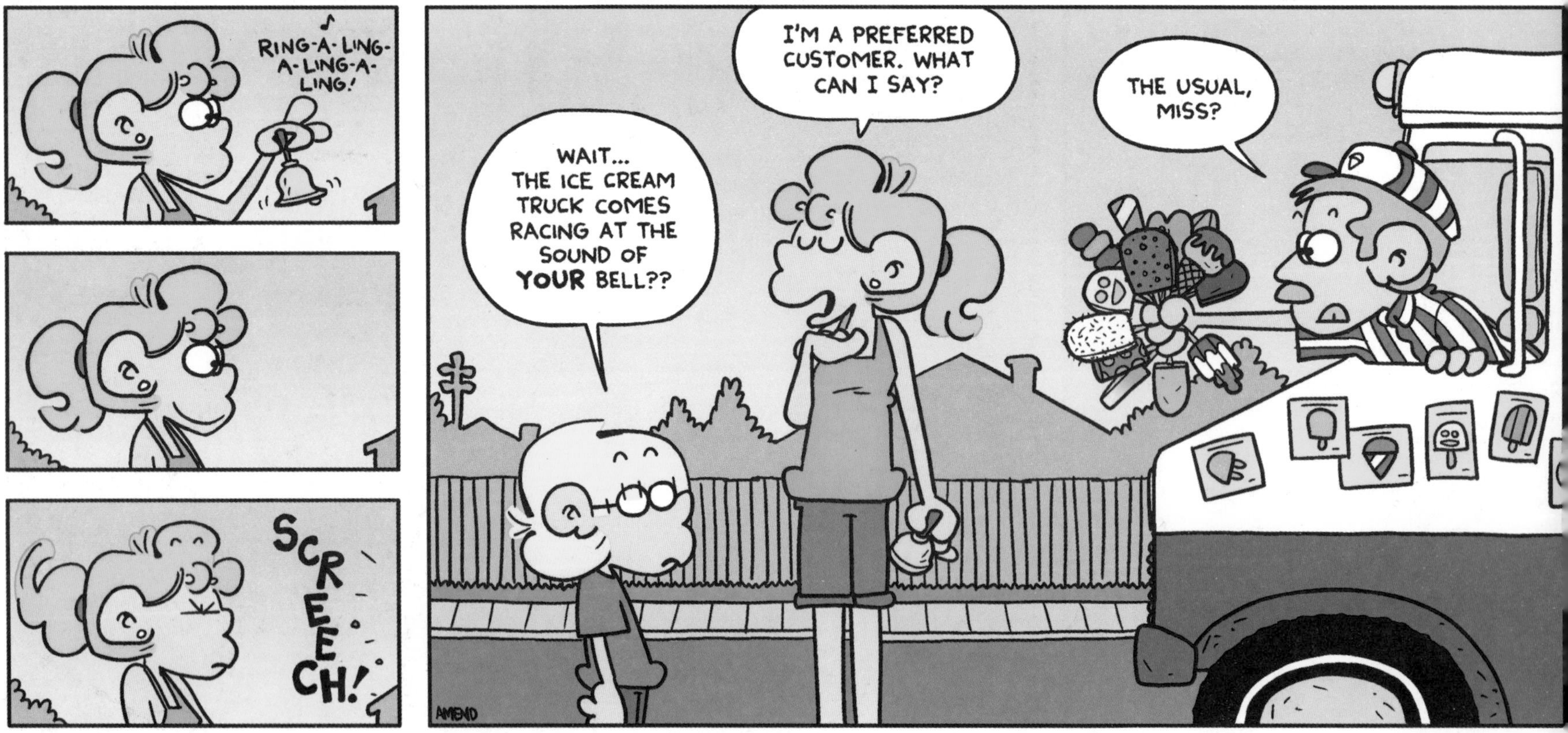
RING-A-LING-A-LING-A-LING!
SCREEECH!
WAIT... THE ICE CREAM TRUCK COMES RACING AT THE SOUND OF YOUR BELL??
I'M A PREFERRED CUSTOMER. WHAT CAN I SAY?
THE USUAL, MISS?
AMEND

The Talk

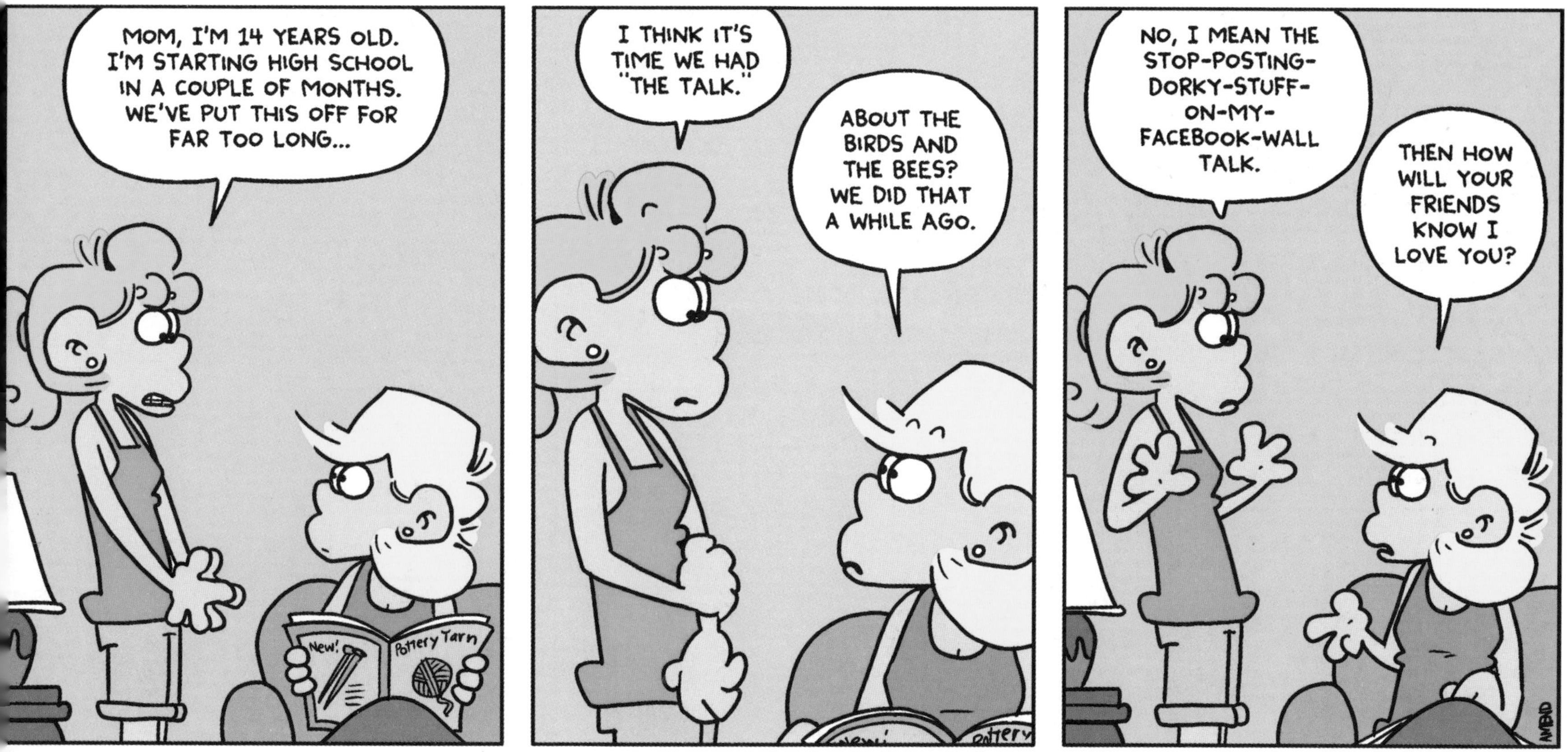
MOM, I'M 14 YEARS OLD. I'M STARTING HIGH SCHOOL IN A COUPLE OF MONTHS. WE'VE PUT THIS OFF FOR FAR TOO LONG...
New!
Pottery Yarn
I THINK IT'S TIME WE HAD "THE TALK."
ABOUT THE BIRDS AND THE BEES? WE DID THAT A WHILE AGO.
NO, I MEAN THE STOP-POSTING-DORKY-STUFF-ON-MY-FACEBOOK-WALL TALK.
THEN HOW WILL YOUR FRIENDS KNOW I LOVE YOU?
AMEND

Backlit

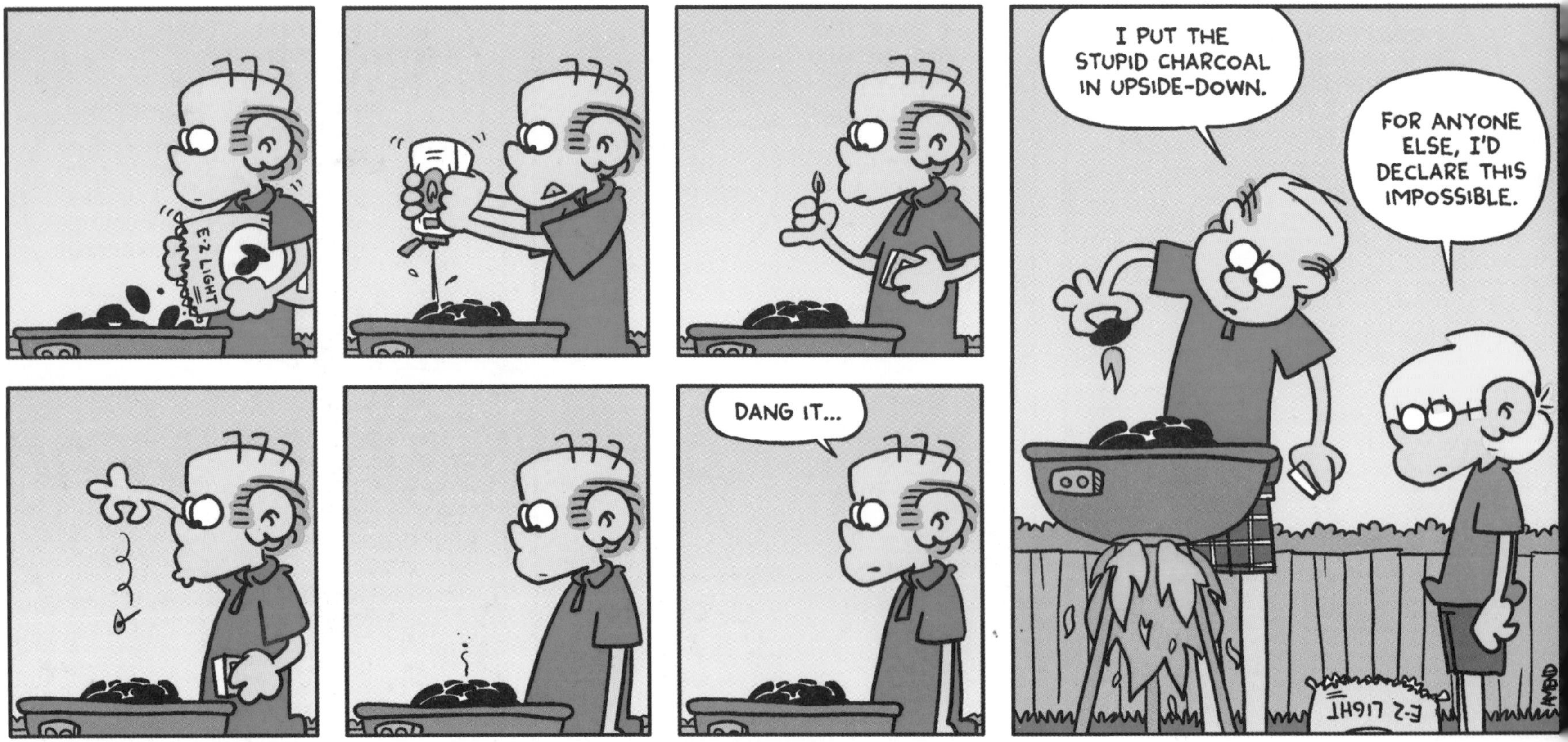
E-Z LIGHT
DANG IT...
I PUT THE STUPID CHARCOAL IN UPSIDE-DOWN.
FOR ANYONE ELSE, I'D DECLARE THIS IMPOSSIBLE.
E-Z LIGHT

Chairway to Heaven

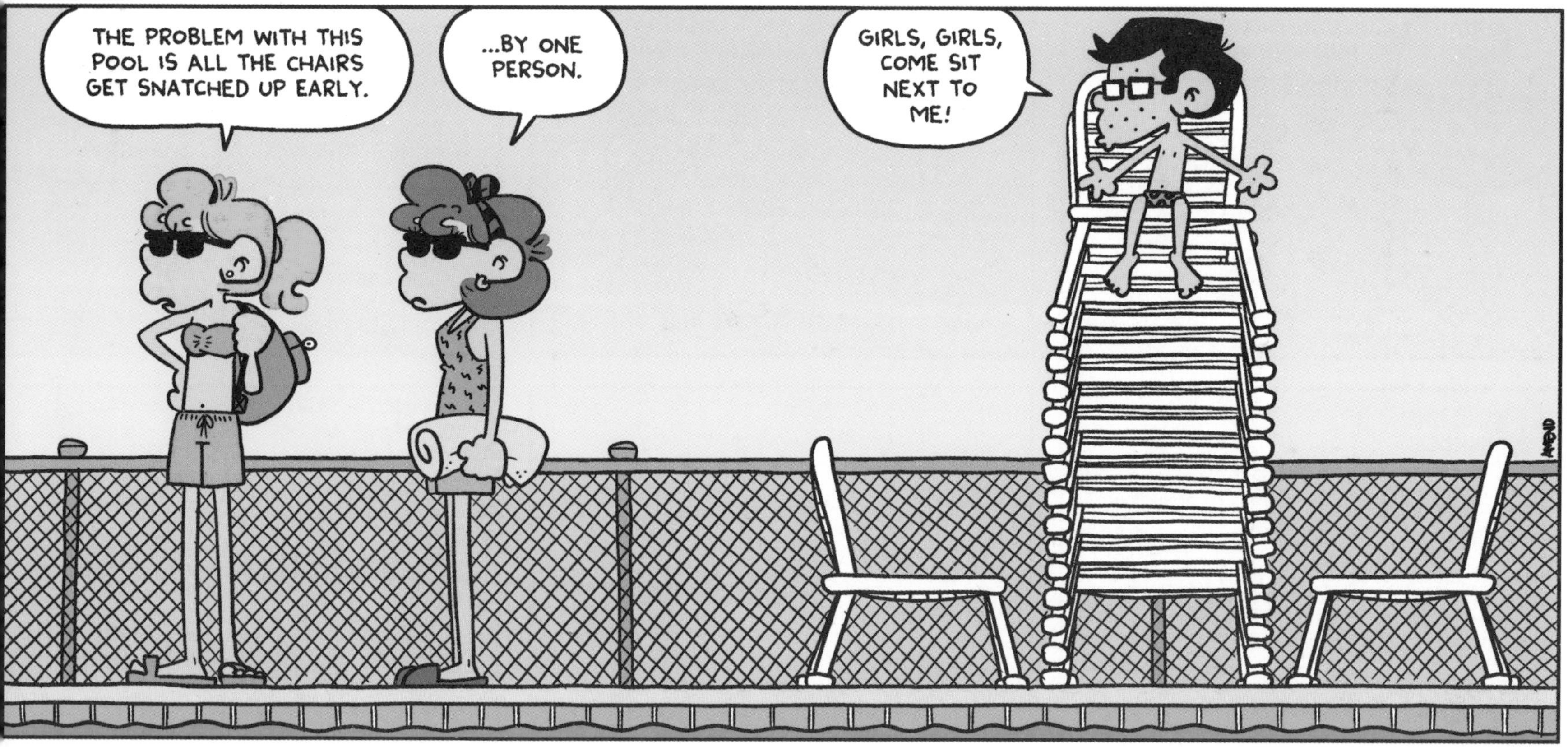
THE PROBLEM WITH THIS POOL IS ALL THE CHAIRS GET SNATCHED UP EARLY.
...BY ONE PERSON.
GIRLS, GIRLS, COME SIT NEXT TO ME!

Dragon Dreams

WHOA, PAIGE! YOU BLEACHED YOUR HAIR?

I'M DAENERYS TARGARYEN, MOTHER OF DRAGONS.

SINCE WHEN DO YOU COSPLAY?

THIS ISN'T COSPLAY. WE'RE IN A DREAM, OBVIOUSLY.

WELL, IT'S NOT **MY** DREAM. I'M ALWAYS A WHITE WALKER IN MY "GAME OF THRONES" DREAMS.

WELL, IT'S CERTAINLY NOT **MY** DREAM. I DON'T EVEN KNOW WHAT A DAENERYS IS.

WELL THEN WHOSE DREAM **IS** THIS?

FHXHXHXXH

QUINCY'S SURE SLEEPING A LOT THESE DAYS.

IS IT JUST ME, OR IS HE SMILING?

AMEND

Getting Close

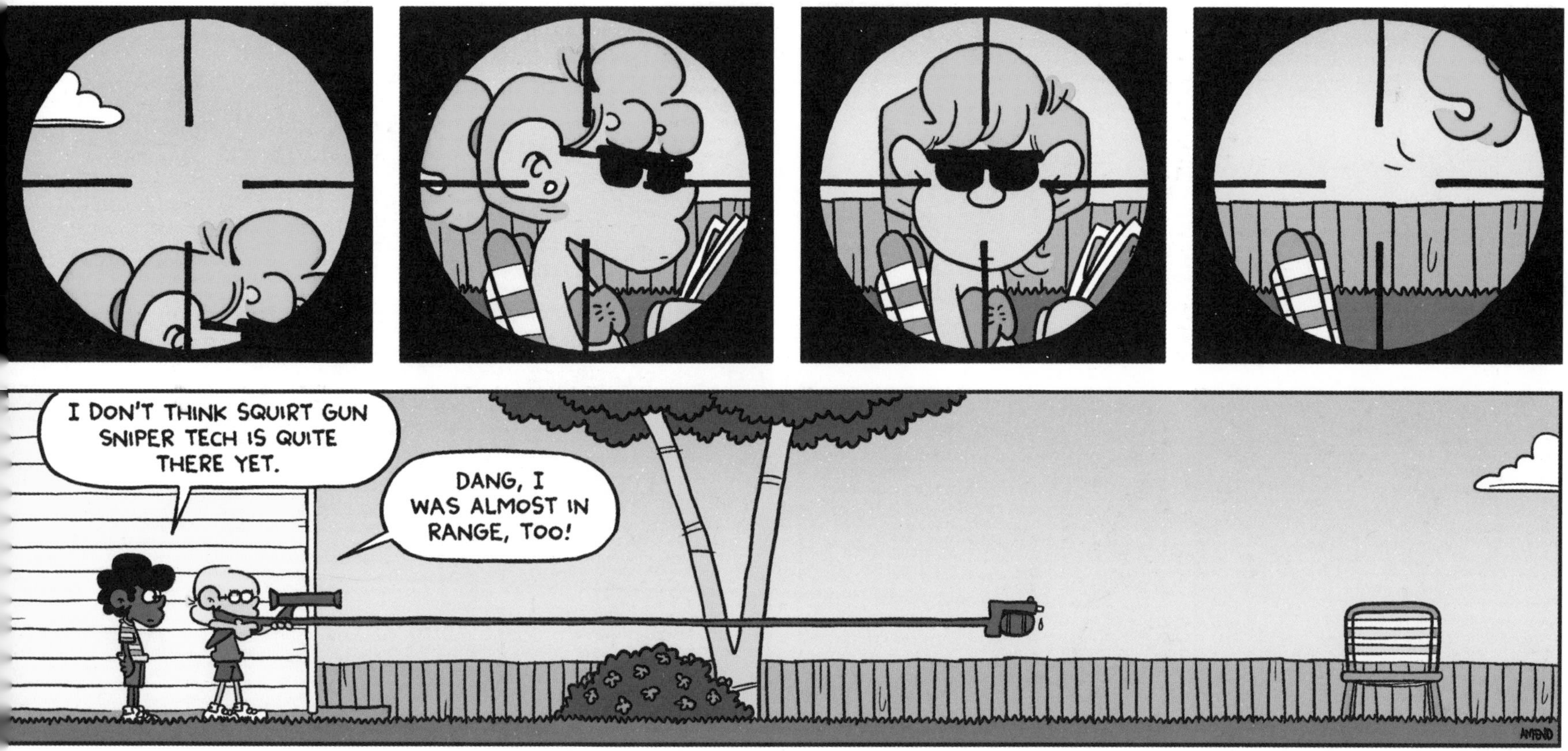
I DON'T THINK SQUIRT GUN SNIPER TECH IS QUITE THERE YET.
DANG, I WAS ALMOST IN RANGE, TOO!

Simnastics

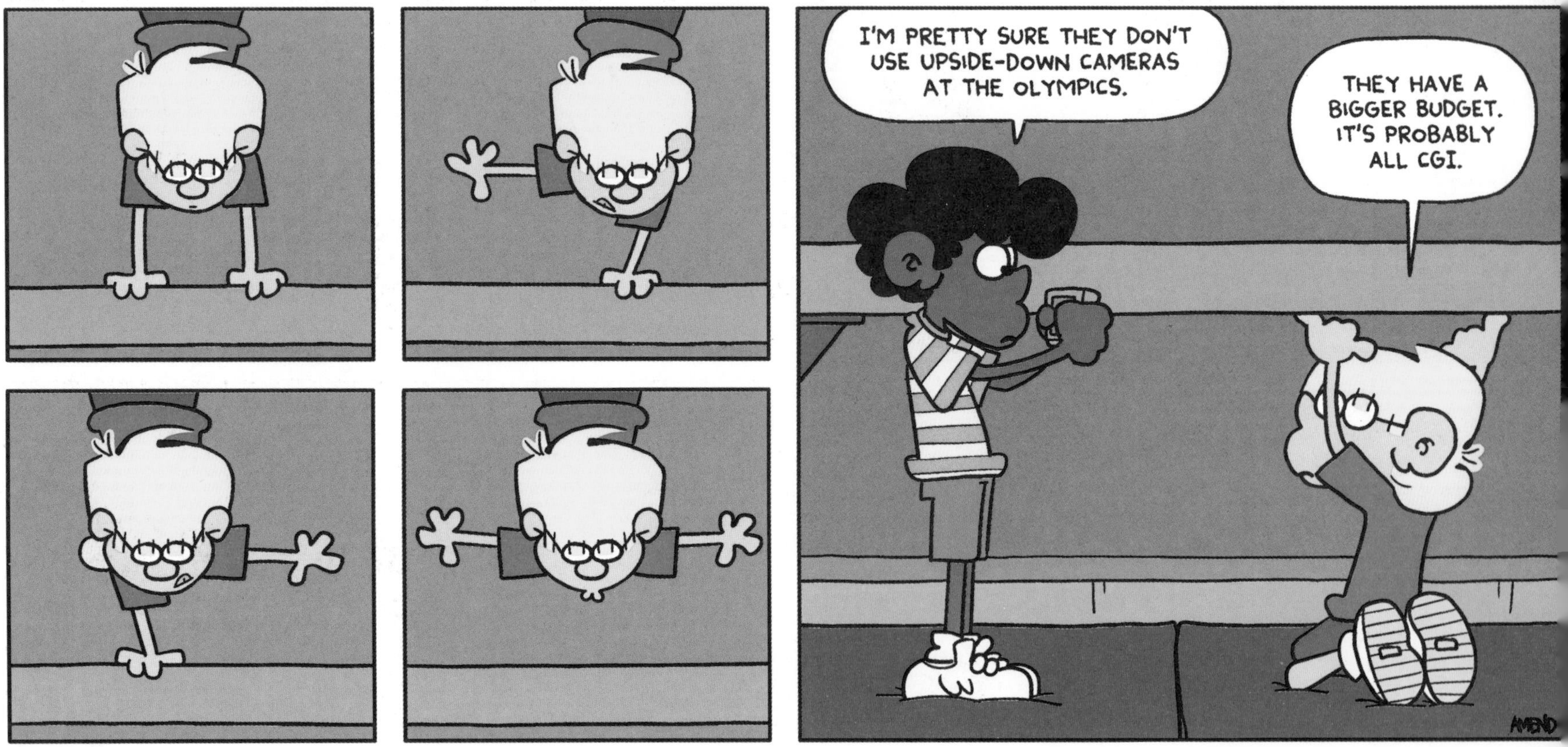
I'M PRETTY SURE THEY DON'T USE UPSIDE-DOWN CAMERAS AT THE OLYMPICS.
THEY HAVE A BIGGER BUDGET. IT'S PROBABLY ALL CGI.
AMEND

Bat Tan

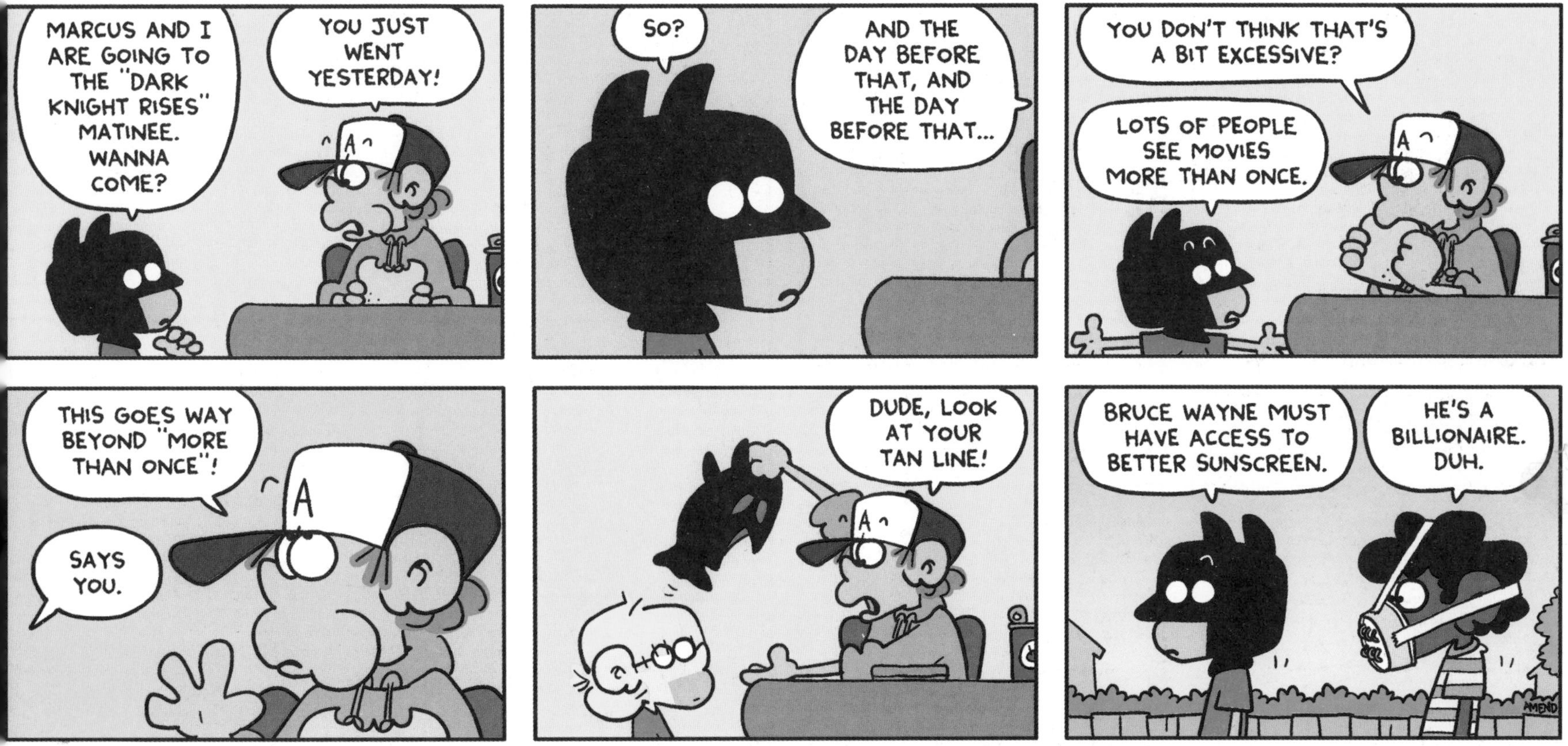

MARCUS AND I ARE GOING TO THE "DARK KNIGHT RISES" MATINEE. WANNA COME?
YOU JUST WENT YESTERDAY!
SO?
AND THE DAY BEFORE THAT, AND THE DAY BEFORE THAT...
YOU DON'T THINK THAT'S A BIT EXCESSIVE?
LOTS OF PEOPLE SEE MOVIES MORE THAN ONCE.
THIS GOES WAY BEYOND "MORE THAN ONCE"!
SAYS YOU.
DUDE, LOOK AT YOUR TAN LINE!
BRUCE WAYNE MUST HAVE ACCESS TO BETTER SUNSCREEN.
HE'S A BILLIONAIRE. DUH.
AMEND

Crock Lobster

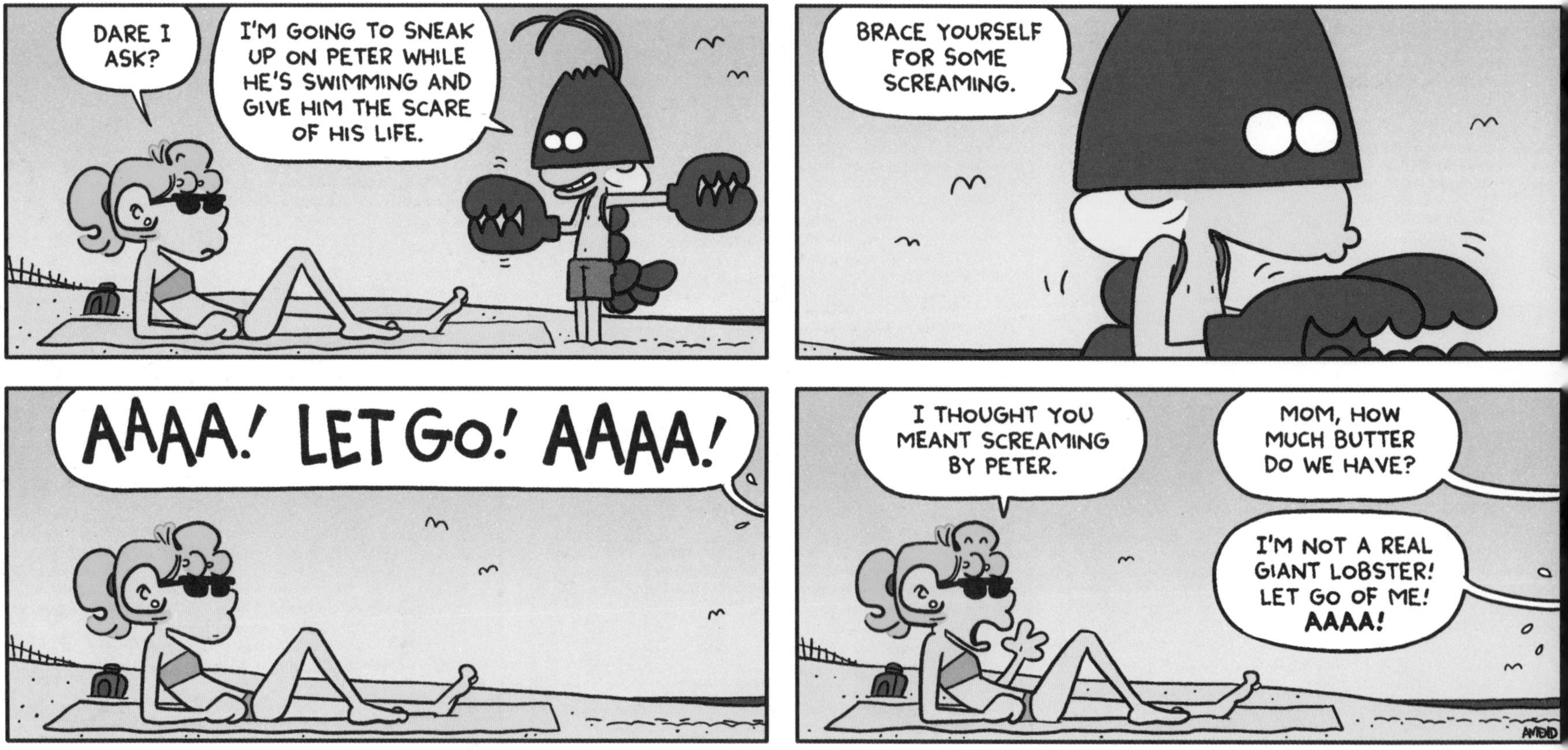

DARE I ASK?
I'M GOING TO SNEAK UP ON PETER WHILE HE'S SWIMMING AND GIVE HIM THE SCARE OF HIS LIFE.
BRACE YOURSELF FOR SOME SCREAMING.
AAAA! LET GO! AAAA!
I THOUGHT YOU MEANT SCREAMING BY PETER.
MOM, HOW MUCH BUTTER DO WE HAVE?
I'M NOT A REAL GIANT LOBSTER! LET GO OF ME! AAAA!
AMEND

Beach Fauxtos

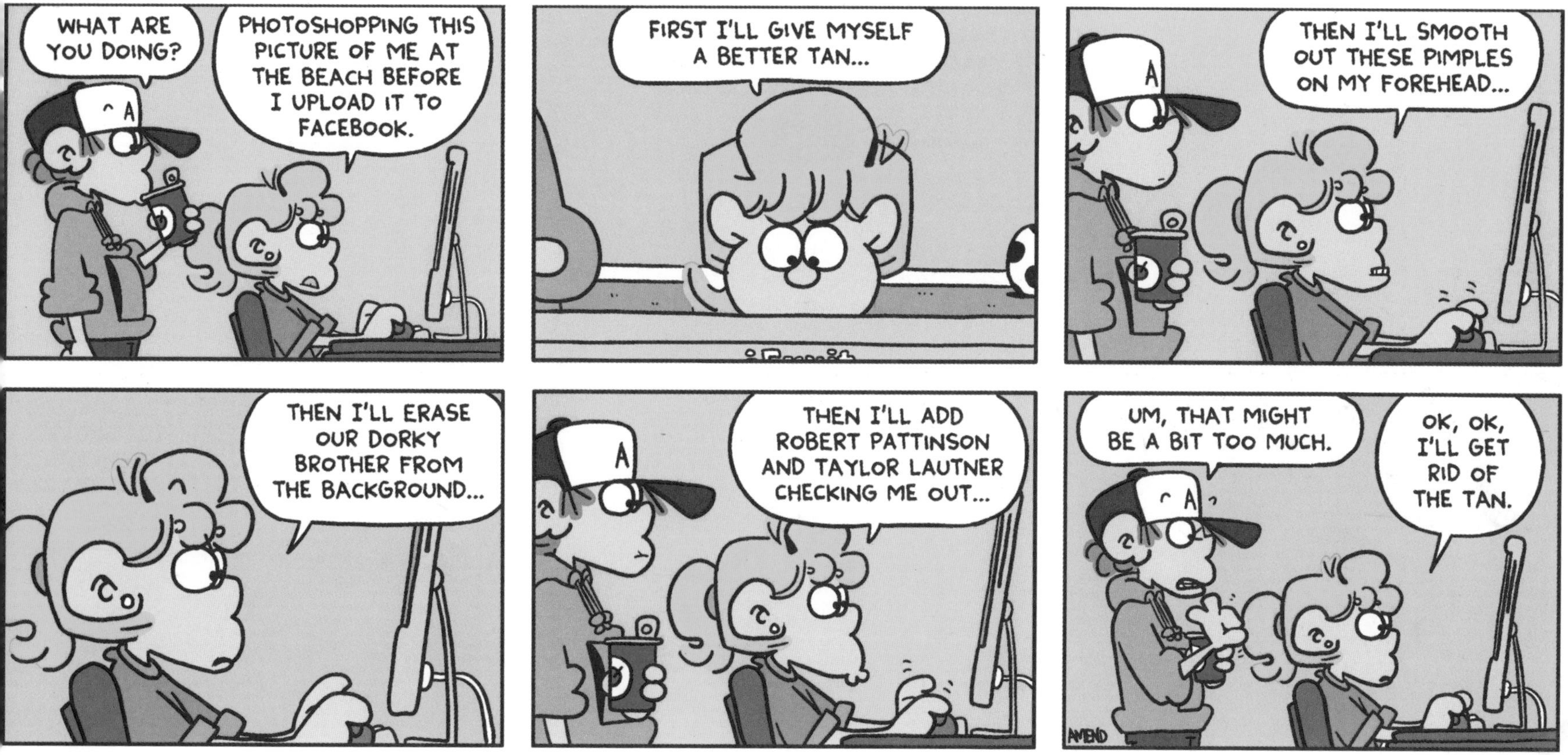
WHAT ARE YOU DOING?
PHOTOSHOPPING THIS PICTURE OF ME AT THE BEACH BEFORE I UPLOAD IT TO FACEBOOK.
FIRST I'LL GIVE MYSELF A BETTER TAN...
THEN I'LL SMOOTH OUT THESE PIMPLES ON MY FOREHEAD...
THEN I'LL ERASE OUR DORKY BROTHER FROM THE BACKGROUND...
THEN I'LL ADD ROBERT PATTINSON AND TAYLOR LAUTNER CHECKING ME OUT...
UM, THAT MIGHT BE A BIT TOO MUCH.
OK, OK, I'LL GET RID OF THE TAN.
AMEND

Prepping for School

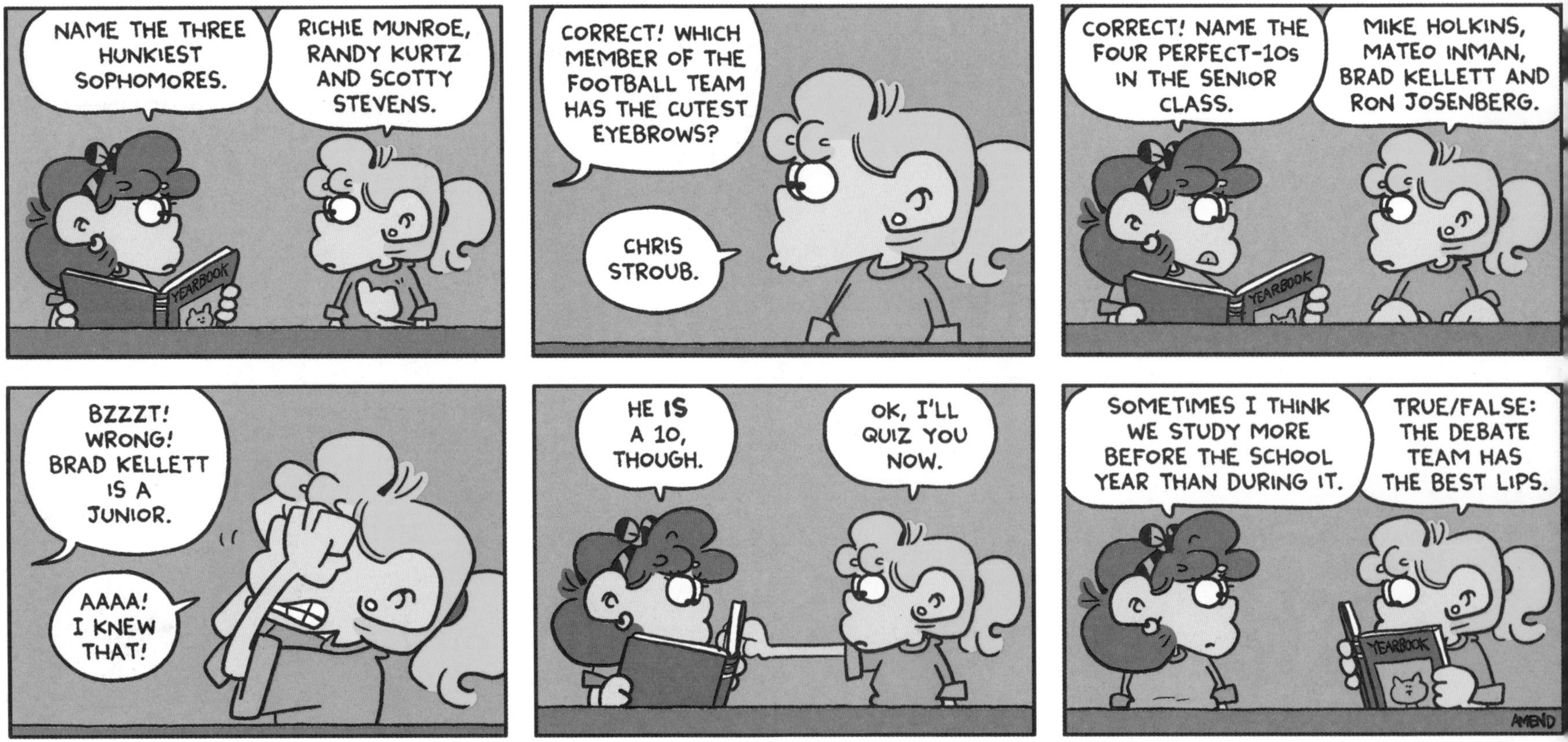
NAME THE THREE HUNKIEST SOPHOMORES.
RICHIE MUNROE, RANDY KURTZ AND SCOTTY STEVENS.
YEARBOOK
CORRECT! WHICH MEMBER OF THE FOOTBALL TEAM HAS THE CUTEST EYEBROWS?
CHRIS STROUB.
CORRECT! NAME THE FOUR PERFECT-10s IN THE SENIOR CLASS.
MIKE HOLKINS, MATEO INMAN, BRAD KELLETT AND RON JOSENBERG.
YEARBOOK
BZZZT! WRONG! BRAD KELLETT IS A JUNIOR.
AAAA! I KNEW THAT!
HE **IS** A 10, THOUGH.
OK, I'LL QUIZ YOU NOW.
SOMETIMES I THINK WE STUDY MORE BEFORE THE SCHOOL YEAR THAN DURING IT.
TRUE/FALSE: THE DEBATE TEAM HAS THE BEST LIPS.
YEARBOOK
AMEND

Jasonian Ideas

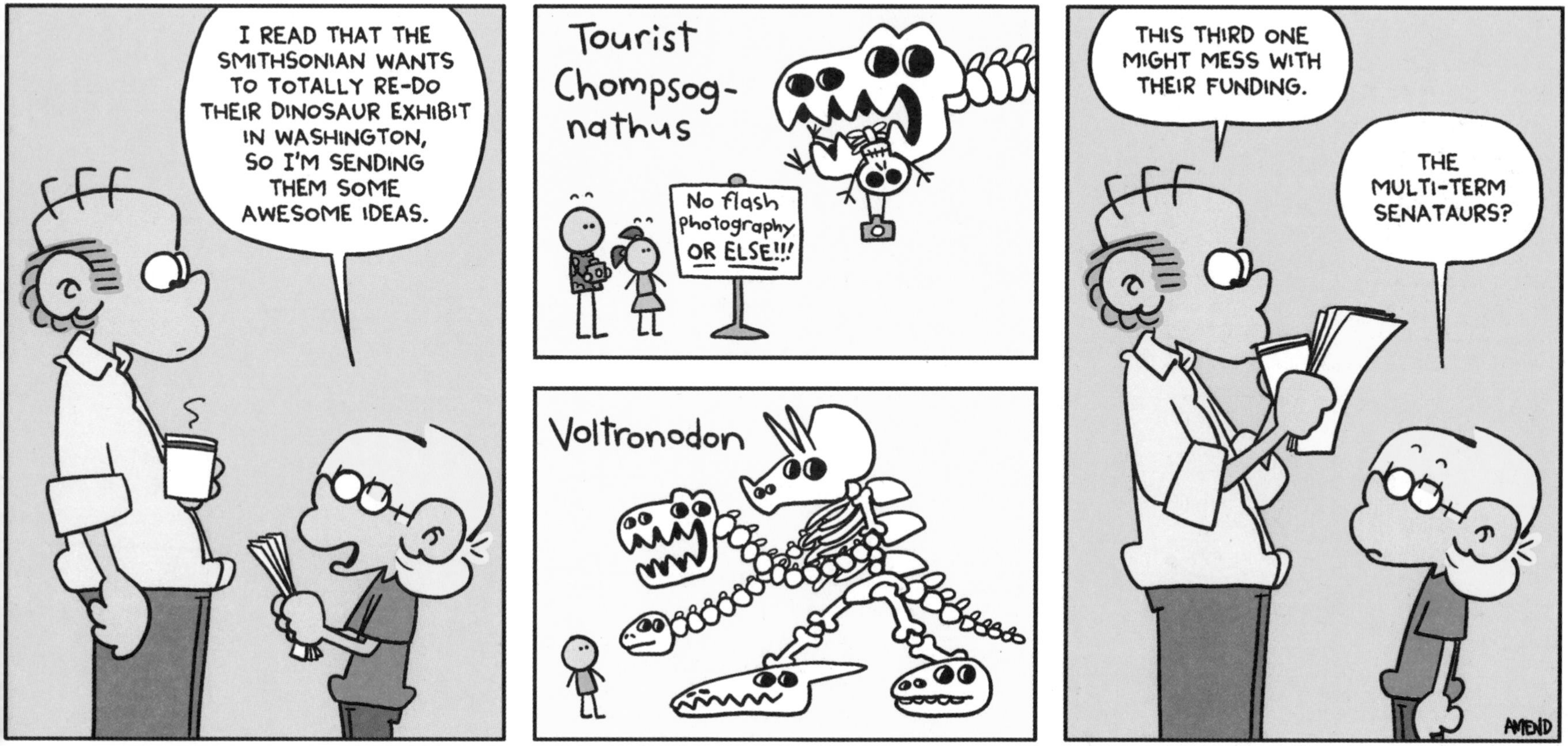
I READ THAT THE SMITHSONIAN WANTS TO TOTALLY RE-DO THEIR DINOSAUR EXHIBIT IN WASHINGTON, SO I'M SENDING THEM SOME AWESOME IDEAS.
Tourist Chompsog-nathus
No flash photography OR ELSE!!!
Voltronodon
THIS THIRD ONE MIGHT MESS WITH THEIR FUNDING.
THE MULTI-TERM SENATAURS?
AMEND

Time Zonked

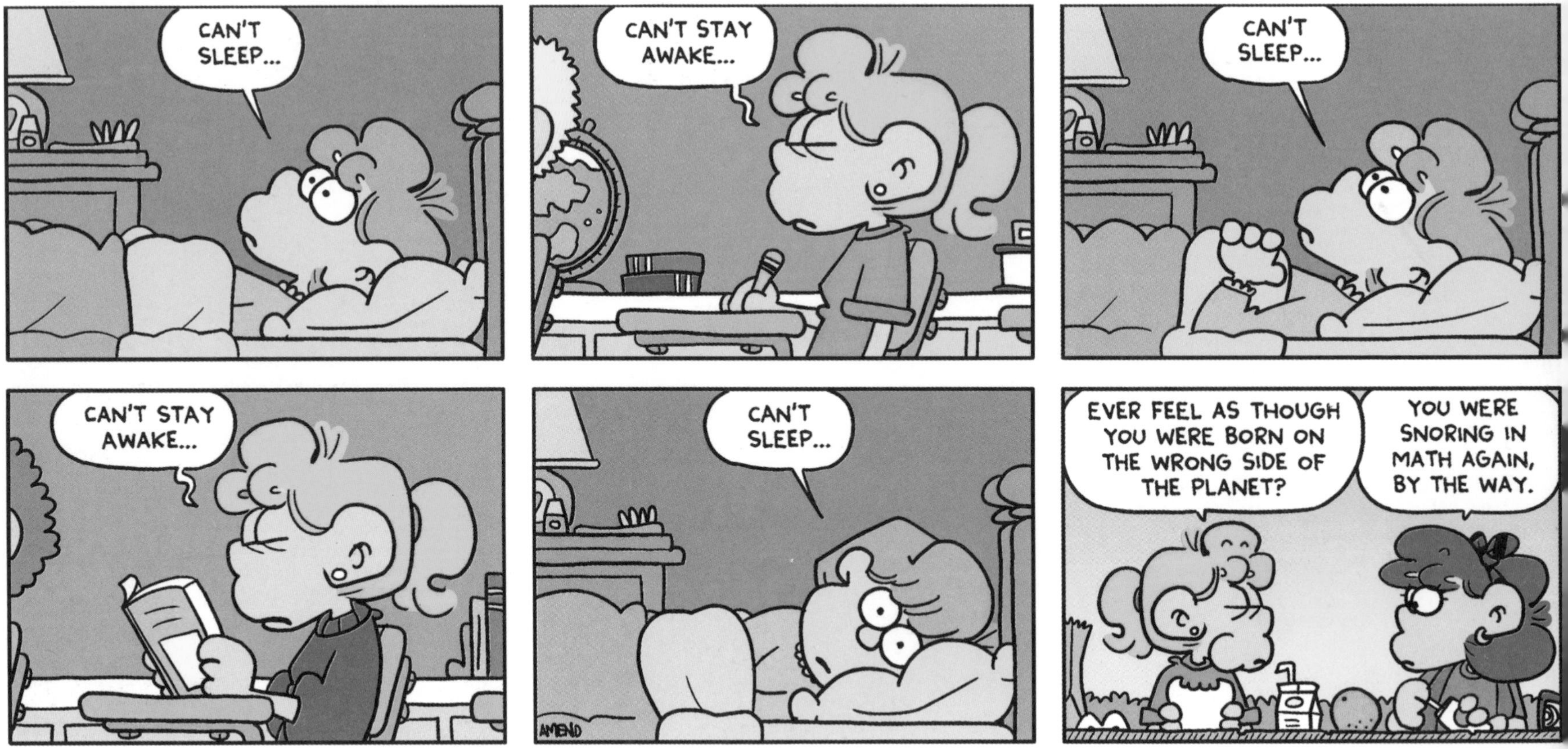
CAN'T SLEEP...
CAN'T STAY AWAKE...
CAN'T SLEEP...
CAN'T STAY AWAKE...
CAN'T SLEEP...
AMEND
EVER FEEL AS THOUGH YOU WERE BORN ON THE WRONG SIDE OF THE PLANET?
YOU WERE SNORING IN MATH AGAIN, BY THE WAY.

B-Positive

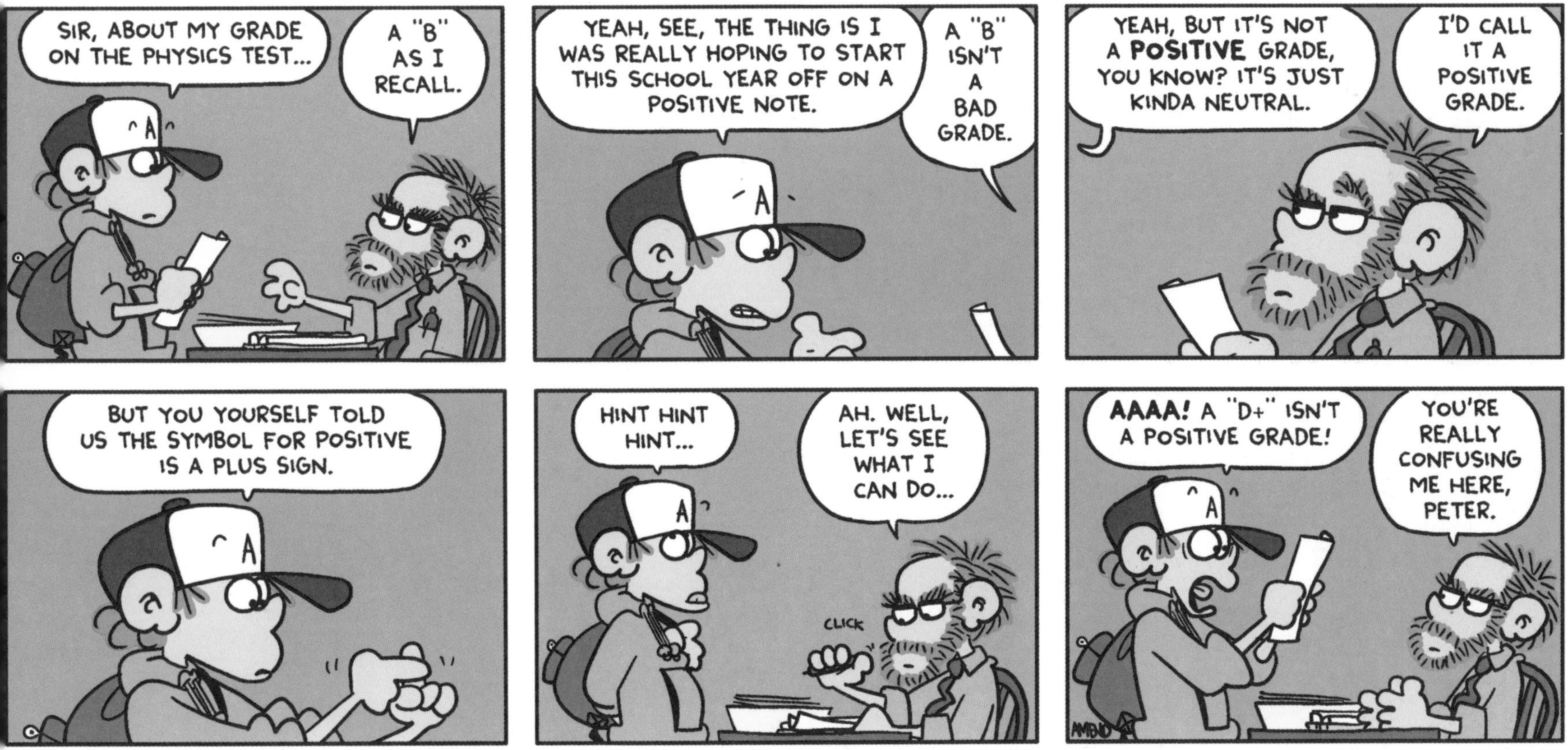
SIR, ABOUT MY GRADE ON THE PHYSICS TEST...
A "B" AS I RECALL.
YEAH, SEE, THE THING IS I WAS REALLY HOPING TO START THIS SCHOOL YEAR OFF ON A POSITIVE NOTE.
A "B" ISN'T A BAD GRADE.
YEAH, BUT IT'S NOT A **POSITIVE** GRADE, YOU KNOW? IT'S JUST KINDA NEUTRAL.
I'D CALL IT A POSITIVE GRADE.
BUT YOU YOURSELF TOLD US THE SYMBOL FOR POSITIVE IS A PLUS SIGN.
HINT HINT HINT...
AH. WELL, LET'S SEE WHAT I CAN DO...
CLICK
AAAA! A "D+" ISN'T A POSITIVE GRADE!
YOU'RE REALLY CONFUSING ME HERE, PETER.

Expansion Blues

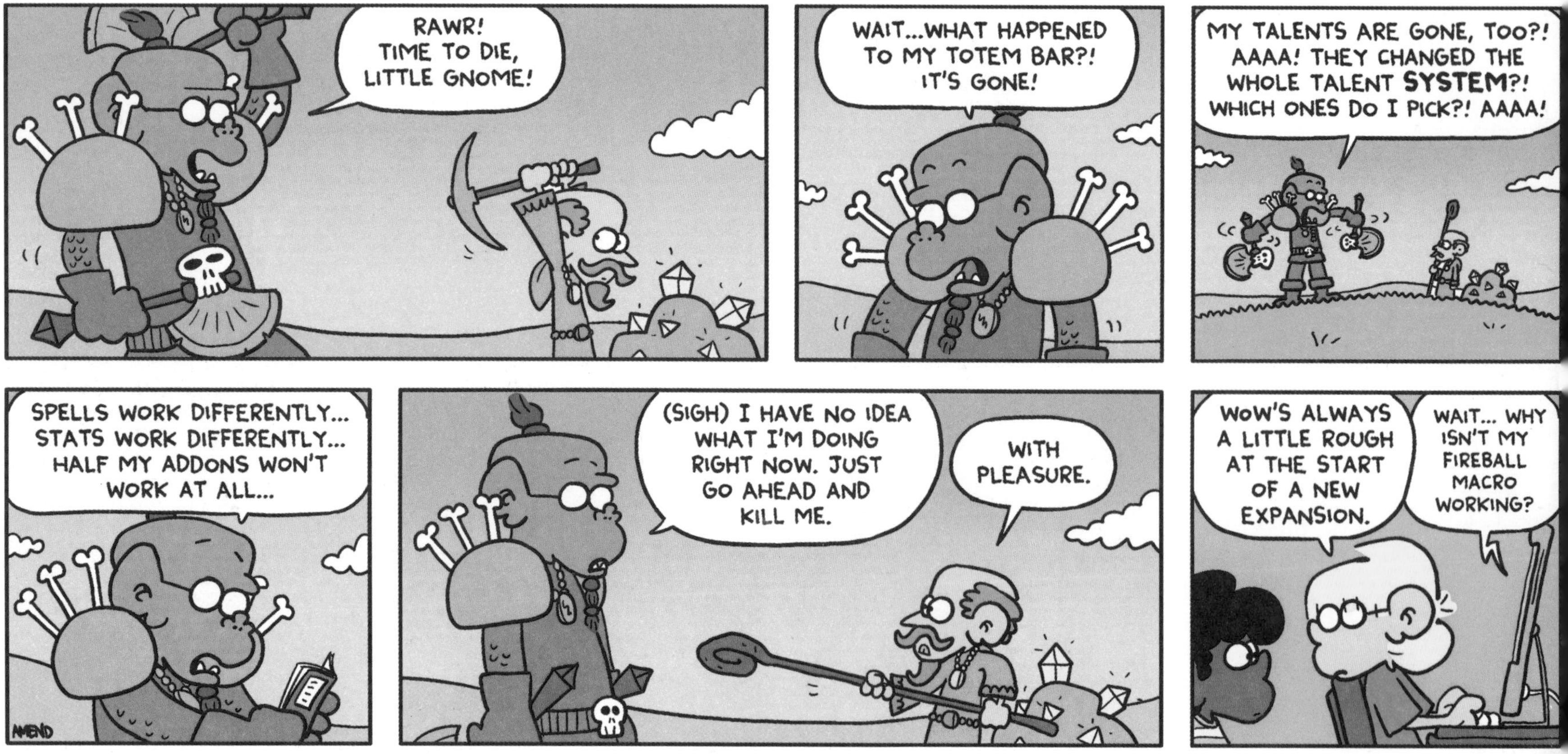

RAWR! TIME TO DIE, LITTLE GNOME!
WAIT...WHAT HAPPENED TO MY TOTEM BAR?! IT'S GONE!
MY TALENTS ARE GONE, TOO?! AAAA! THEY CHANGED THE WHOLE TALENT **SYSTEM**?! WHICH ONES DO I PICK?! AAAA!
SPELLS WORK DIFFERENTLY... STATS WORK DIFFERENTLY... HALF MY ADDONS WON'T WORK AT ALL...
AMEND
(SIGH) I HAVE NO IDEA WHAT I'M DOING RIGHT NOW. JUST GO AHEAD AND KILL ME.
WITH PLEASURE.
WoW'S ALWAYS A LITTLE ROUGH AT THE START OF A NEW EXPANSION.
WAIT... WHY ISN'T MY FIREBALL MACRO WORKING?

Dexterous

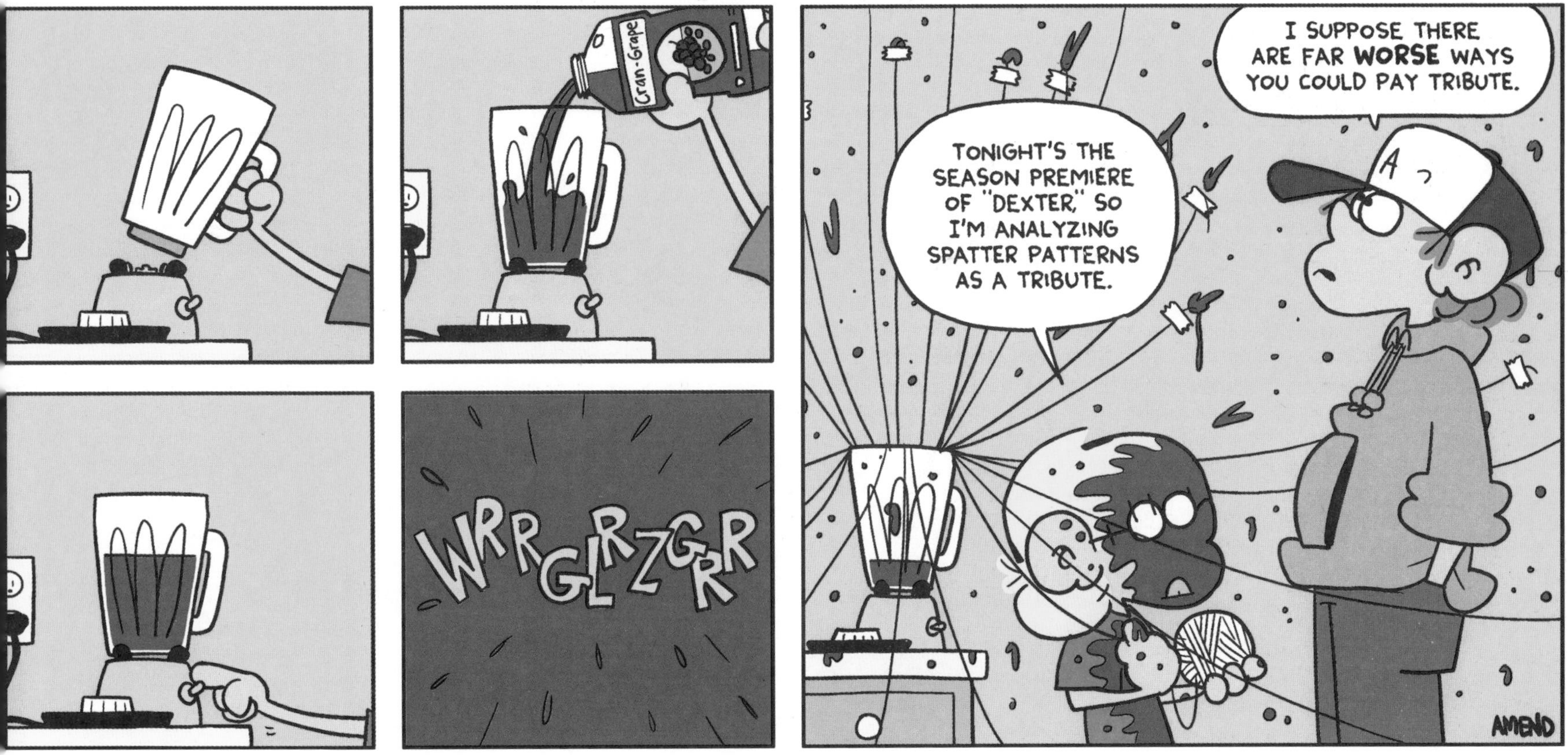
Cran-Grape
WRRGLRZGRR
TONIGHT'S THE SEASON PREMIERE OF "DEXTER," SO I'M ANALYZING SPATTER PATTERNS AS A TRIBUTE.
I SUPPOSE THERE ARE FAR **WORSE** WAYS YOU COULD PAY TRIBUTE.
AMEND

Pattern Recognition

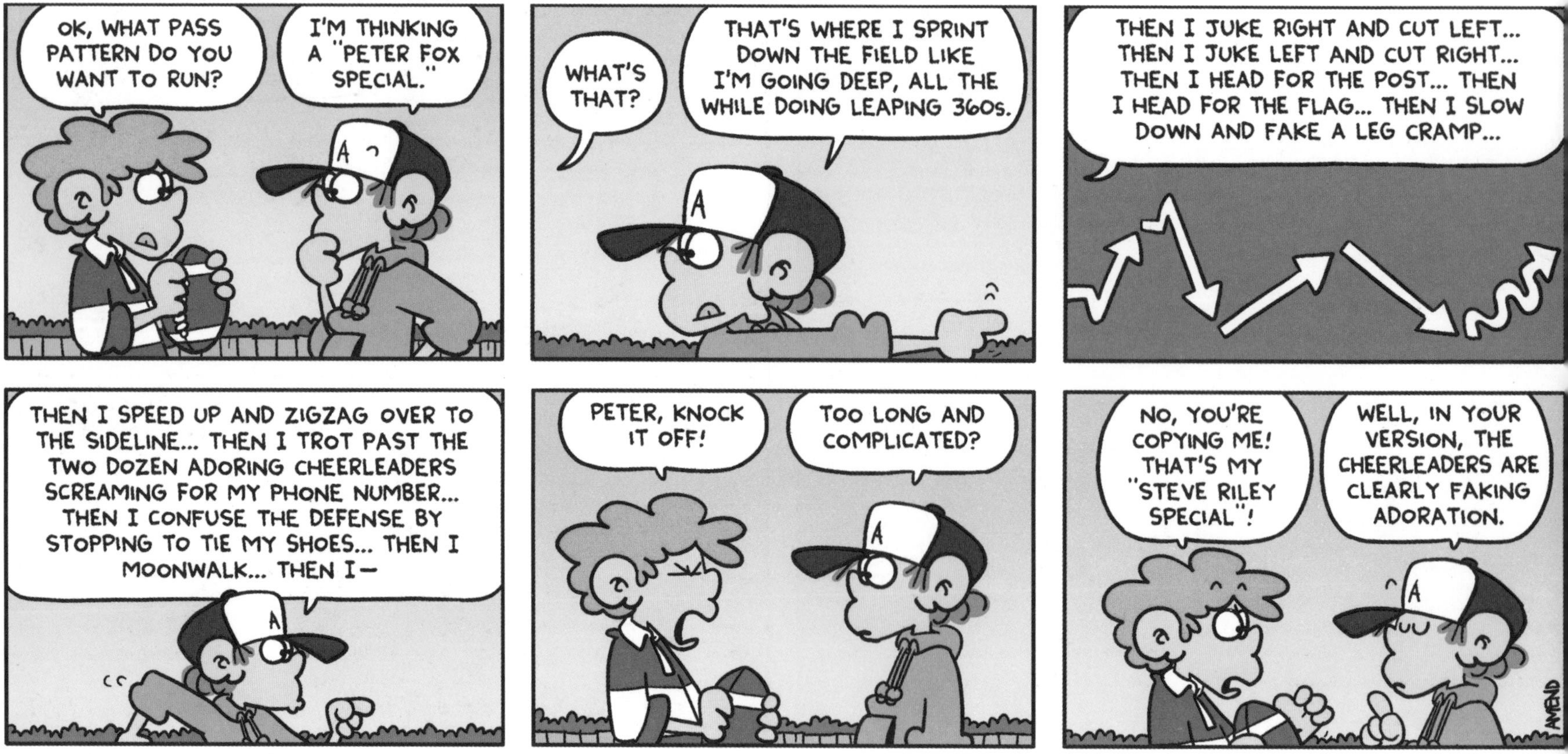

OK, WHAT PASS PATTERN DO YOU WANT TO RUN?
I'M THINKING A "PETER FOX SPECIAL."
WHAT'S THAT?
THAT'S WHERE I SPRINT DOWN THE FIELD LIKE I'M GOING DEEP, ALL THE WHILE DOING LEAPING 360s.
THEN I JUKE RIGHT AND CUT LEFT... THEN I JUKE LEFT AND CUT RIGHT... THEN I HEAD FOR THE POST... THEN I HEAD FOR THE FLAG... THEN I SLOW DOWN AND FAKE A LEG CRAMP...
THEN I SPEED UP AND ZIGZAG OVER TO THE SIDELINE... THEN I TROT PAST THE TWO DOZEN ADORING CHEERLEADERS SCREAMING FOR MY PHONE NUMBER... THEN I CONFUSE THE DEFENSE BY STOPPING TO TIE MY SHOES... THEN I MOONWALK... THEN I—
PETER, KNOCK IT OFF!
TOO LONG AND COMPLICATED?
NO, YOU'RE COPYING ME! THAT'S MY "STEVE RILEY SPECIAL"!
WELL, IN YOUR VERSION, THE CHEERLEADERS ARE CLEARLY FAKING ADORATION.
AMEND

Fancy Pancakes

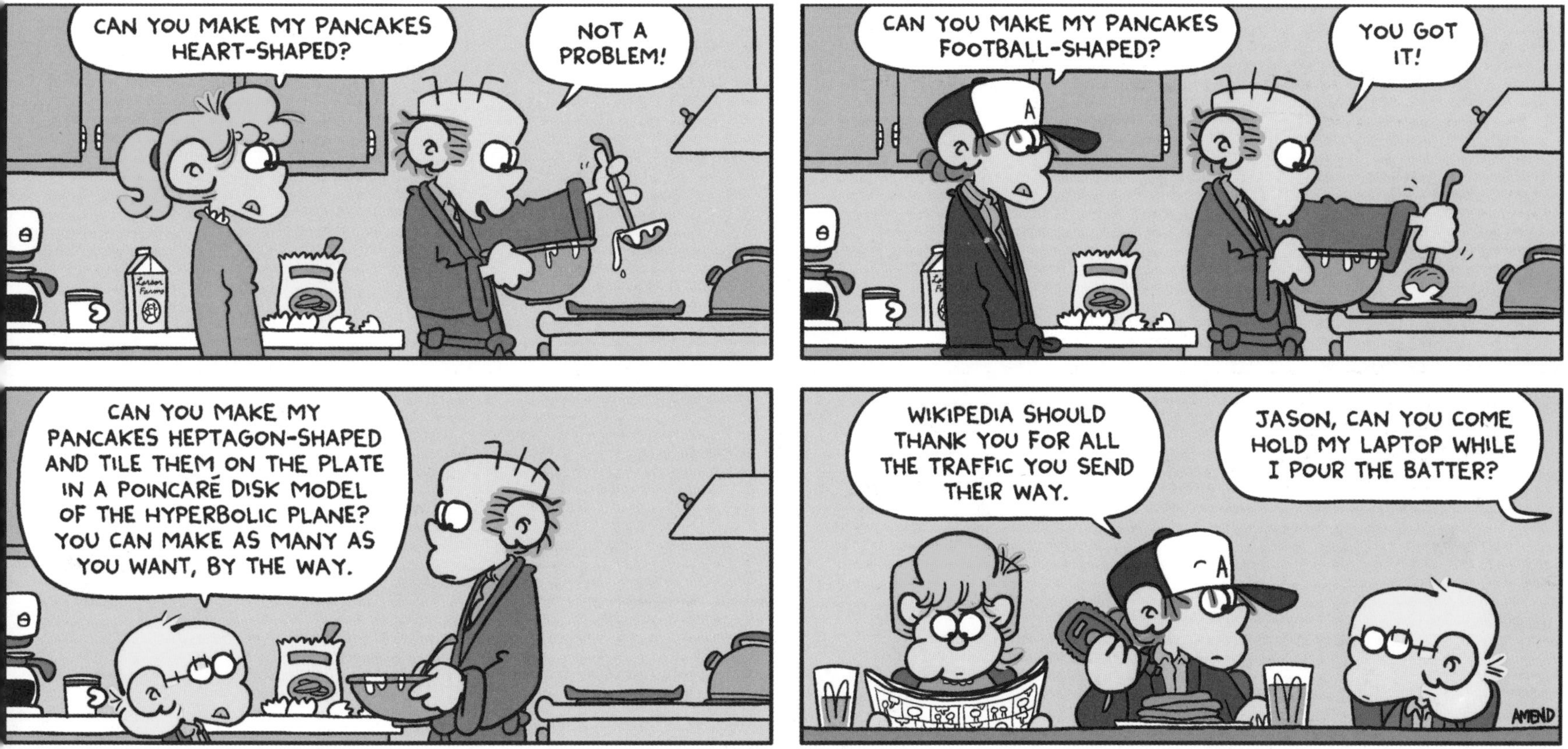

CAN YOU MAKE MY PANCAKES HEART-SHAPED?
NOT A PROBLEM!
CAN YOU MAKE MY PANCAKES FOOTBALL-SHAPED?
YOU GOT IT!
CAN YOU MAKE MY PANCAKES HEPTAGON-SHAPED AND TILE THEM ON THE PLATE IN A POINCARÉ DISK MODEL OF THE HYPERBOLIC PLANE? YOU CAN MAKE AS MANY AS YOU WANT, BY THE WAY.
WIKIPEDIA SHOULD THANK YOU FOR ALL THE TRAFFIC YOU SEND THEIR WAY.
JASON, CAN YOU COME HOLD MY LAPTOP WHILE I POUR THE BATTER?
AMEND

Scaredcrows

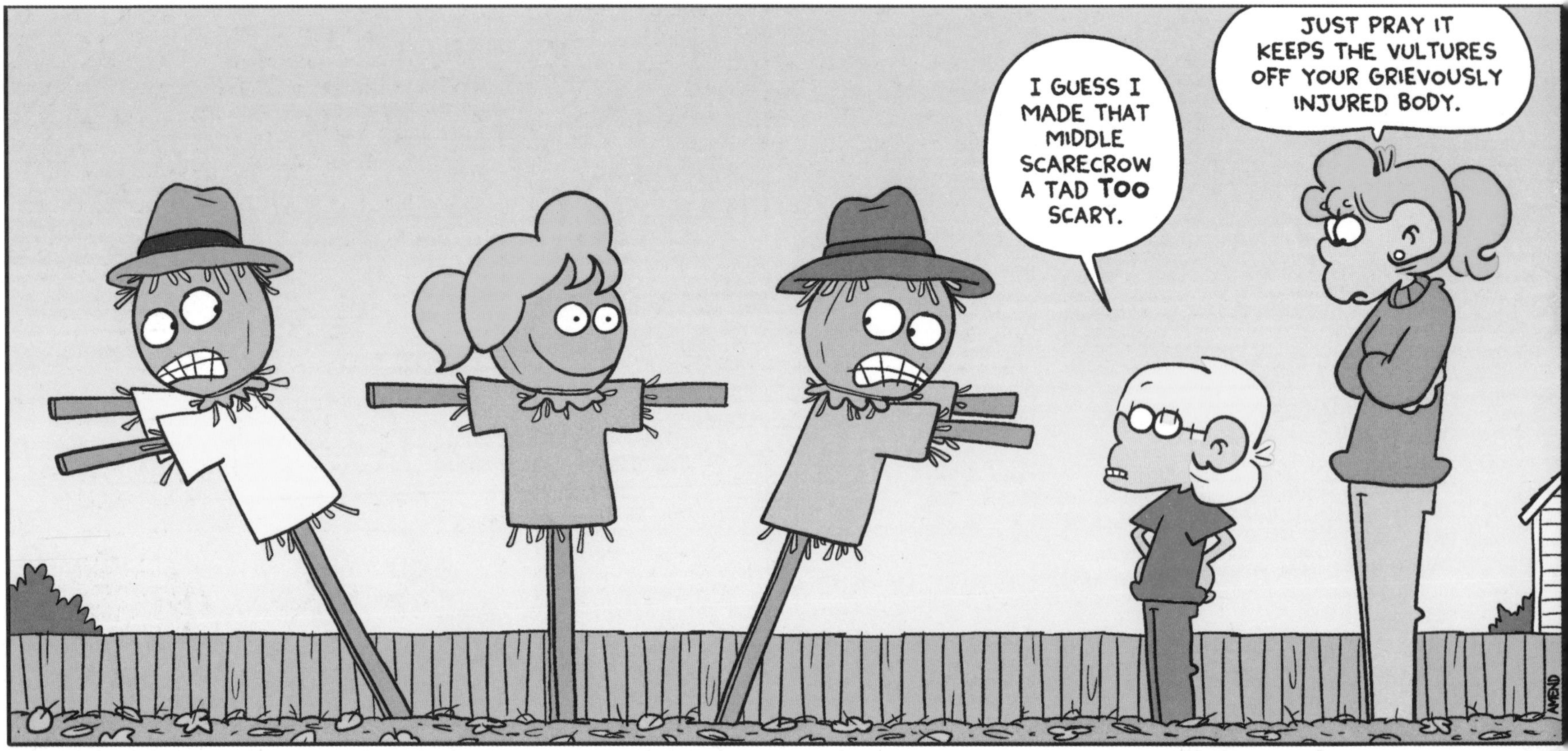
I GUESS I MADE THAT MIDDLE SCARECROW A TAD TOO SCARY.
JUST PRAY IT KEEPS THE VULTURES OFF YOUR GRIEVOUSLY INJURED BODY.
AMEND

Don't Spoil It

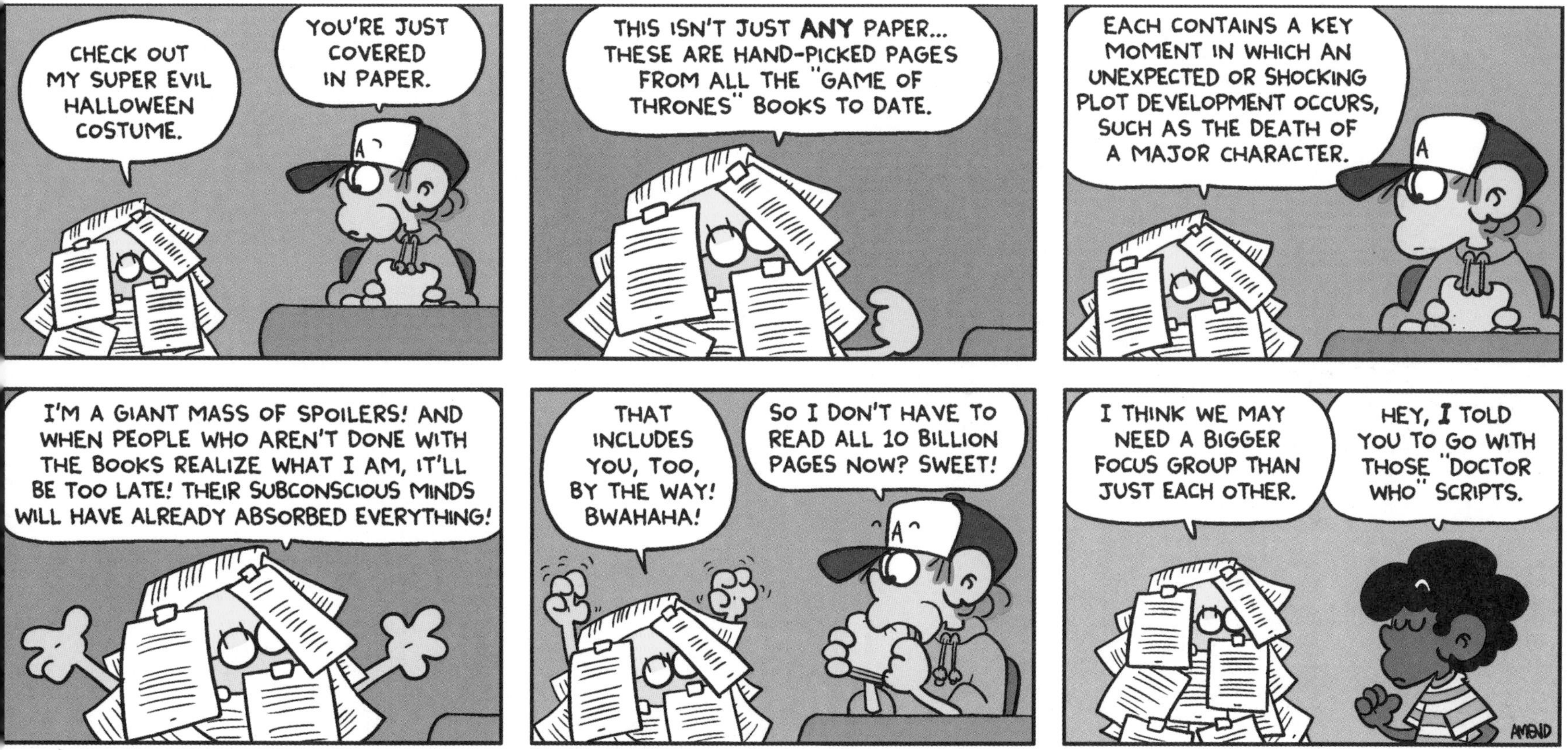
CHECK OUT MY SUPER EVIL HALLOWEEN COSTUME.
YOU'RE JUST COVERED IN PAPER.
THIS ISN'T JUST ANY PAPER... THESE ARE HAND-PICKED PAGES FROM ALL THE "GAME OF THRONES" BOOKS TO DATE.
EACH CONTAINS A KEY MOMENT IN WHICH AN UNEXPECTED OR SHOCKING PLOT DEVELOPMENT OCCURS, SUCH AS THE DEATH OF A MAJOR CHARACTER.
I'M A GIANT MASS OF SPOILERS! AND WHEN PEOPLE WHO AREN'T DONE WITH THE BOOKS REALIZE WHAT I AM, IT'LL BE TOO LATE! THEIR SUBCONSCIOUS MINDS WILL HAVE ALREADY ABSORBED EVERYTHING!
THAT INCLUDES YOU, TOO, BY THE WAY! BWAHAHA!
SO I DON'T HAVE TO READ ALL 10 BILLION PAGES NOW? SWEET!
I THINK WE MAY NEED A BIGGER FOCUS GROUP THAN JUST EACH OTHER.
HEY, I TOLD YOU TO GO WITH THOSE "DOCTOR WHO" SCRIPTS.
AMEND

Greatness Takes a While

Eleven Eleven Eleven

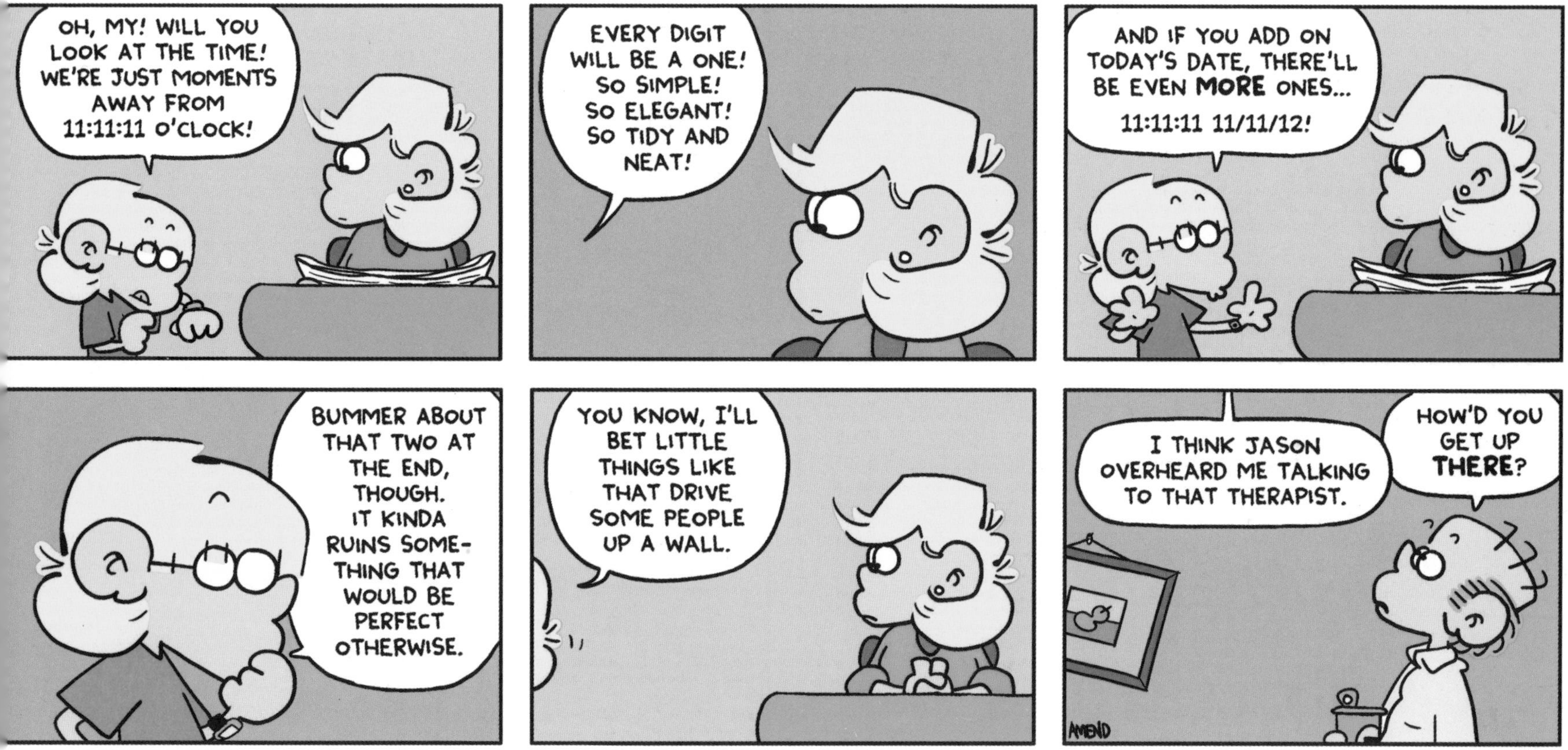

OH, MY! WILL YOU LOOK AT THE TIME! WE'RE JUST MOMENTS AWAY FROM 11:11:11 O'CLOCK!
EVERY DIGIT WILL BE A ONE! SO SIMPLE! SO ELEGANT! SO TIDY AND NEAT!
AND IF YOU ADD ON TODAY'S DATE, THERE'LL BE EVEN **MORE** ONES... 11:11:11 11/11/12!
BUMMER ABOUT THAT TWO AT THE END, THOUGH. IT KINDA RUINS SOME-THING THAT WOULD BE PERFECT OTHERWISE.
YOU KNOW, I'LL BET LITTLE THINGS LIKE THAT DRIVE SOME PEOPLE UP A WALL.
I THINK JASON OVERHEARD ME TALKING TO THAT THERAPIST.
HOW'D YOU GET UP **THERE**?
AMEND

Fast Times

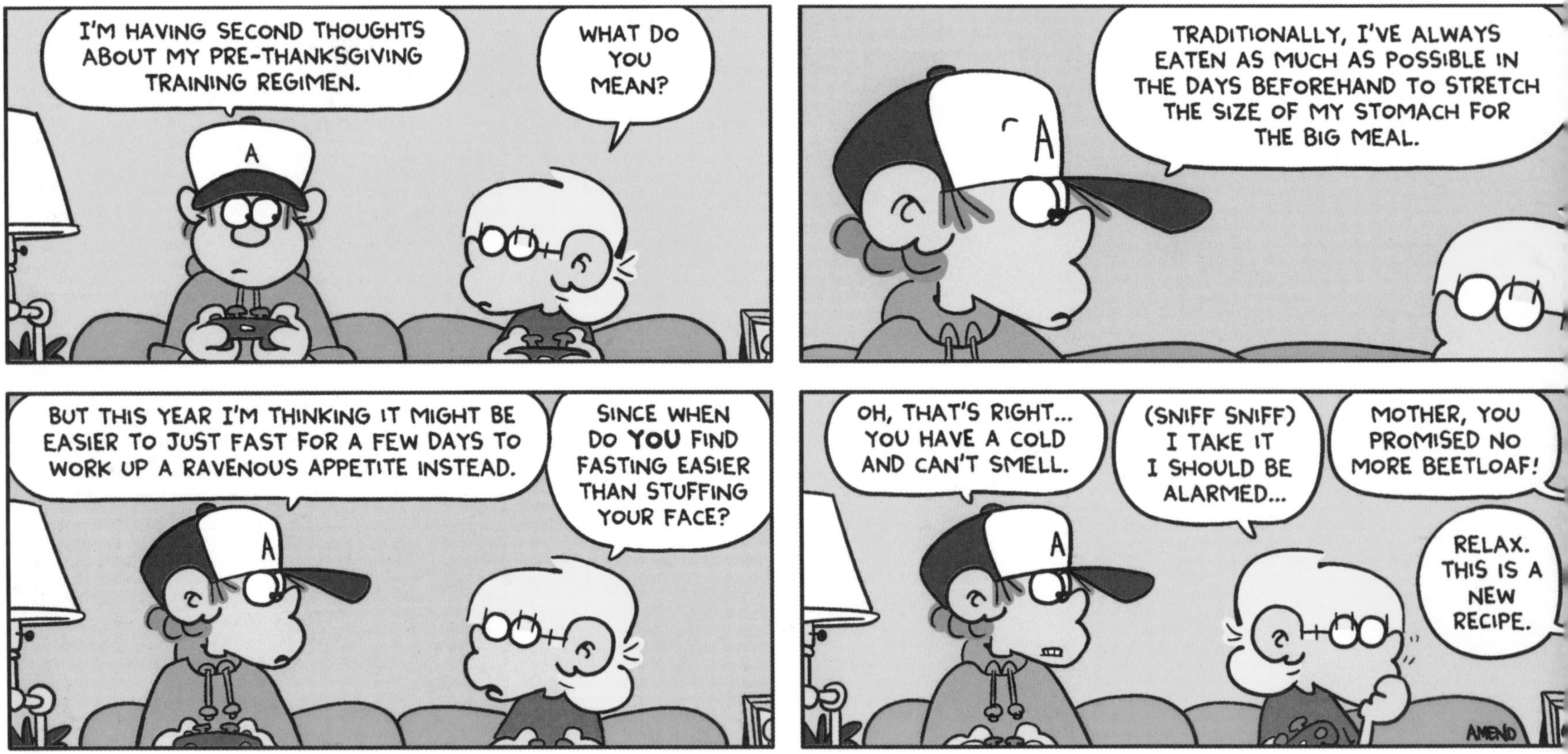

I'M HAVING SECOND THOUGHTS ABOUT MY PRE-THANKSGIVING TRAINING REGIMEN.
WHAT DO YOU MEAN?
A
TRADITIONALLY, I'VE ALWAYS EATEN AS MUCH AS POSSIBLE IN THE DAYS BEFOREHAND TO STRETCH THE SIZE OF MY STOMACH FOR THE BIG MEAL.
A
BUT THIS YEAR I'M THINKING IT MIGHT BE EASIER TO JUST FAST FOR A FEW DAYS TO WORK UP A RAVENOUS APPETITE INSTEAD.
SINCE WHEN DO **YOU** FIND FASTING EASIER THAN STUFFING YOUR FACE?
A
OH, THAT'S RIGHT... YOU HAVE A COLD AND CAN'T SMELL.
(SNIFF SNIFF) I TAKE IT I SHOULD BE ALARMED...
MOTHER, YOU PROMISED NO MORE BEETLOAF!
RELAX. THIS IS A NEW RECIPE.
A
AMEND

Nutwork Effect

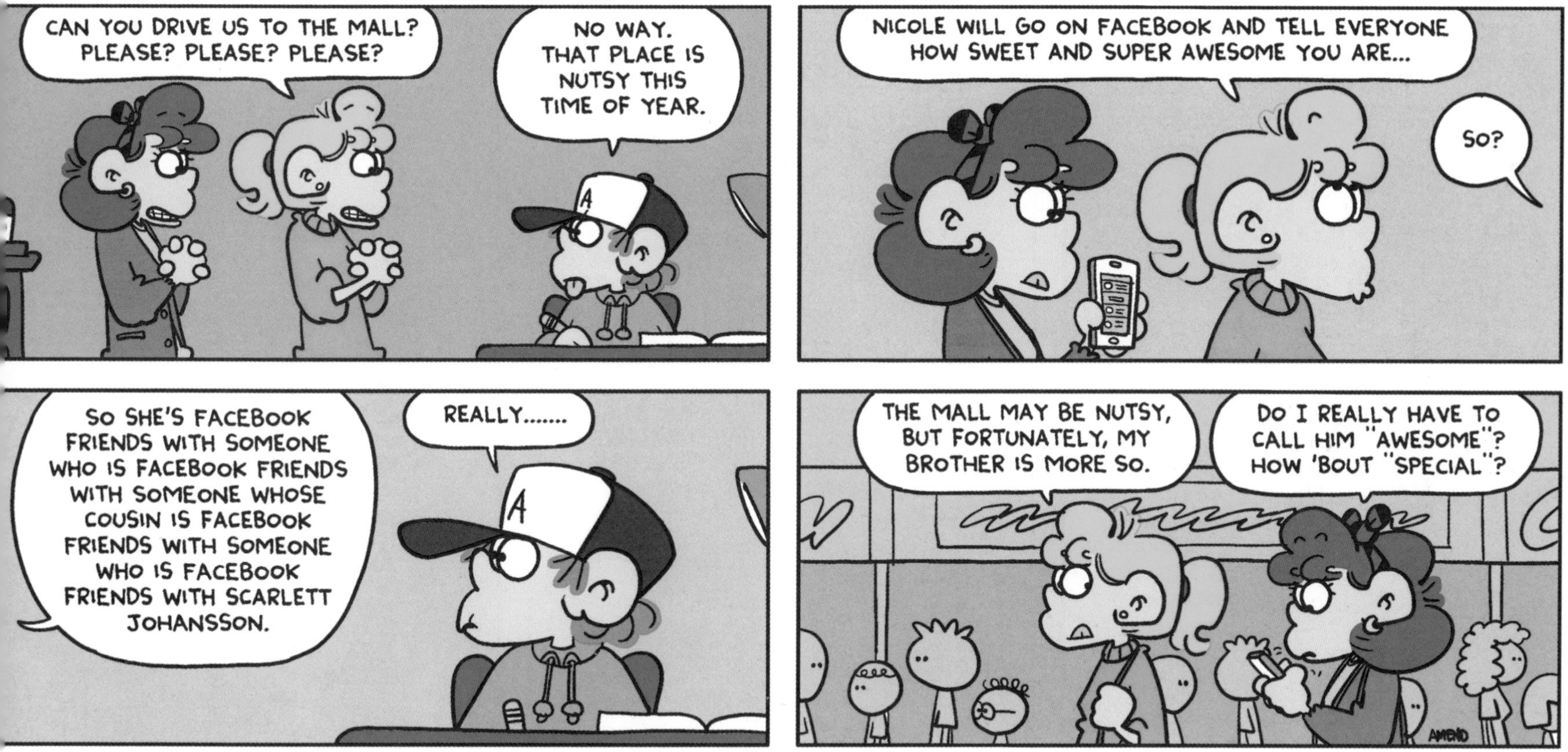

CAN YOU DRIVE US TO THE MALL? PLEASE? PLEASE? PLEASE?
NO WAY. THAT PLACE IS NUTSY THIS TIME OF YEAR.
NICOLE WILL GO ON FACEBOOK AND TELL EVERYONE HOW SWEET AND SUPER AWESOME YOU ARE...
SO?
SO SHE'S FACEBOOK FRIENDS WITH SOMEONE WHO IS FACEBOOK FRIENDS WITH SOMEONE WHOSE COUSIN IS FACEBOOK FRIENDS WITH SOMEONE WHO IS FACEBOOK FRIENDS WITH SCARLETT JOHANSSON.
REALLY.......
THE MALL MAY BE NUTSY, BUT FORTUNATELY, MY BROTHER IS MORE SO.
DO I REALLY HAVE TO CALL HIM "AWESOME"? HOW 'BOUT "SPECIAL"?
AMEND

Dungeon Division

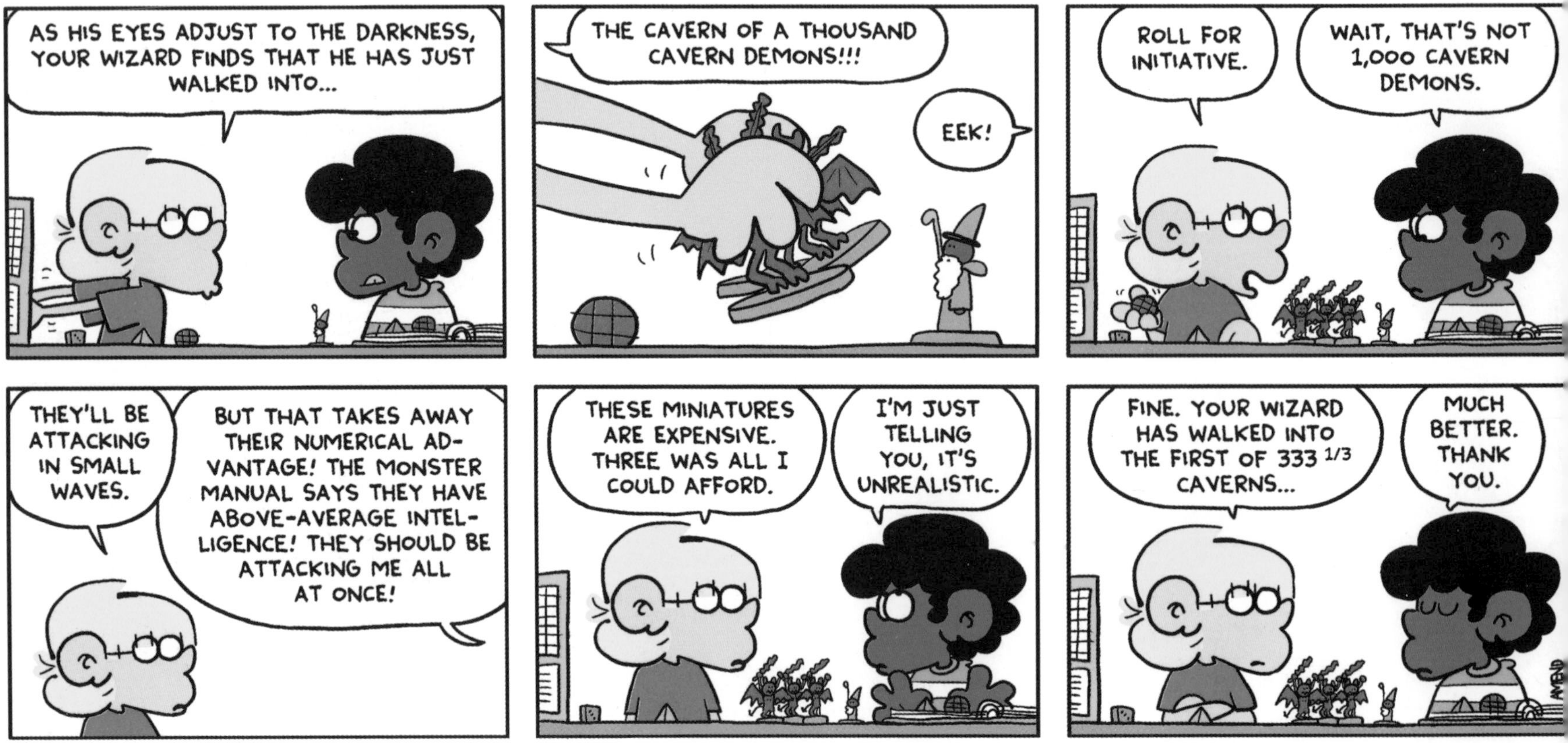
AS HIS EYES ADJUST TO THE DARKNESS, YOUR WIZARD FINDS THAT HE HAS JUST WALKED INTO...
THE CAVERN OF A THOUSAND CAVERN DEMONS!!!
EEK!
ROLL FOR INITIATIVE.
WAIT, THAT'S NOT 1,000 CAVERN DEMONS.
THEY'LL BE ATTACKING IN SMALL WAVES.
BUT THAT TAKES AWAY THEIR NUMERICAL AD-VANTAGE! THE MONSTER MANUAL SAYS THEY HAVE ABOVE-AVERAGE INTEL-LIGENCE! THEY SHOULD BE ATTACKING ME ALL AT ONCE!
THESE MINIATURES ARE EXPENSIVE. THREE WAS ALL I COULD AFFORD.
I'M JUST TELLING YOU, IT'S UNREALISTIC.
FINE. YOUR WIZARD HAS WALKED INTO THE FIRST OF 333 1/3 CAVERNS...
MUCH BETTER. THANK YOU.

Stung

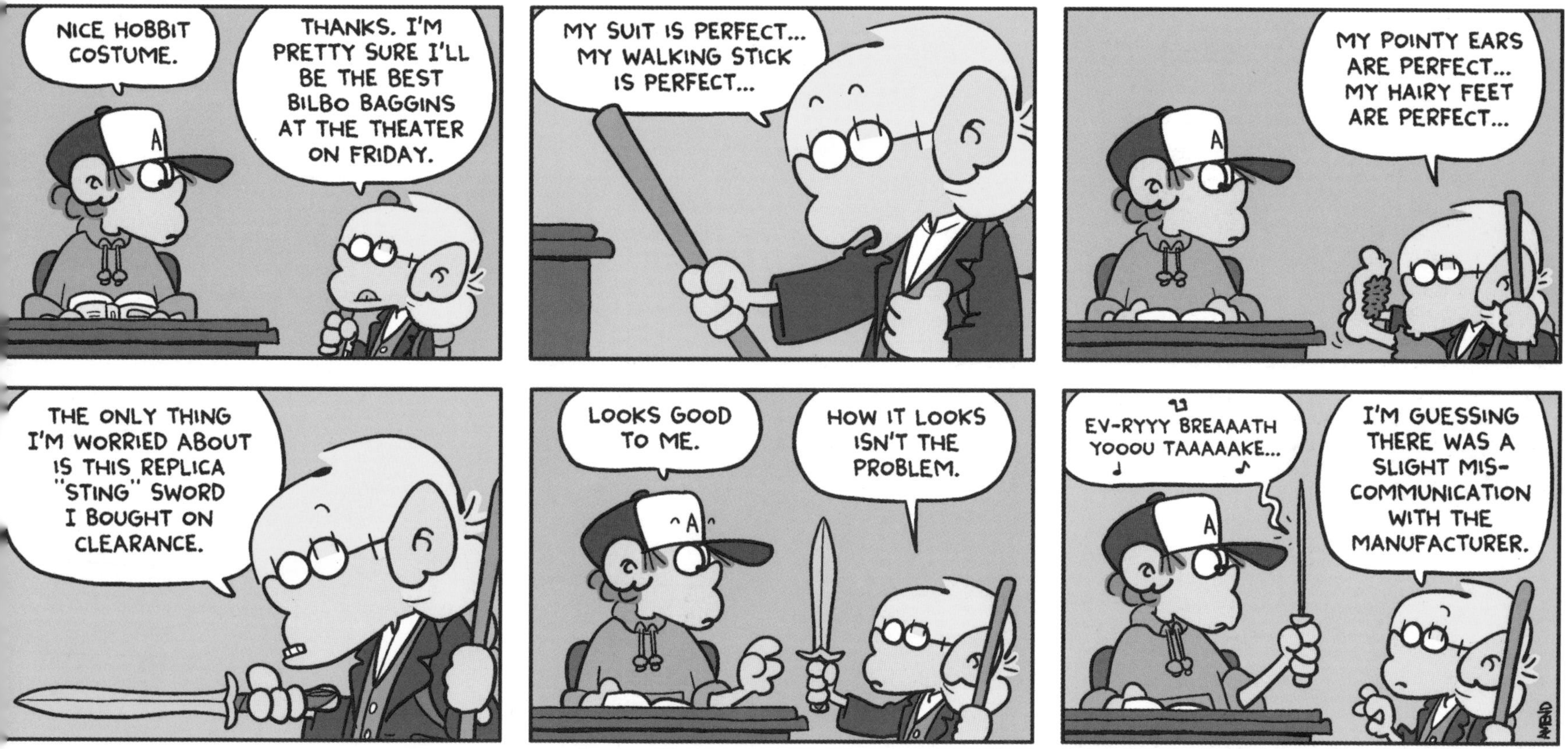
NICE HOBBIT COSTUME.
THANKS. I'M PRETTY SURE I'LL BE THE BEST BILBO BAGGINS AT THE THEATER ON FRIDAY.
MY SUIT IS PERFECT... MY WALKING STICK IS PERFECT...
MY POINTY EARS ARE PERFECT... MY HAIRY FEET ARE PERFECT...
THE ONLY THING I'M WORRIED ABOUT IS THIS REPLICA "STING" SWORD I BOUGHT ON CLEARANCE.
LOOKS GOOD TO ME.
HOW IT LOOKS ISN'T THE PROBLEM.
EV-RYYY BREAAATH YOOOU TAAAAAKE...
I'M GUESSING THERE WAS A SLIGHT MIS-COMMUNICATION WITH THE MANUFACTURER.

Cookie Science

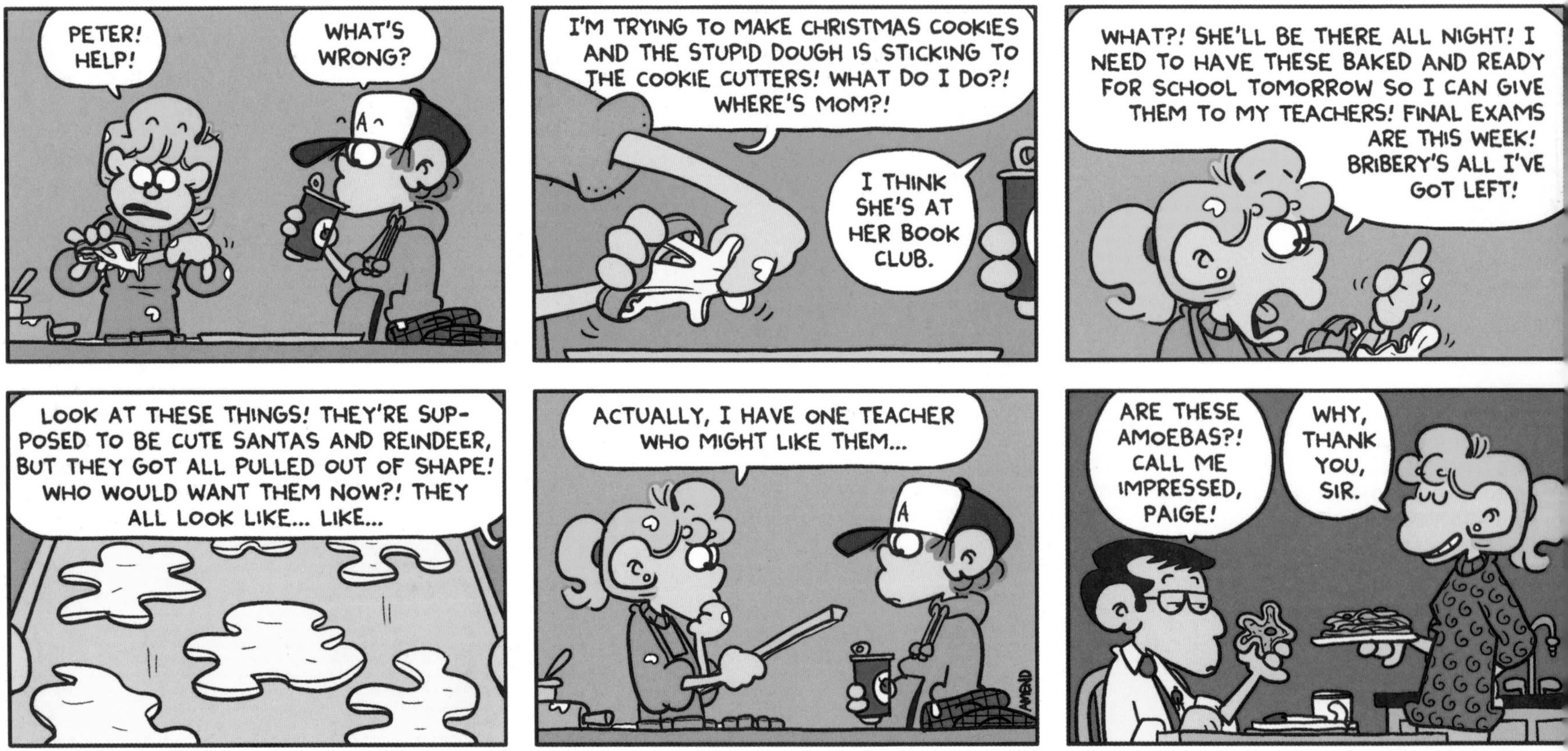
PETER! HELP!
WHAT'S WRONG?
I'M TRYING TO MAKE CHRISTMAS COOKIES AND THE STUPID DOUGH IS STICKING TO THE COOKIE CUTTERS! WHAT DO I DO?! WHERE'S MOM?!
I THINK SHE'S AT HER BOOK CLUB.
WHAT?! SHE'LL BE THERE ALL NIGHT! I NEED TO HAVE THESE BAKED AND READY FOR SCHOOL TOMORROW SO I CAN GIVE THEM TO MY TEACHERS! FINAL EXAMS ARE THIS WEEK! BRIBERY'S ALL I'VE GOT LEFT!
LOOK AT THESE THINGS! THEY'RE SUP-POSED TO BE CUTE SANTAS AND REINDEER, BUT THEY GOT ALL PULLED OUT OF SHAPE! WHO WOULD WANT THEM NOW?! THEY ALL LOOK LIKE... LIKE...
ACTUALLY, I HAVE ONE TEACHER WHO MIGHT LIKE THEM...
AMEND
ARE THESE AMOEBAS?! CALL ME IMPRESSED, PAIGE!
WHY, THANK YOU, SIR.

Packet Analysis

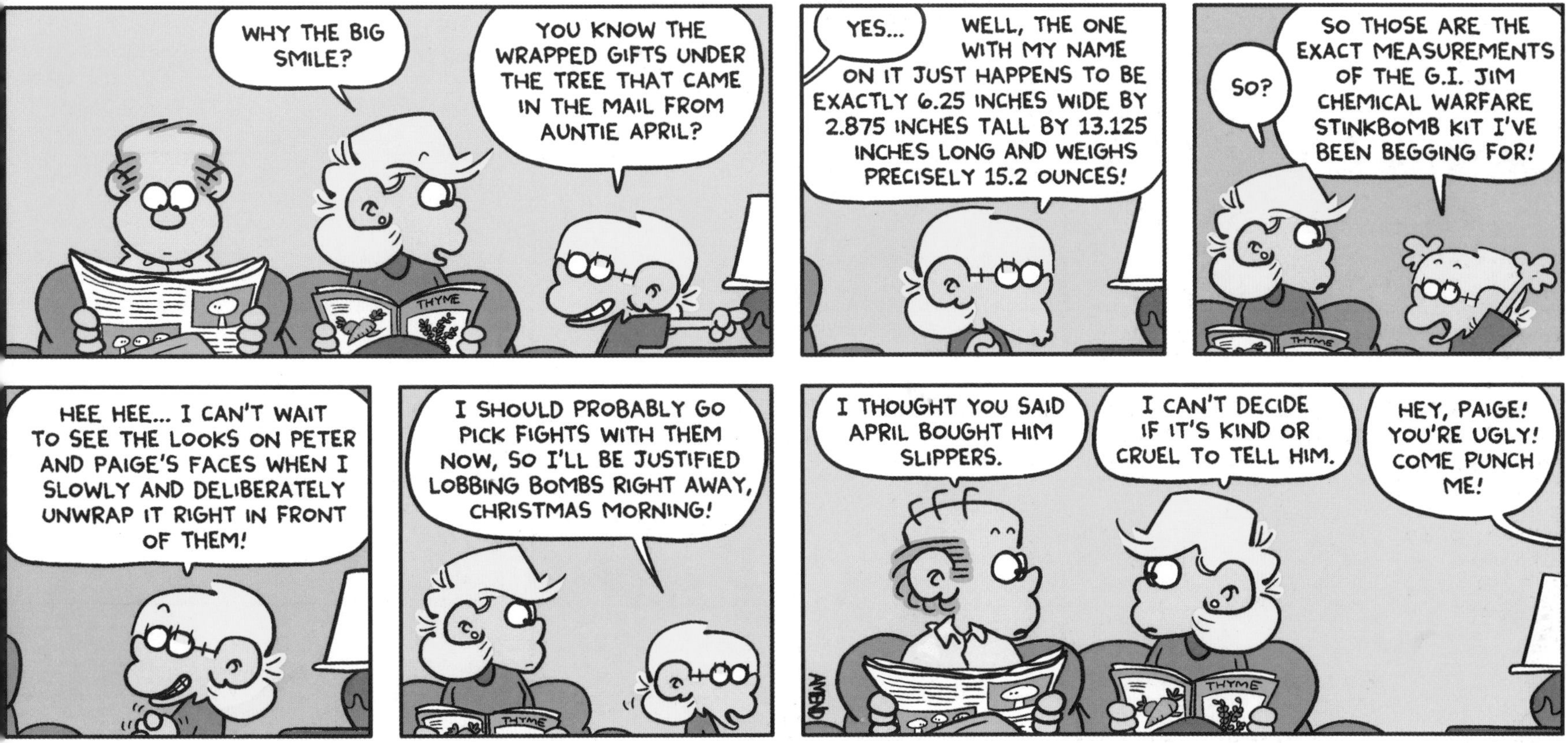
WHY THE BIG SMILE?
YOU KNOW THE WRAPPED GIFTS UNDER THE TREE THAT CAME IN THE MAIL FROM AUNTIE APRIL?
YES...
WELL, THE ONE WITH MY NAME ON IT JUST HAPPENS TO BE EXACTLY 6.25 INCHES WIDE BY 2.875 INCHES TALL BY 13.125 INCHES LONG AND WEIGHS PRECISELY 15.2 OUNCES!
SO?
SO THOSE ARE THE EXACT MEASUREMENTS OF THE G.I. JIM CHEMICAL WARFARE STINKBOMB KIT I'VE BEEN BEGGING FOR!
HEE HEE... I CAN'T WAIT TO SEE THE LOOKS ON PETER AND PAIGE'S FACES WHEN I SLOWLY AND DELIBERATELY UNWRAP IT RIGHT IN FRONT OF THEM!
I SHOULD PROBABLY GO PICK FIGHTS WITH THEM NOW, SO I'LL BE JUSTIFIED LOBBING BOMBS RIGHT AWAY, CHRISTMAS MORNING!
I THOUGHT YOU SAID APRIL BOUGHT HIM SLIPPERS.
I CAN'T DECIDE IF IT'S KIND OR CRUEL TO TELL HIM.
HEY, PAIGE! YOU'RE UGLY! COME PUNCH ME!

Resolute

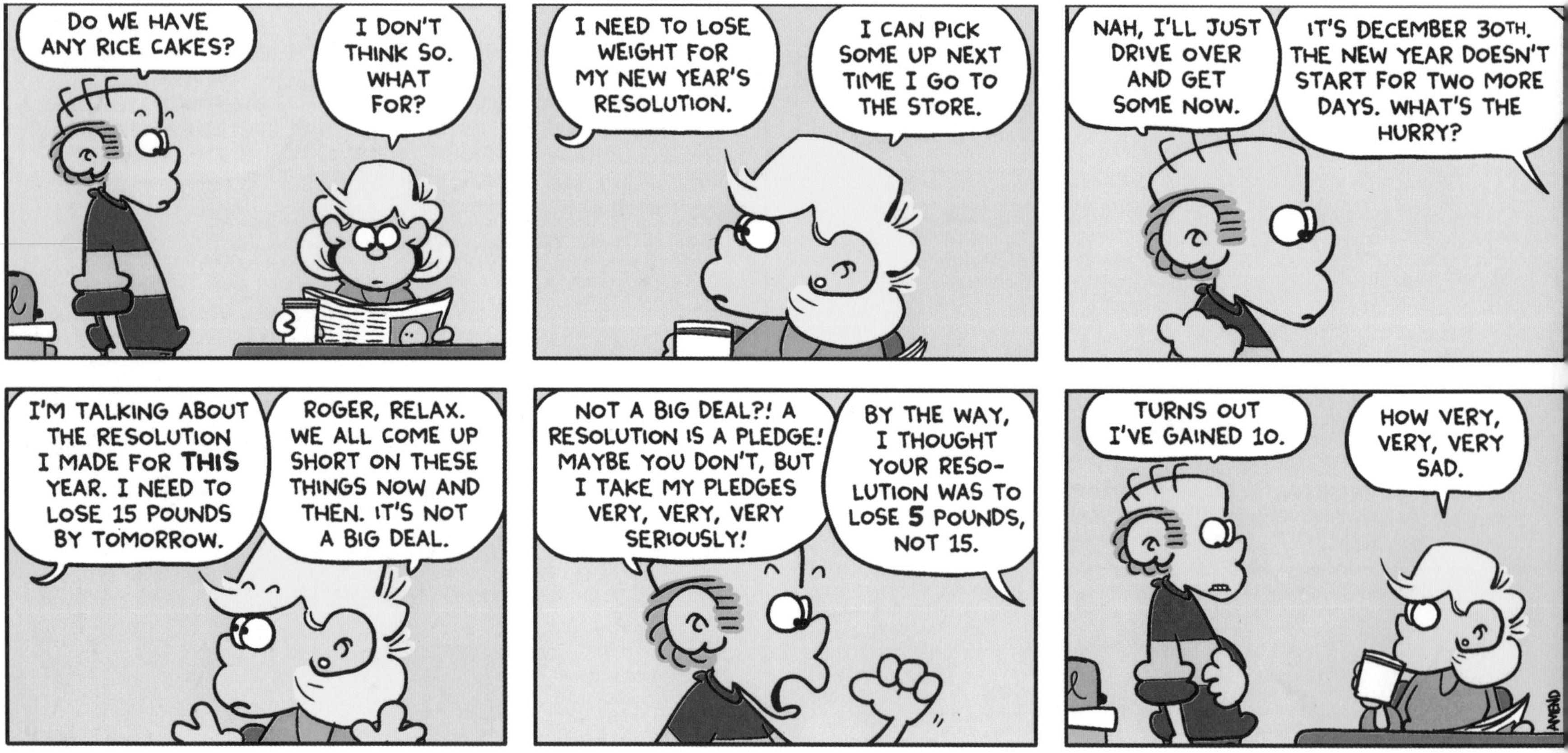
DO WE HAVE ANY RICE CAKES?
I DON'T THINK SO. WHAT FOR?
I NEED TO LOSE WEIGHT FOR MY NEW YEAR'S RESOLUTION.
I CAN PICK SOME UP NEXT TIME I GO TO THE STORE.
NAH, I'LL JUST DRIVE OVER AND GET SOME NOW.
IT'S DECEMBER 30TH. THE NEW YEAR DOESN'T START FOR TWO MORE DAYS. WHAT'S THE HURRY?
I'M TALKING ABOUT THE RESOLUTION I MADE FOR **THIS** YEAR. I NEED TO LOSE 15 POUNDS BY TOMORROW.
ROGER, RELAX. WE ALL COME UP SHORT ON THESE THINGS NOW AND THEN. IT'S NOT A BIG DEAL.
NOT A BIG DEAL?! A RESOLUTION IS A PLEDGE! MAYBE YOU DON'T, BUT I TAKE MY PLEDGES VERY, VERY, VERY SERIOUSLY!
BY THE WAY, I THOUGHT YOUR RESO-LUTION WAS TO LOSE **5** POUNDS, NOT 15.
TURNS OUT I'VE GAINED 10.
HOW VERY, VERY, VERY SAD.
AMEND

Team Player

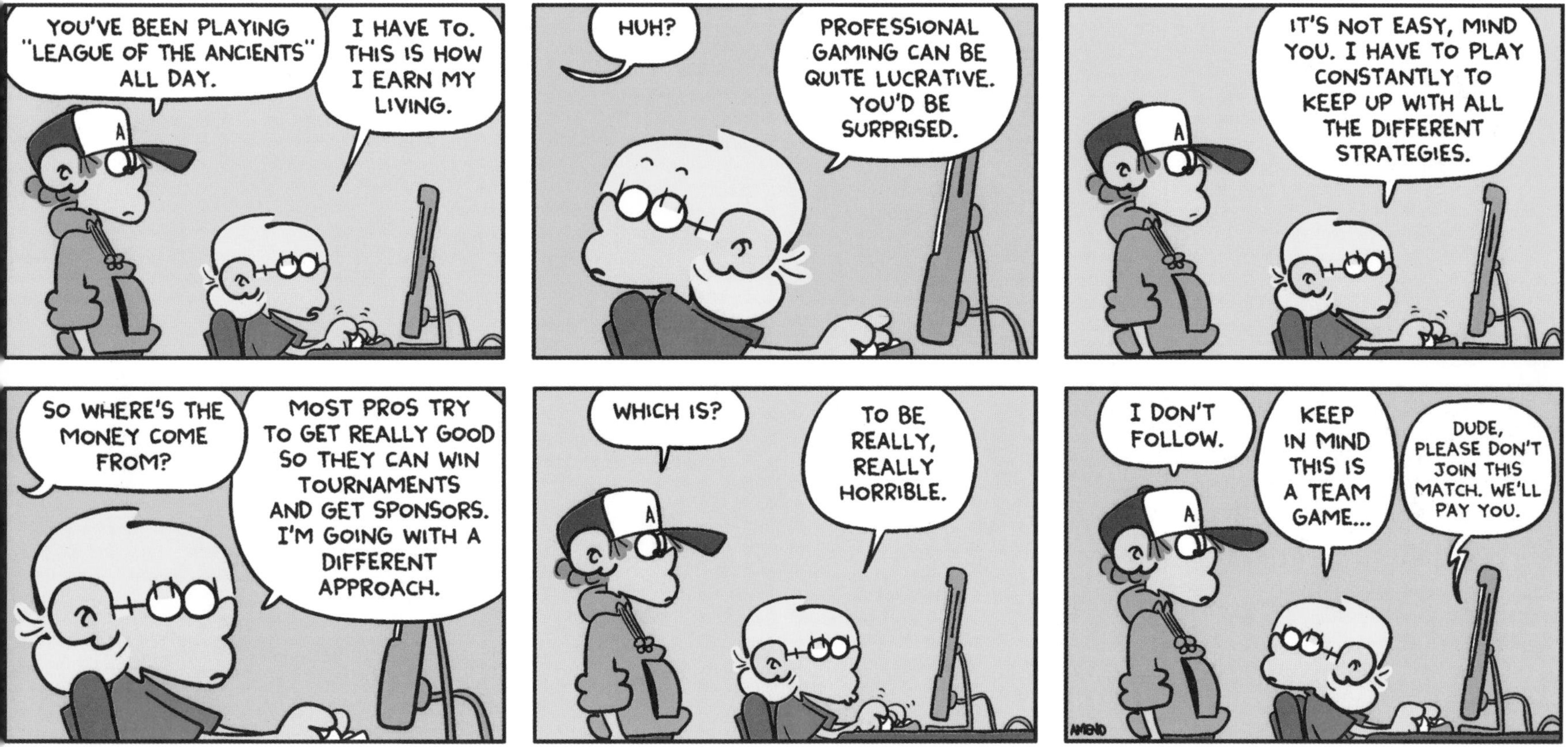
YOU'VE BEEN PLAYING "LEAGUE OF THE ANCIENTS" ALL DAY.
I HAVE TO. THIS IS HOW I EARN MY LIVING.
HUH?
PROFESSIONAL GAMING CAN BE QUITE LUCRATIVE. YOU'D BE SURPRISED.
IT'S NOT EASY, MIND YOU. I HAVE TO PLAY CONSTANTLY TO KEEP UP WITH ALL THE DIFFERENT STRATEGIES.
SO WHERE'S THE MONEY COME FROM?
MOST PROS TRY TO GET REALLY GOOD SO THEY CAN WIN TOURNAMENTS AND GET SPONSORS. I'M GOING WITH A DIFFERENT APPROACH.
WHICH IS?
TO BE REALLY, REALLY HORRIBLE.
I DON'T FOLLOW.
KEEP IN MIND THIS IS A TEAM GAME...
DUDE, PLEASE DON'T JOIN THIS MATCH. WE'LL PAY YOU.
AMEND

Snow More Vegetables

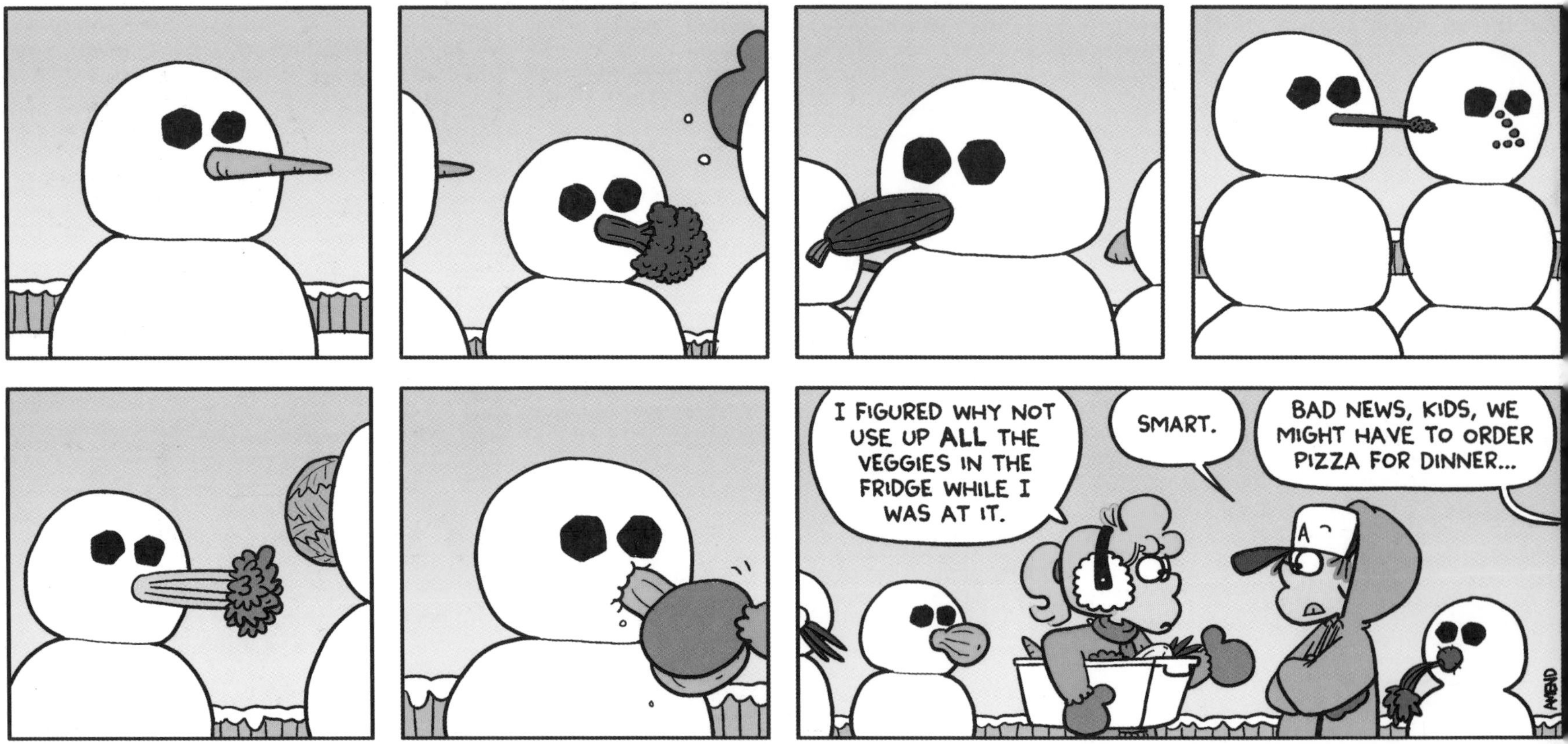
I FIGURED WHY NOT USE UP ALL THE VEGGIES IN THE FRIDGE WHILE I WAS AT IT.
SMART.
BAD NEWS, KIDS, WE MIGHT HAVE TO ORDER PIZZA FOR DINNER...
AMEND

Google Mapping

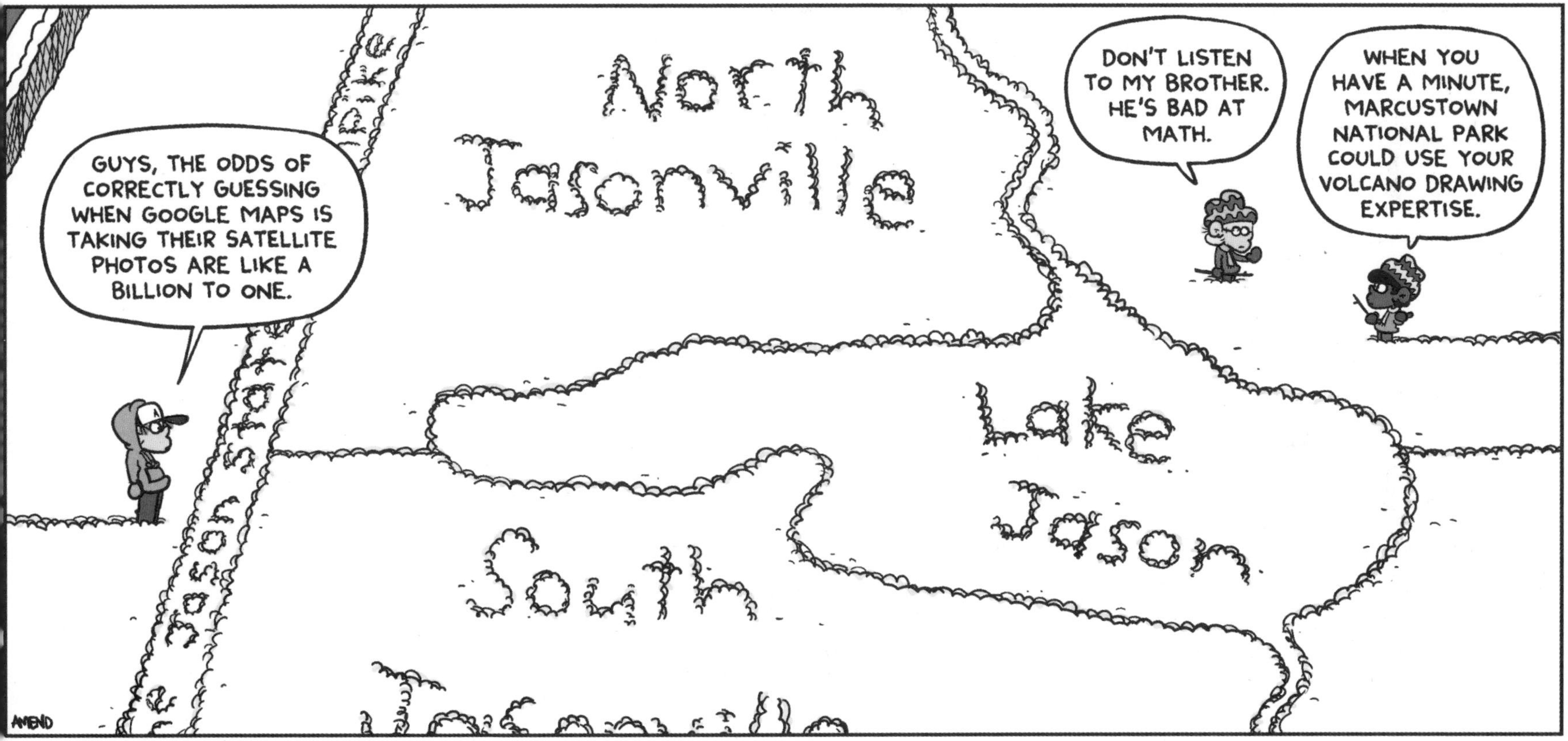

GUYS, THE ODDS OF CORRECTLY GUESSING WHEN GOOGLE MAPS IS TAKING THEIR SATELLITE PHOTOS ARE LIKE A BILLION TO ONE.
DON'T LISTEN TO MY BROTHER. HE'S BAD AT MATH.
WHEN YOU HAVE A MINUTE, MARCUSTOWN NATIONAL PARK COULD USE YOUR VOLCANO DRAWING EXPERTISE.
North Jasonville
Lake Jason
South
AMEND

Don't Ask

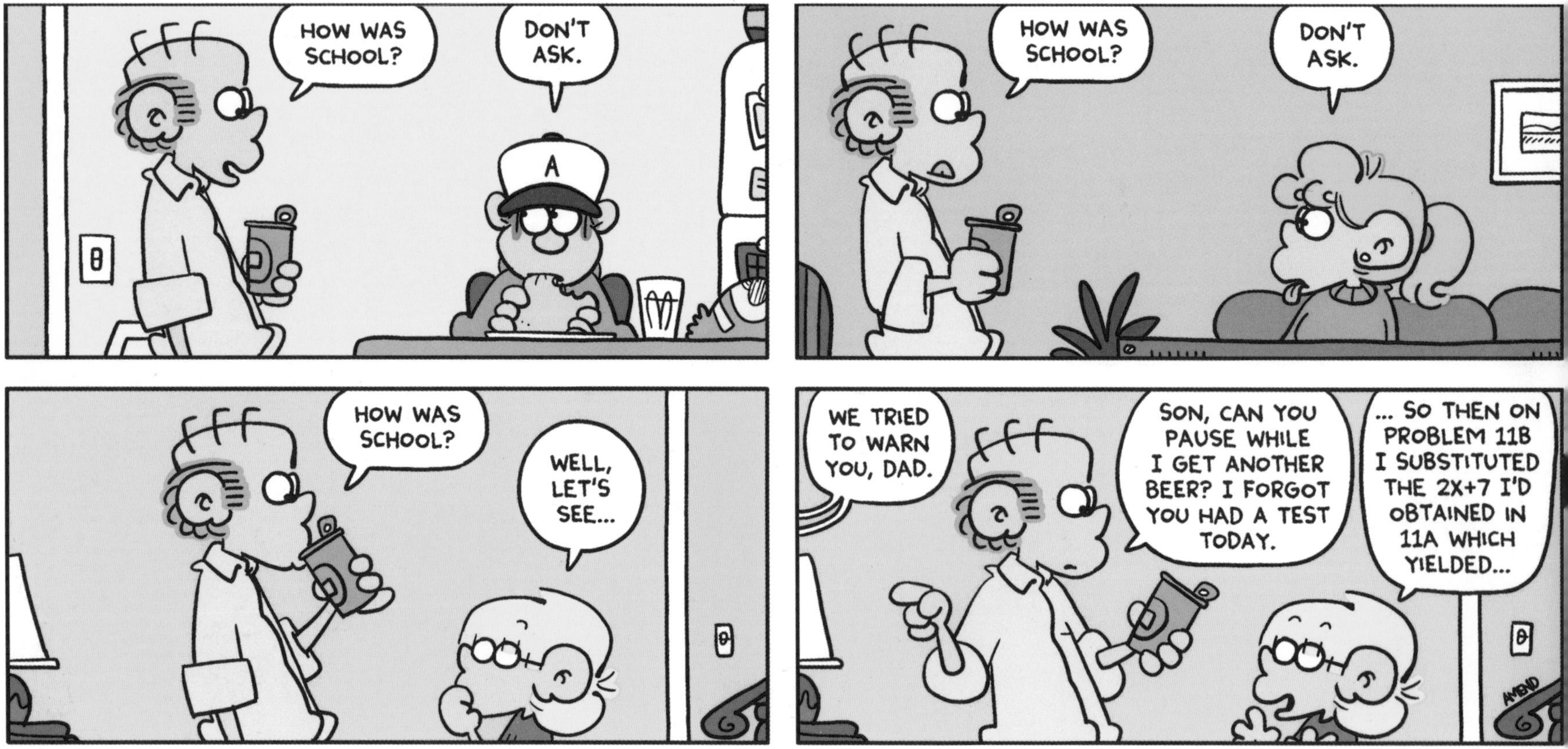
HOW WAS SCHOOL?
DON'T ASK.
HOW WAS SCHOOL?
DON'T ASK.
HOW WAS SCHOOL?
WELL, LET'S SEE...
WE TRIED TO WARN YOU, DAD.
SON, CAN YOU PAUSE WHILE I GET ANOTHER BEER? I FORGOT YOU HAD A TEST TODAY.
... SO THEN ON PROBLEM 11B I SUBSTITUTED THE 2X+7 I'D OBTAINED IN 11A WHICH YIELDED...

Jason and the Beanstalk

Heart Attack

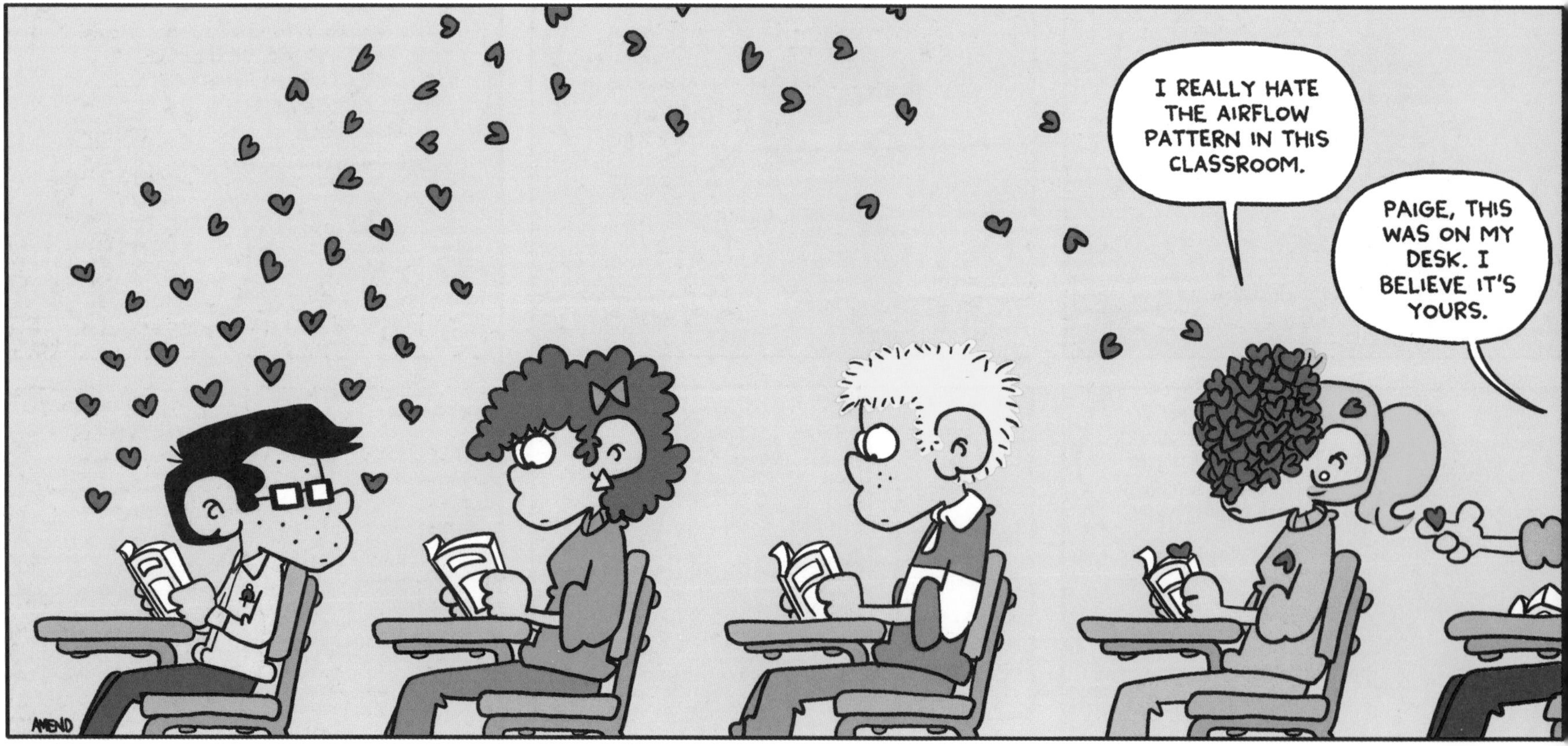
I REALLY HATE THE AIRFLOW PATTERN IN THIS CLASSROOM.
PAIGE, THIS WAS ON MY DESK. I BELIEVE IT'S YOURS.
AMEND

Lucky Guess

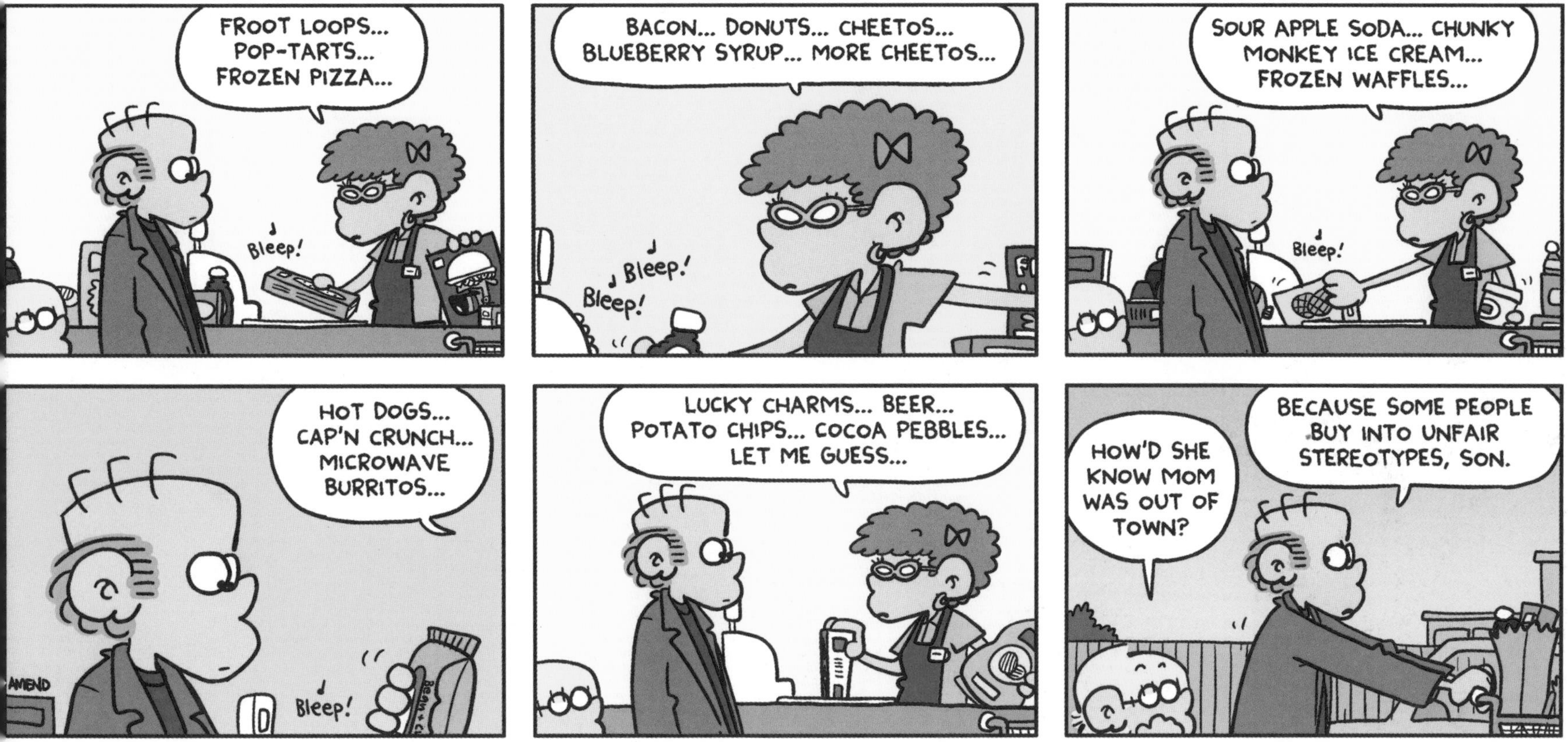
FROOT LOOPS... POP-TARTS... FROZEN PIZZA...
Bleep!
BACON... DONUTS... CHEETOS... BLUEBERRY SYRUP... MORE CHEETOS...
Bleep!
Bleep!
SOUR APPLE SODA... CHUNKY MONKEY ICE CREAM... FROZEN WAFFLES...
Bleep!
HOT DOGS... CAP'N CRUNCH... MICROWAVE BURRITOS...
AMEND
Bleep!
LUCKY CHARMS... BEER... POTATO CHIPS... COCOA PEBBLES... LET ME GUESS...
HOW'D SHE KNOW MOM WAS OUT OF TOWN?
BECAUSE SOME PEOPLE BUY INTO UNFAIR STEREOTYPES, SON.

Higher Achiever

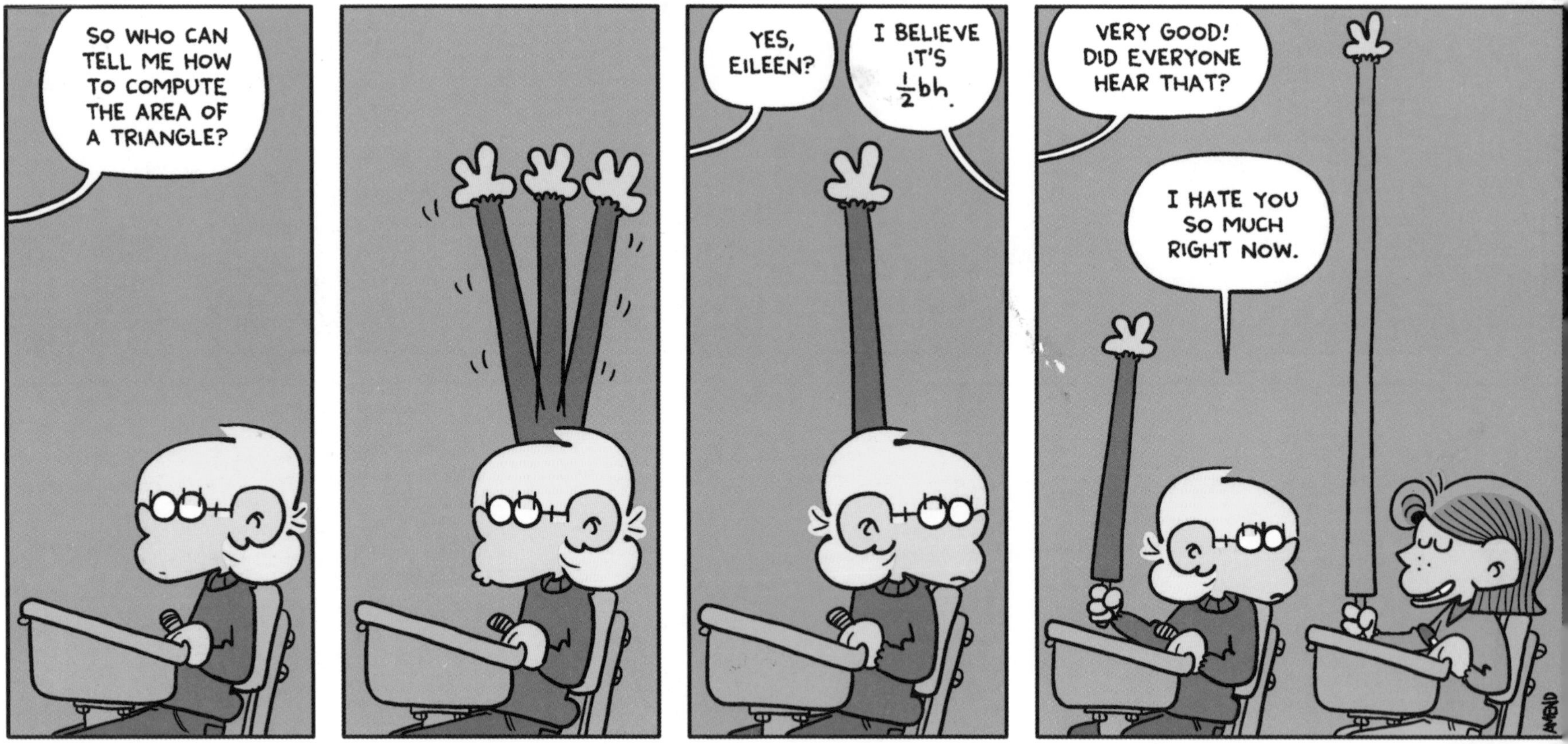
SO WHO CAN TELL ME HOW TO COMPUTE THE AREA OF A TRIANGLE?
YES, EILEEN?
I BELIEVE IT'S $\frac{1}{2}bh$.
VERY GOOD! DID EVERYONE HEAR THAT?
I HATE YOU SO MUCH RIGHT NOW.
AMEND

Dial T for Twitter

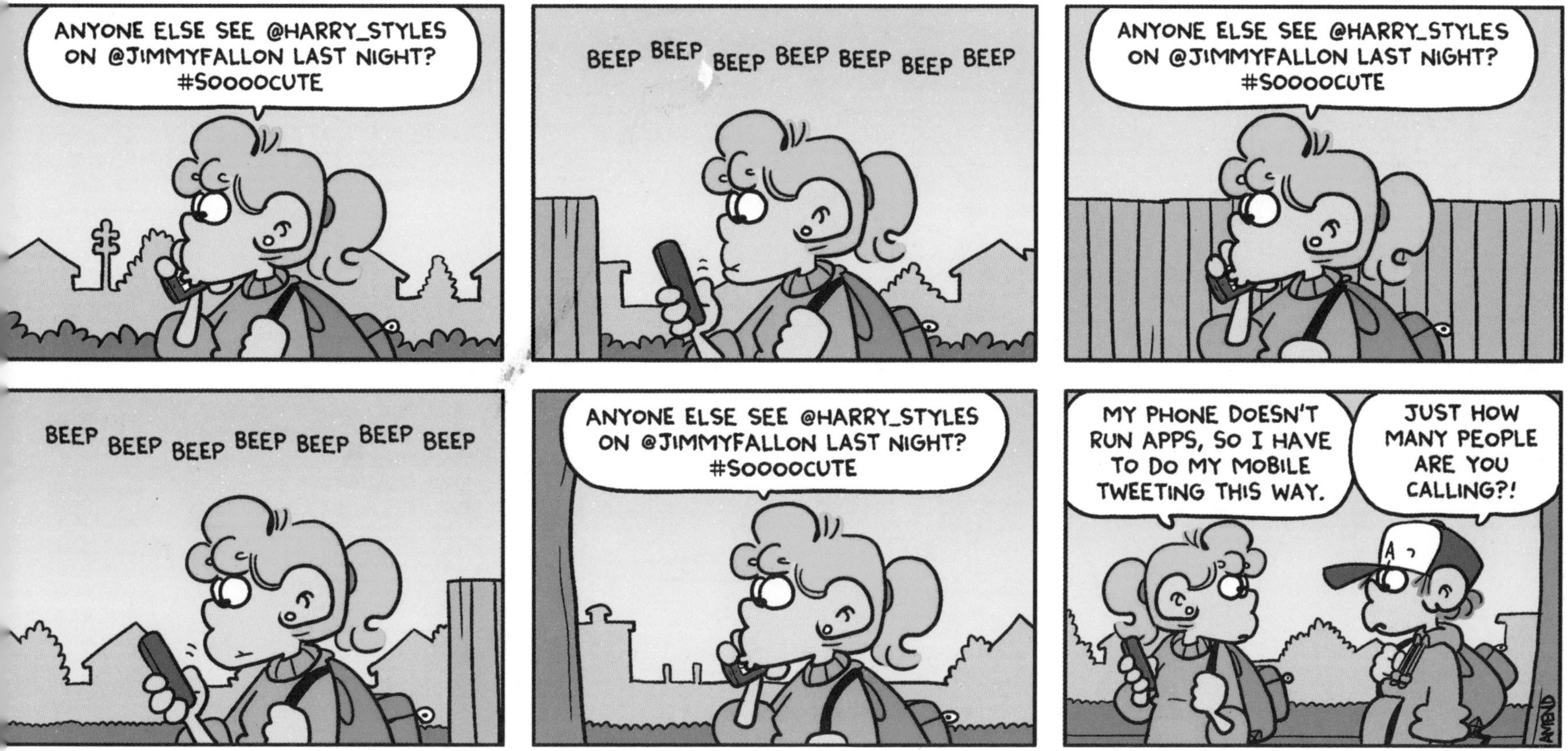

ANYONE ELSE SEE @HARRY_STYLES ON @JIMMYFALLON LAST NIGHT? #SOOOOCUTE
BEEP BEEP BEEP BEEP BEEP BEEP BEEP
ANYONE ELSE SEE @HARRY_STYLES ON @JIMMYFALLON LAST NIGHT? #SOOOOCUTE
BEEP BEEP BEEP BEEP BEEP BEEP BEEP
ANYONE ELSE SEE @HARRY_STYLES ON @JIMMYFALLON LAST NIGHT? #SOOOOCUTE
MY PHONE DOESN'T RUN APPS, SO I HAVE TO DO MY MOBILE TWEETING THIS WAY.
JUST HOW MANY PEOPLE ARE YOU CALLING?!

Starcraft Gibberish

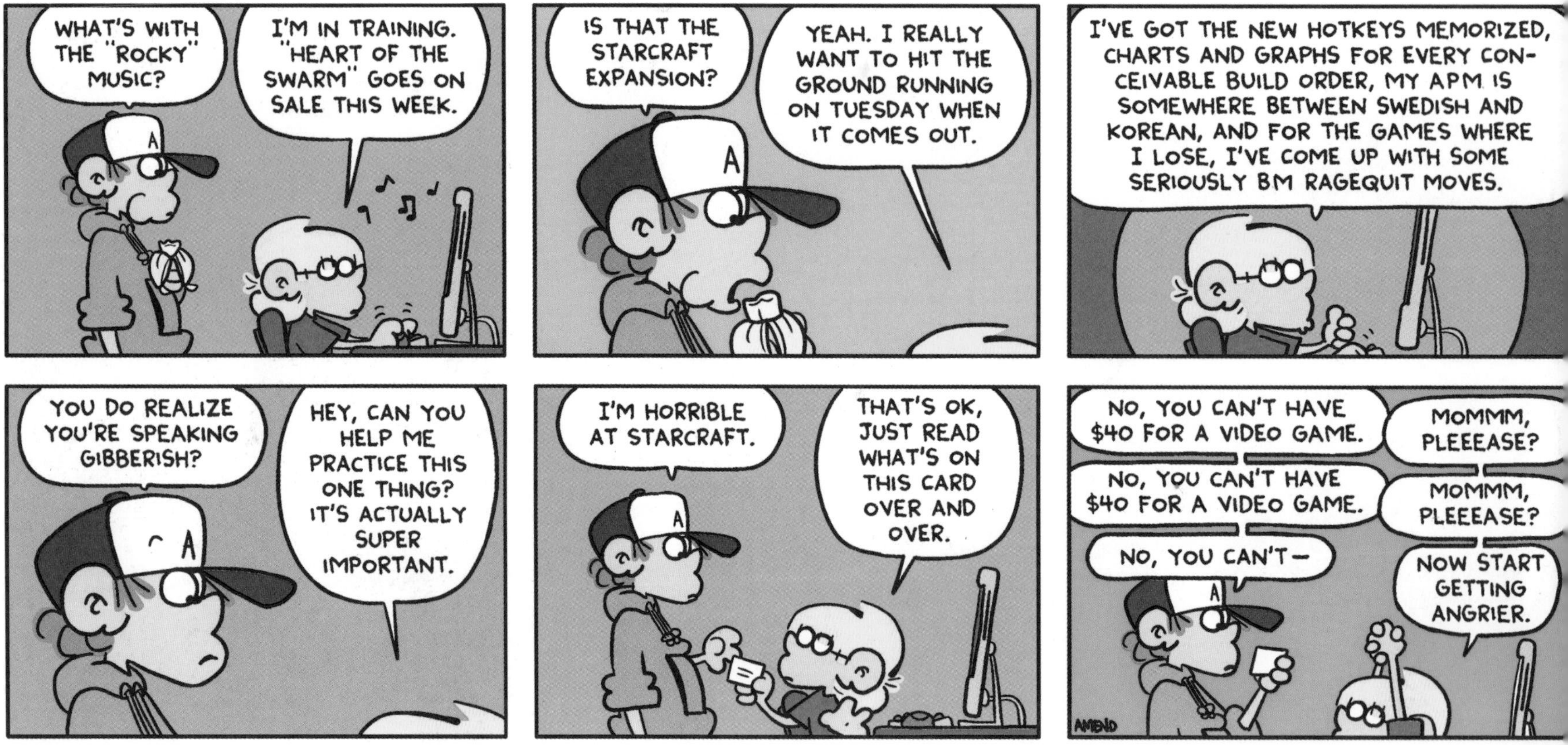
WHAT'S WITH THE "ROCKY" MUSIC?
I'M IN TRAINING. "HEART OF THE SWARM" GOES ON SALE THIS WEEK.
IS THAT THE STARCRAFT EXPANSION?
YEAH. I REALLY WANT TO HIT THE GROUND RUNNING ON TUESDAY WHEN IT COMES OUT.
I'VE GOT THE NEW HOTKEYS MEMORIZED, CHARTS AND GRAPHS FOR EVERY CONCEIVABLE BUILD ORDER, MY APM IS SOMEWHERE BETWEEN SWEDISH AND KOREAN, AND FOR THE GAMES WHERE I LOSE, I'VE COME UP WITH SOME SERIOUSLY BM RAGEQUIT MOVES.
YOU DO REALIZE YOU'RE SPEAKING GIBBERISH?
HEY, CAN YOU HELP ME PRACTICE THIS ONE THING? IT'S ACTUALLY SUPER IMPORTANT.
I'M HORRIBLE AT STARCRAFT.
THAT'S OK, JUST READ WHAT'S ON THIS CARD OVER AND OVER.
NO, YOU CAN'T HAVE $40 FOR A VIDEO GAME.
MOMMM, PLEEEASE?
NO, YOU CAN'T HAVE $40 FOR A VIDEO GAME.
MOMMM, PLEEEASE?
NO, YOU CAN'T—
NOW START GETTING ANGRIER.
AMEND

Hot Tips

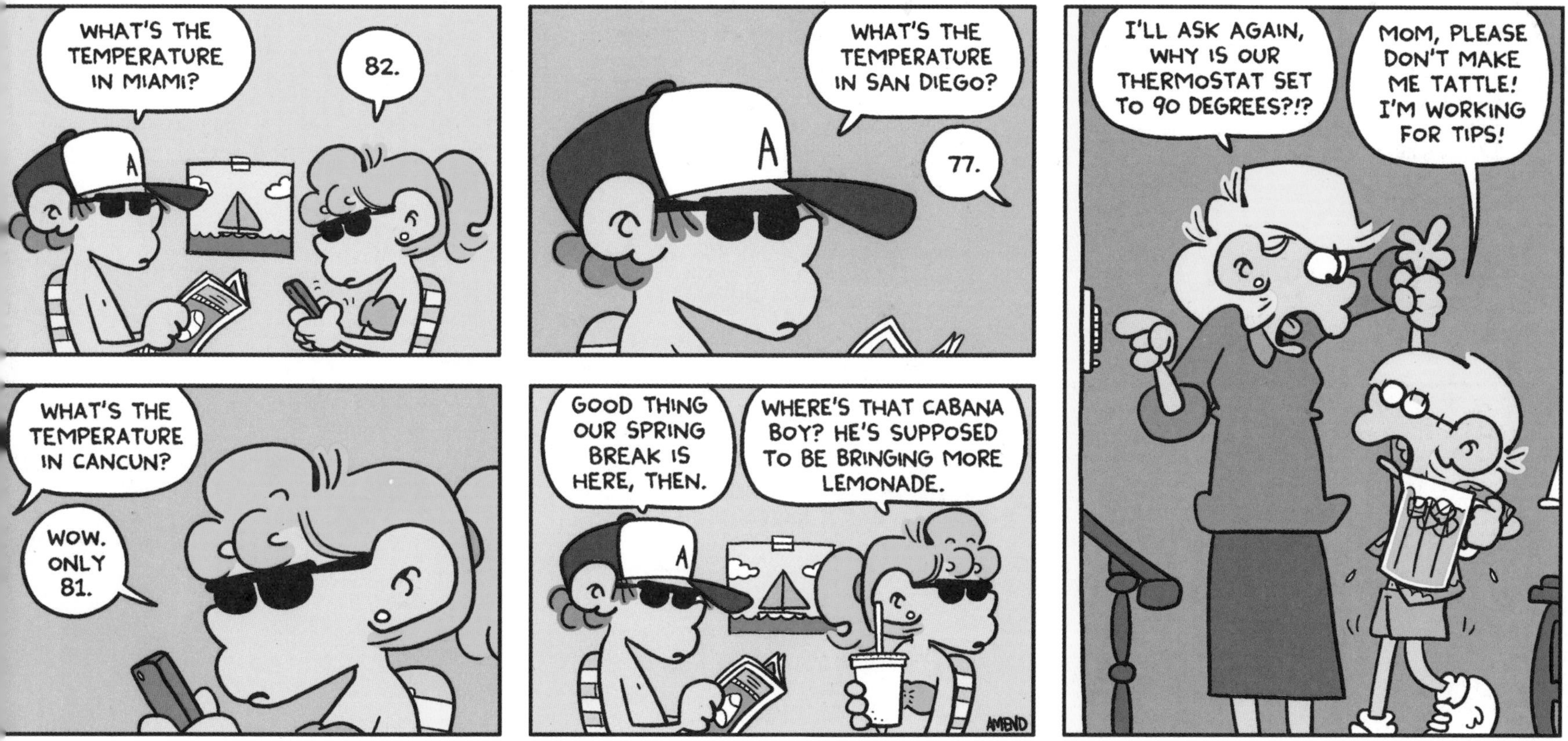
WHAT'S THE TEMPERATURE IN MIAMI?
82.
WHAT'S THE TEMPERATURE IN SAN DIEGO?
77.
WHAT'S THE TEMPERATURE IN CANCUN?
WOW. ONLY 81.
GOOD THING OUR SPRING BREAK IS HERE, THEN.
WHERE'S THAT CABANA BOY? HE'S SUPPOSED TO BE BRINGING MORE LEMONADE.
AMEND
I'LL ASK AGAIN, WHY IS OUR THERMOSTAT SET TO 90 DEGREES?!?
MOM, PLEASE DON'T MAKE ME TATTLE! I'M WORKING FOR TIPS!

Am I Okay?

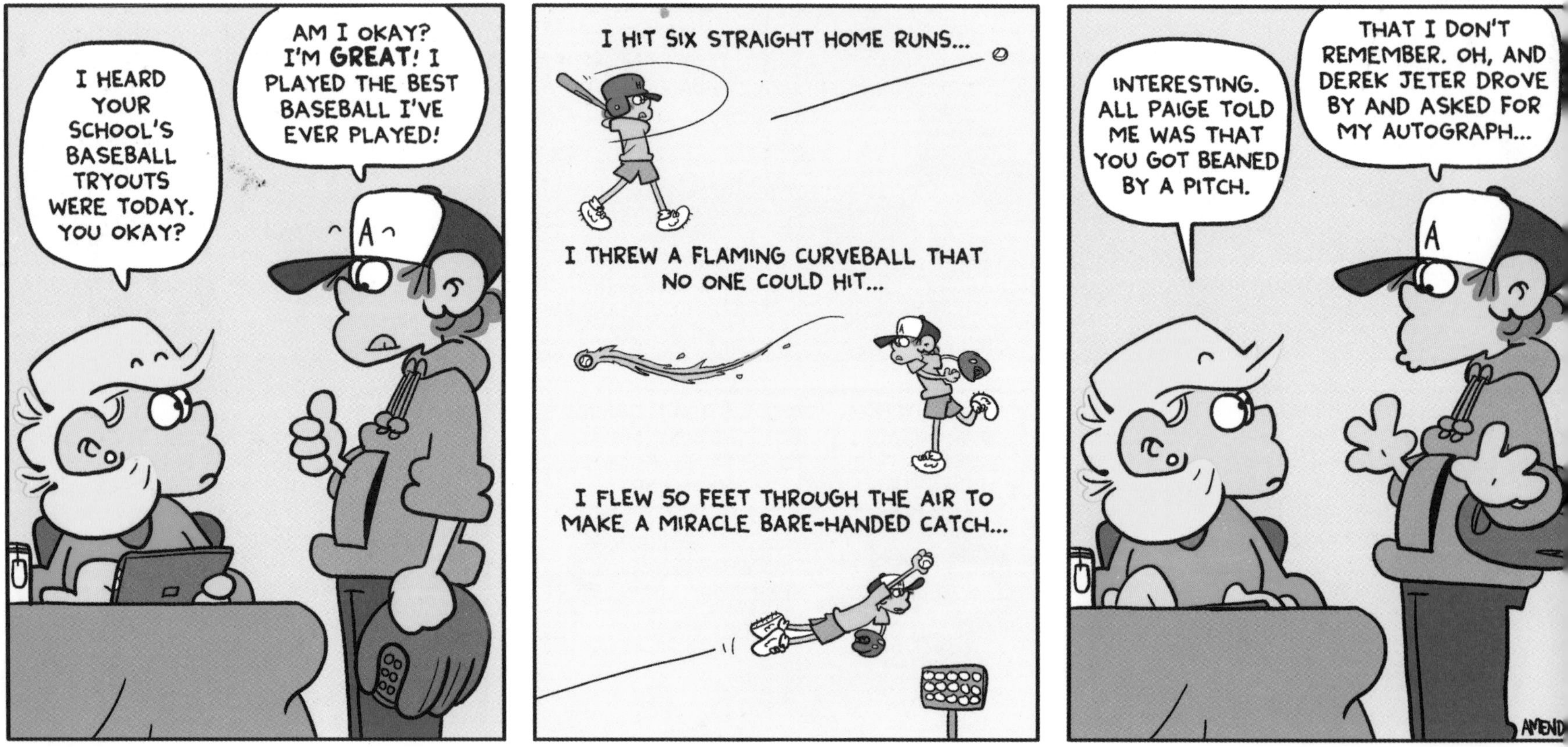
I HEARD YOUR SCHOOL'S BASEBALL TRYOUTS WERE TODAY. YOU OKAY?
AM I OKAY? I'M **GREAT**! I PLAYED THE BEST BASEBALL I'VE EVER PLAYED!
I HIT SIX STRAIGHT HOME RUNS...
I THREW A FLAMING CURVEBALL THAT NO ONE COULD HIT...
I FLEW 50 FEET THROUGH THE AIR TO MAKE A MIRACLE BARE-HANDED CATCH...
INTERESTING. ALL PAIGE TOLD ME WAS THAT YOU GOT BEANED BY A PITCH.
THAT I DON'T REMEMBER. OH, AND DEREK JETER DROVE BY AND ASKED FOR MY AUTOGRAPH...
AMEND

Pent-up Demand

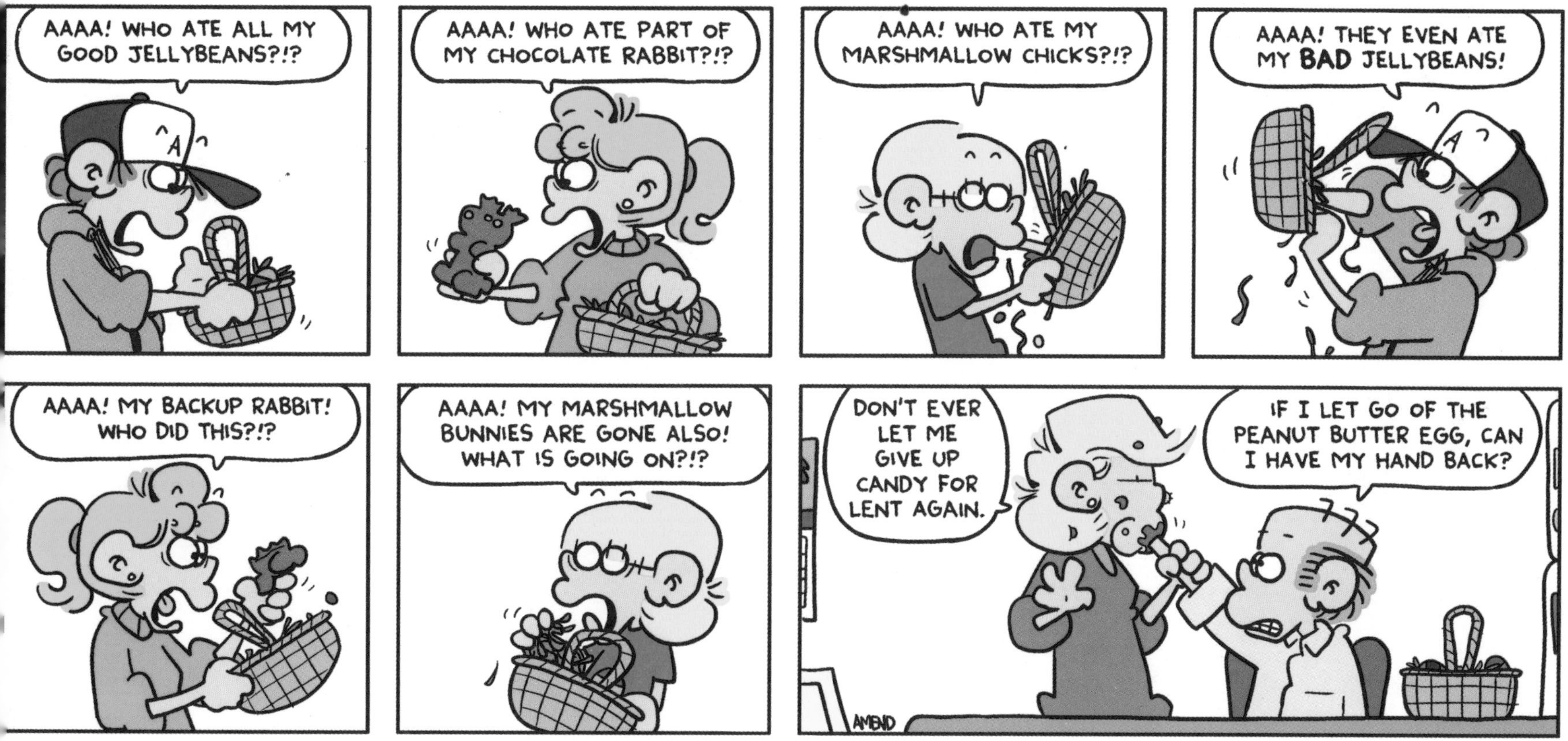
AAAA! WHO ATE ALL MY GOOD JELLYBEANS?!?
AAAA! WHO ATE PART OF MY CHOCOLATE RABBIT?!?
AAAA! WHO ATE MY MARSHMALLOW CHICKS?!?
AAAA! THEY EVEN ATE MY **BAD** JELLYBEANS!
AAAA! MY BACKUP RABBIT! WHO DID THIS?!?
AAAA! MY MARSHMALLOW BUNNIES ARE GONE ALSO! WHAT IS GOING ON?!?
DON'T EVER LET ME GIVE UP CANDY FOR LENT AGAIN.
IF I LET GO OF THE PEANUT BUTTER EGG, CAN I HAVE MY HAND BACK?
AMEND

Comics Trip

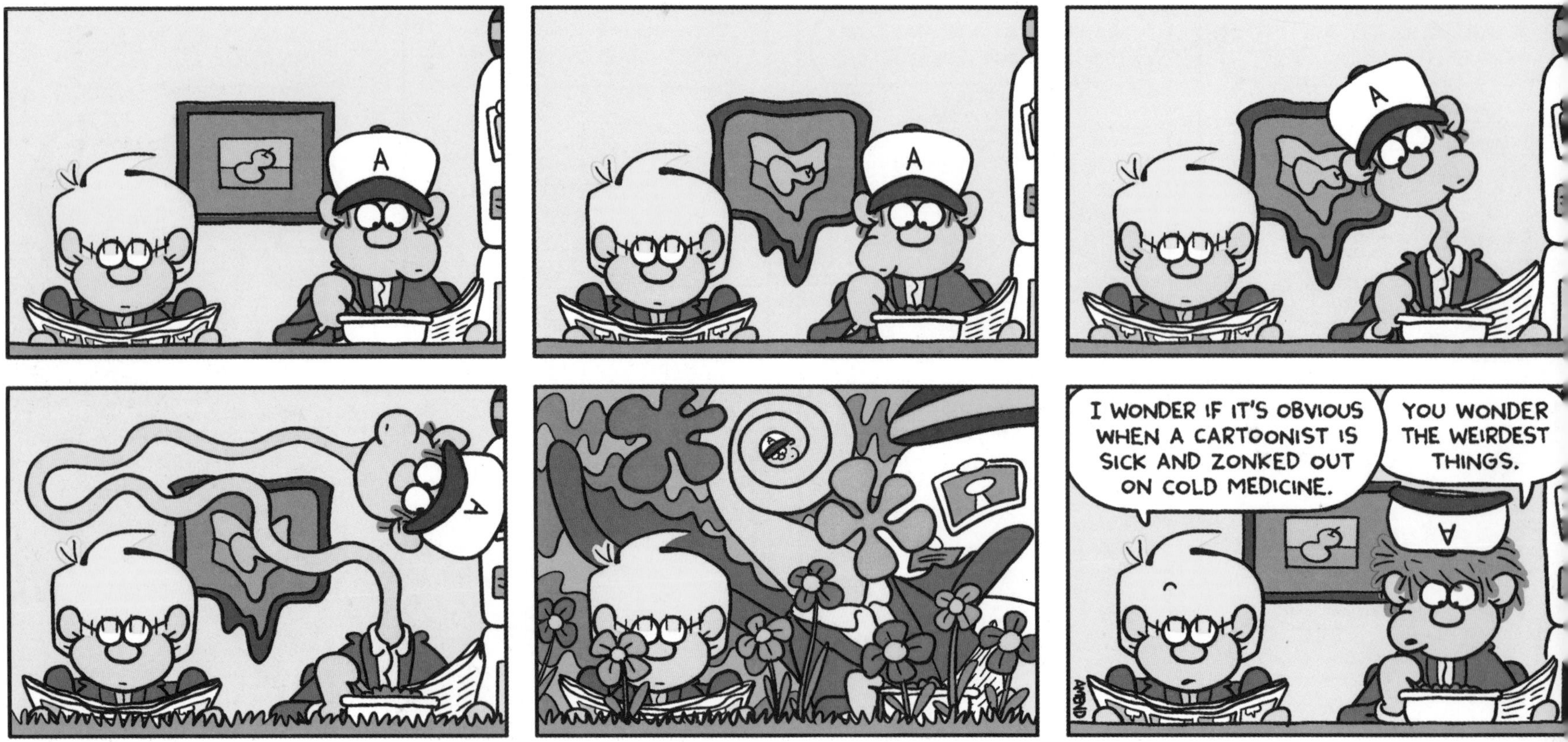

I WONDER IF IT'S OBVIOUS WHEN A CARTOONIST IS SICK AND ZONKED OUT ON COLD MEDICINE.
YOU WONDER THE WEIRDEST THINGS.

Form 1040-PUZ

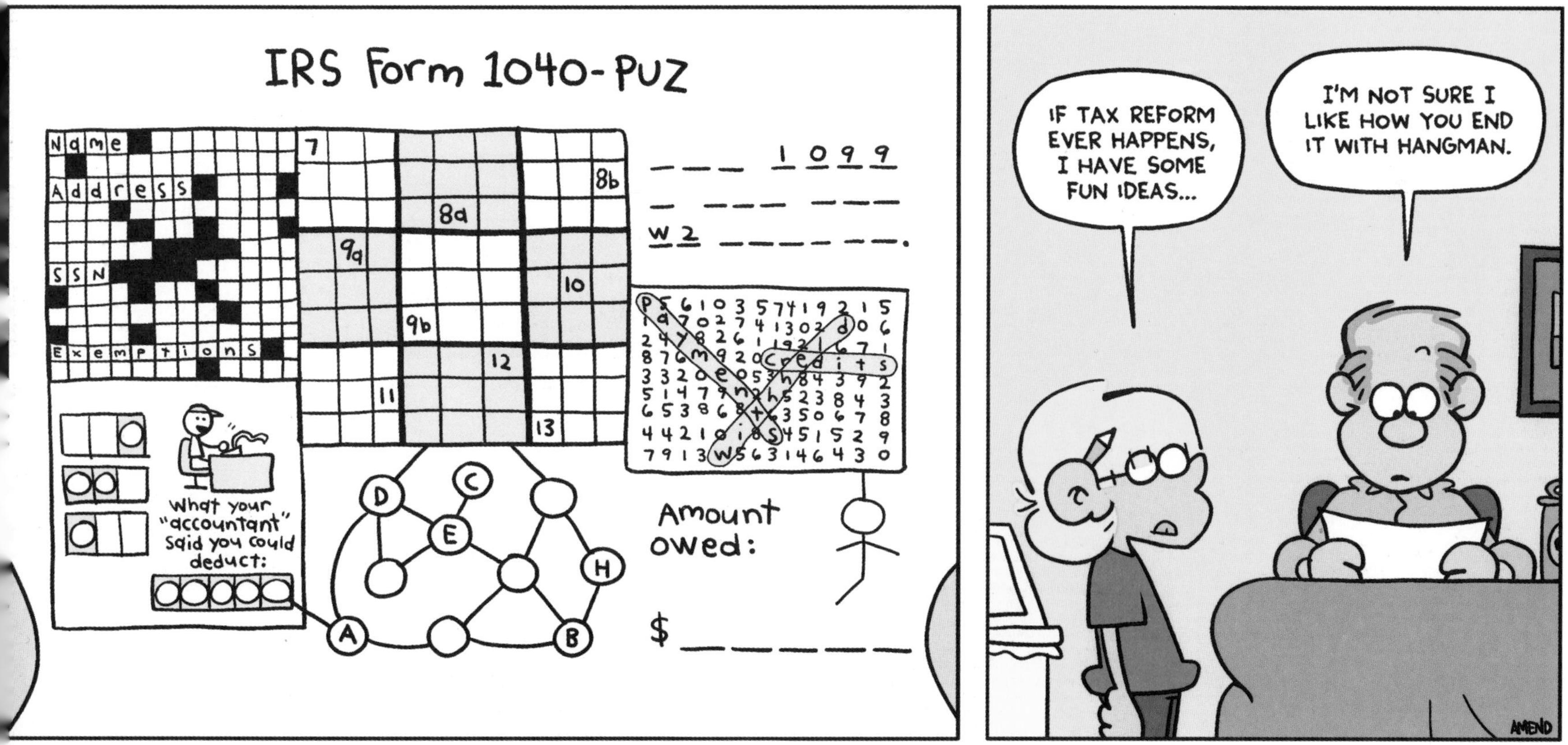
IRS Form 1040-PUZ
Name
Address
SSN
Exemptions
What your "accountant" said you could deduct:
1099
W2
credits
Amount owed:
$
IF TAX REFORM EVER HAPPENS, I HAVE SOME FUN IDEAS...
I'M NOT SURE I LIKE HOW YOU END IT WITH HANGMAN.
AMEND

Mulligan and Again

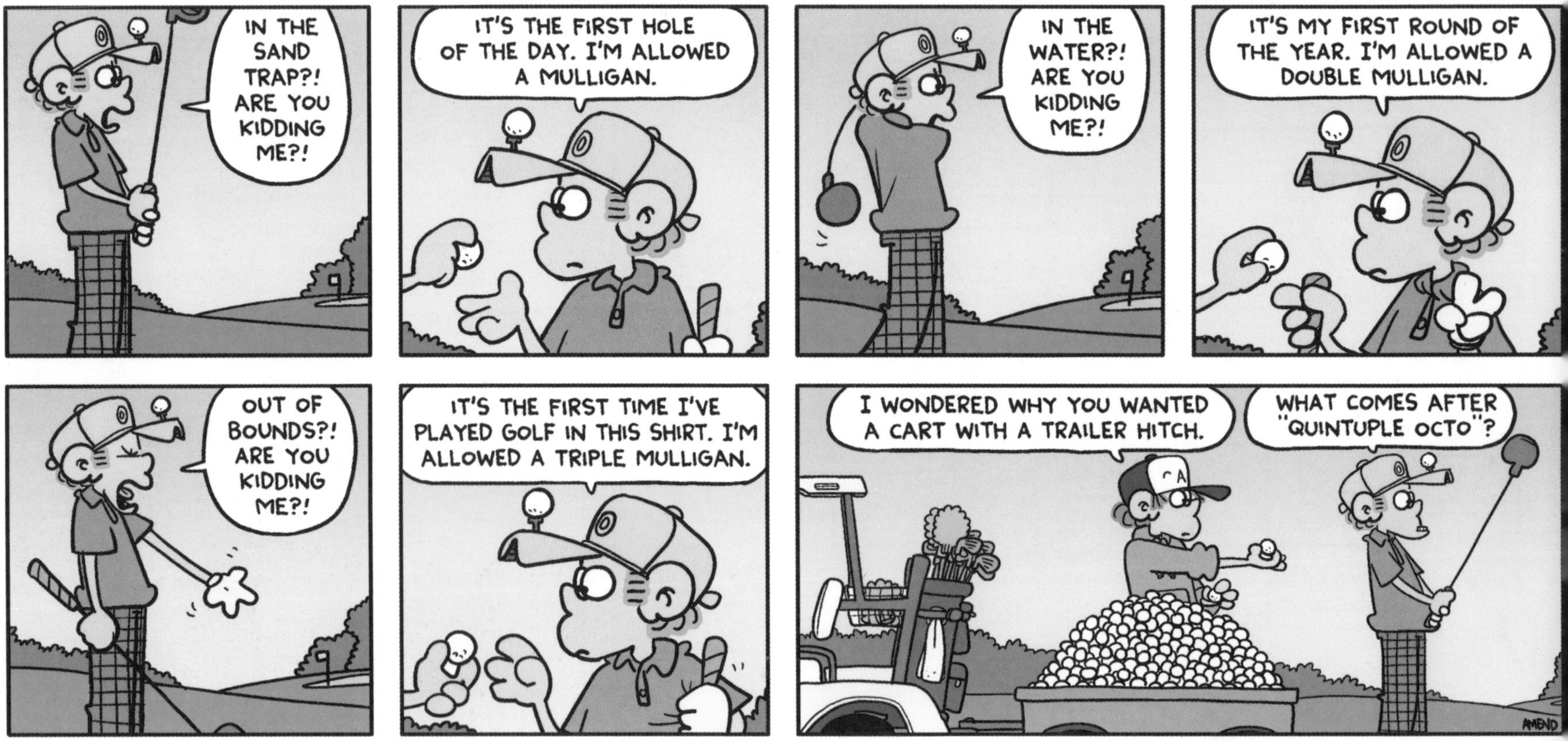
IN THE SAND TRAP?! ARE YOU KIDDING ME?!
IT'S THE FIRST HOLE OF THE DAY. I'M ALLOWED A MULLIGAN.
IN THE WATER?! ARE YOU KIDDING ME?!
IT'S MY FIRST ROUND OF THE YEAR. I'M ALLOWED A DOUBLE MULLIGAN.
OUT OF BOUNDS?! ARE YOU KIDDING ME?!
IT'S THE FIRST TIME I'VE PLAYED GOLF IN THIS SHIRT. I'M ALLOWED A TRIPLE MULLIGAN.
I WONDERED WHY YOU WANTED A CART WITH A TRAILER HITCH.
WHAT COMES AFTER "QUINTUPLE OCTO"?
AMEND

Held as Evidence

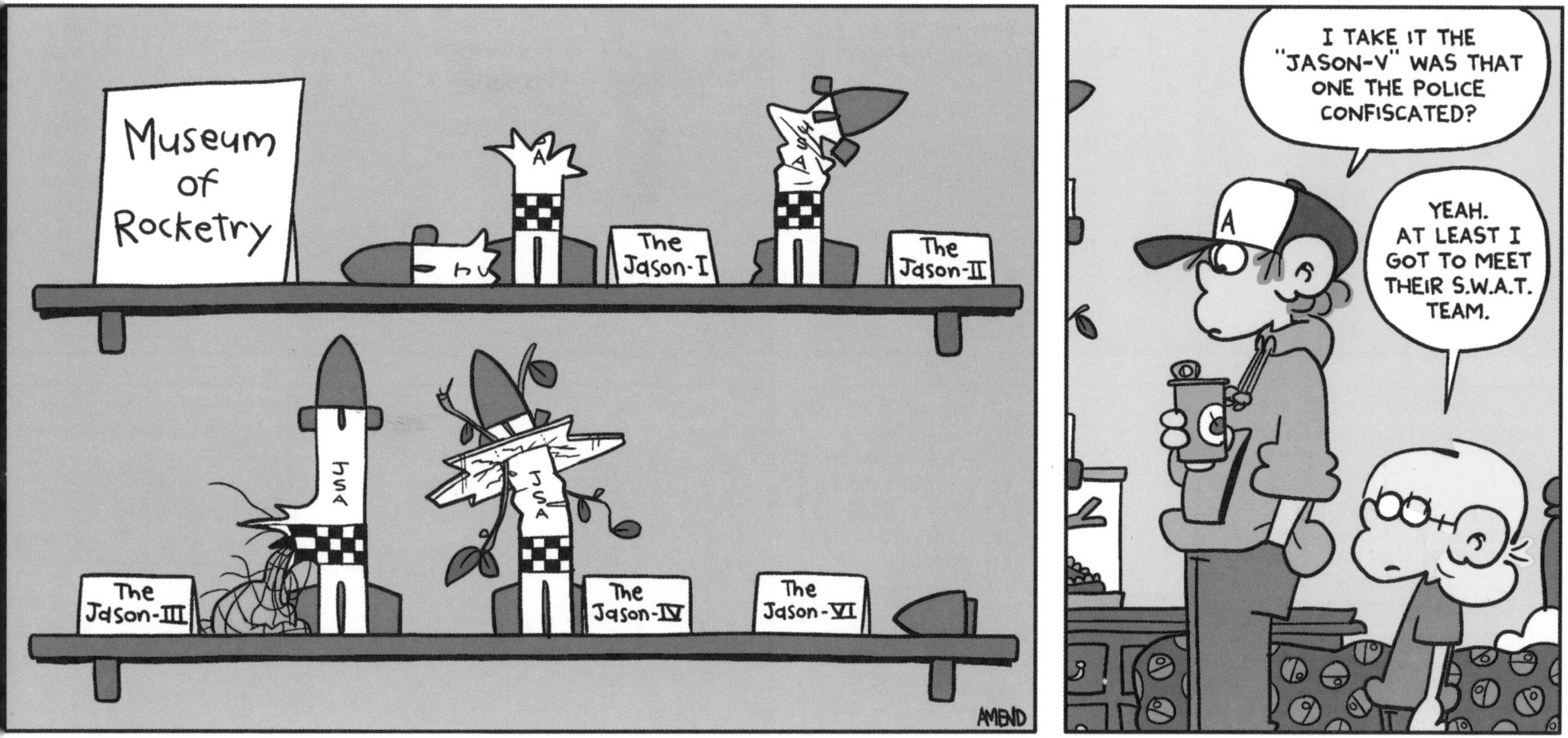
Museum of Rocketry
The Jason-I
The Jason-II
The Jason-III
The Jason-IV
The Jason-VI
AMEND
I TAKE IT THE "JASON-V" WAS THAT ONE THE POLICE CONFISCATED?
YEAH. AT LEAST I GOT TO MEET THEIR S.W.A.T. TEAM.

NDA Tryouts

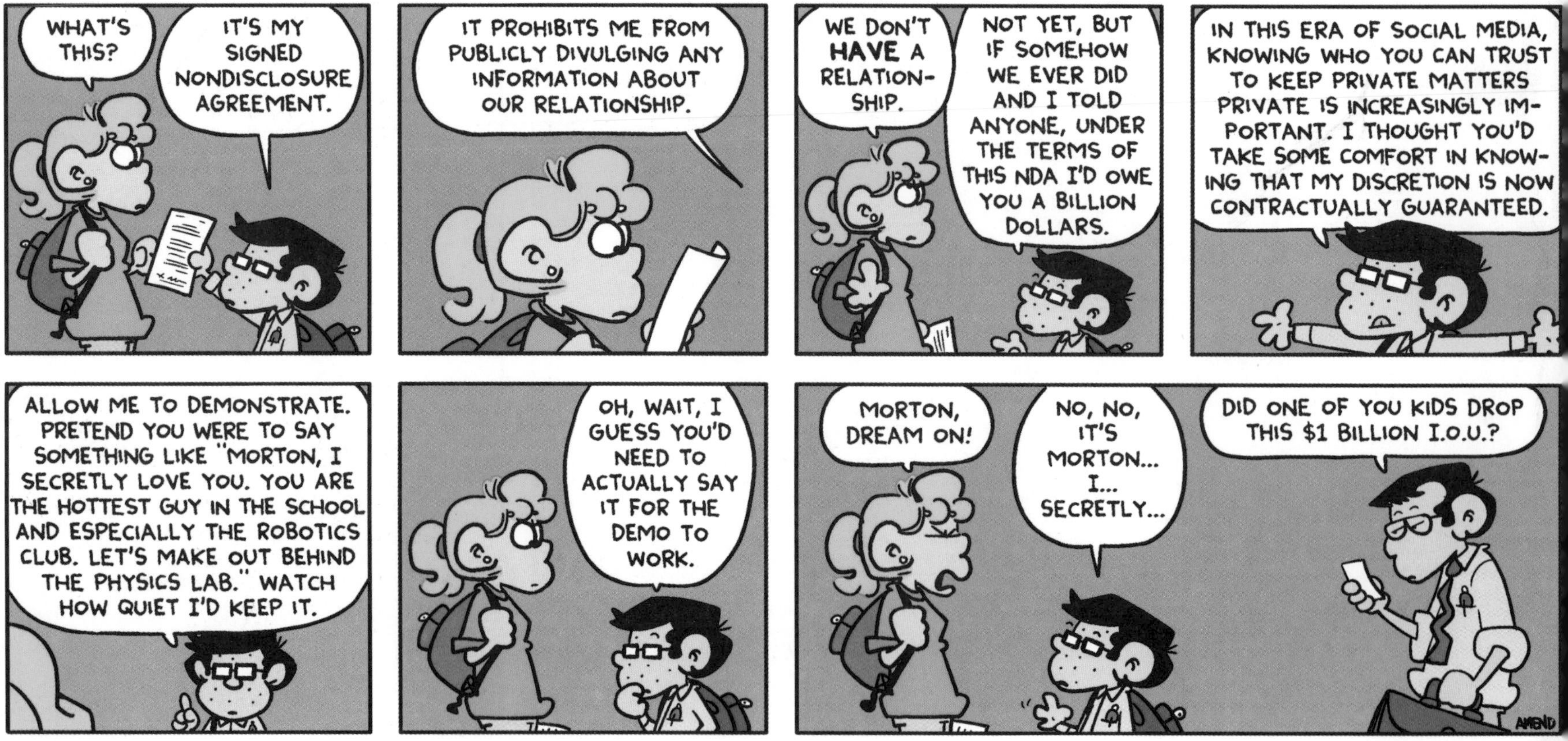
WHAT'S THIS?
IT'S MY SIGNED NONDISCLOSURE AGREEMENT.
IT PROHIBITS ME FROM PUBLICLY DIVULGING ANY INFORMATION ABOUT OUR RELATIONSHIP.
WE DON'T HAVE A RELATION-SHIP.
NOT YET, BUT IF SOMEHOW WE EVER DID AND I TOLD ANYONE, UNDER THE TERMS OF THIS NDA I'D OWE YOU A BILLION DOLLARS.
IN THIS ERA OF SOCIAL MEDIA, KNOWING WHO YOU CAN TRUST TO KEEP PRIVATE MATTERS PRIVATE IS INCREASINGLY IM-PORTANT. I THOUGHT YOU'D TAKE SOME COMFORT IN KNOW-ING THAT MY DISCRETION IS NOW CONTRACTUALLY GUARANTEED.
ALLOW ME TO DEMONSTRATE. PRETEND YOU WERE TO SAY SOMETHING LIKE "MORTON, I SECRETLY LOVE YOU. YOU ARE THE HOTTEST GUY IN THE SCHOOL AND ESPECIALLY THE ROBOTICS CLUB. LET'S MAKE OUT BEHIND THE PHYSICS LAB." WATCH HOW QUIET I'D KEEP IT.
OH, WAIT, I GUESS YOU'D NEED TO ACTUALLY SAY IT FOR THE DEMO TO WORK.
MORTON, DREAM ON!
NO, NO, IT'S MORTON... I... SECRETLY...
DID ONE OF YOU KIDS DROP THIS $1 BILLION I.O.U.?
AMEND

Field Trips

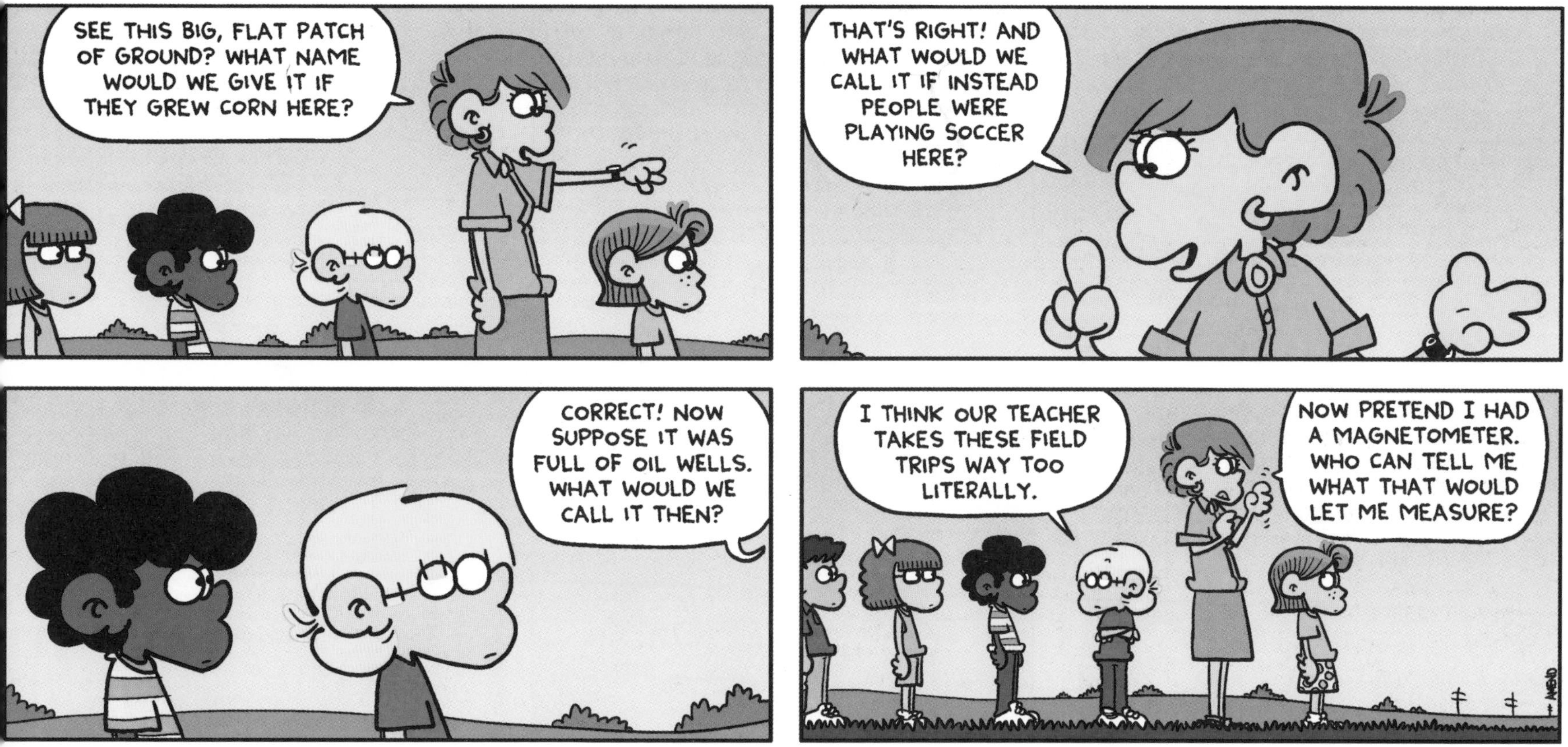

SEE THIS BIG, FLAT PATCH OF GROUND? WHAT NAME WOULD WE GIVE IT IF THEY GREW CORN HERE?
THAT'S RIGHT! AND WHAT WOULD WE CALL IT IF INSTEAD PEOPLE WERE PLAYING SOCCER HERE?
CORRECT! NOW SUPPOSE IT WAS FULL OF OIL WELLS. WHAT WOULD WE CALL IT THEN?
I THINK OUR TEACHER TAKES THESE FIELD TRIPS WAY TOO LITERALLY.
NOW PRETEND I HAD A MAGNETOMETER. WHO CAN TELL ME WHAT THAT WOULD LET ME MEASURE?

Finals Simulator

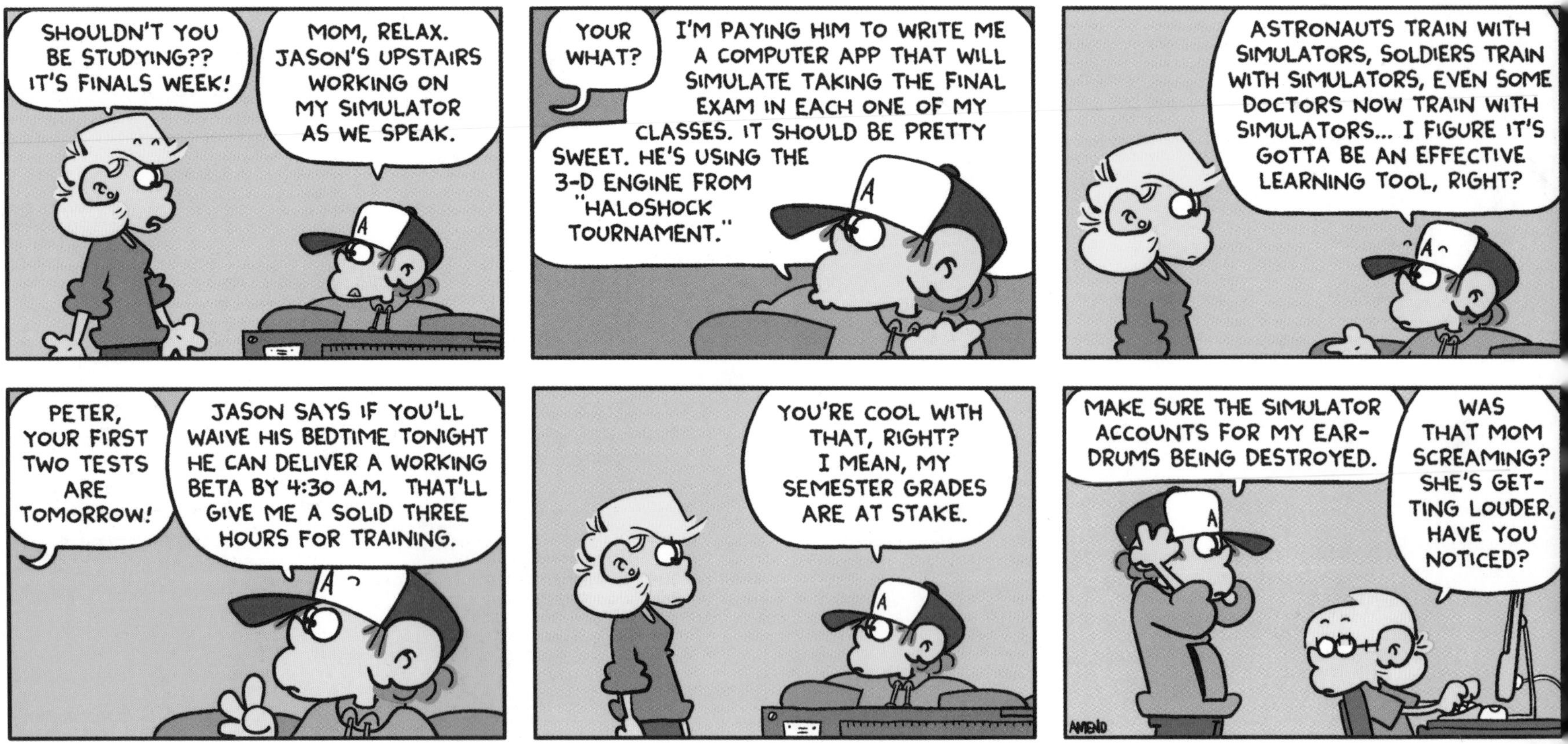

SHOULDN'T YOU BE STUDYING?? IT'S FINALS WEEK!
MOM, RELAX. JASON'S UPSTAIRS WORKING ON MY SIMULATOR AS WE SPEAK.
YOUR WHAT?
I'M PAYING HIM TO WRITE ME A COMPUTER APP THAT WILL SIMULATE TAKING THE FINAL EXAM IN EACH ONE OF MY CLASSES. IT SHOULD BE PRETTY SWEET. HE'S USING THE 3-D ENGINE FROM "HALOSHOCK TOURNAMENT."
ASTRONAUTS TRAIN WITH SIMULATORS, SOLDIERS TRAIN WITH SIMULATORS, EVEN SOME DOCTORS NOW TRAIN WITH SIMULATORS... I FIGURE IT'S GOTTA BE AN EFFECTIVE LEARNING TOOL, RIGHT?
PETER, YOUR FIRST TWO TESTS ARE TOMORROW!
JASON SAYS IF YOU'LL WAIVE HIS BEDTIME TONIGHT HE CAN DELIVER A WORKING BETA BY 4:30 A.M. THAT'LL GIVE ME A SOLID THREE HOURS FOR TRAINING.
YOU'RE COOL WITH THAT, RIGHT? I MEAN, MY SEMESTER GRADES ARE AT STAKE.
MAKE SURE THE SIMULATOR ACCOUNTS FOR MY EAR-DRUMS BEING DESTROYED.
WAS THAT MOM SCREAMING? SHE'S GET-TING LOUDER, HAVE YOU NOTICED?
AMEND

Summer Dehydration

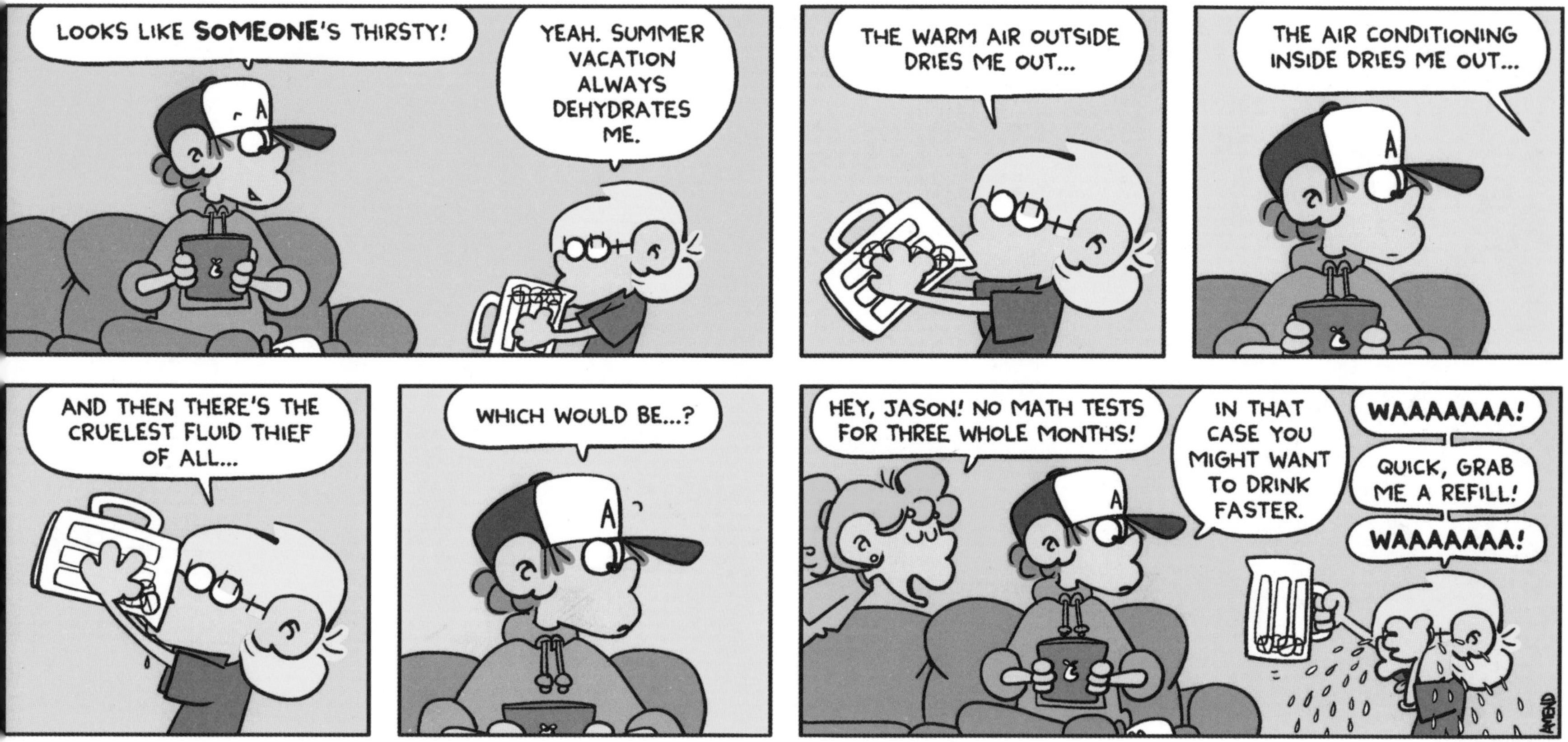
LOOKS LIKE **SOMEONE**'S THIRSTY!
YEAH. SUMMER VACATION ALWAYS DEHYDRATES ME.
THE WARM AIR OUTSIDE DRIES ME OUT...
THE AIR CONDITIONING INSIDE DRIES ME OUT...
AND THEN THERE'S THE CRUELEST FLUID THIEF OF ALL...
WHICH WOULD BE...?
HEY, JASON! NO MATH TESTS FOR THREE WHOLE MONTHS!
IN THAT CASE YOU MIGHT WANT TO DRINK FASTER.
WAAAAAAA!
QUICK, GRAB ME A REFILL!
WAAAAAAA!
AMEND

Don't Be Sour

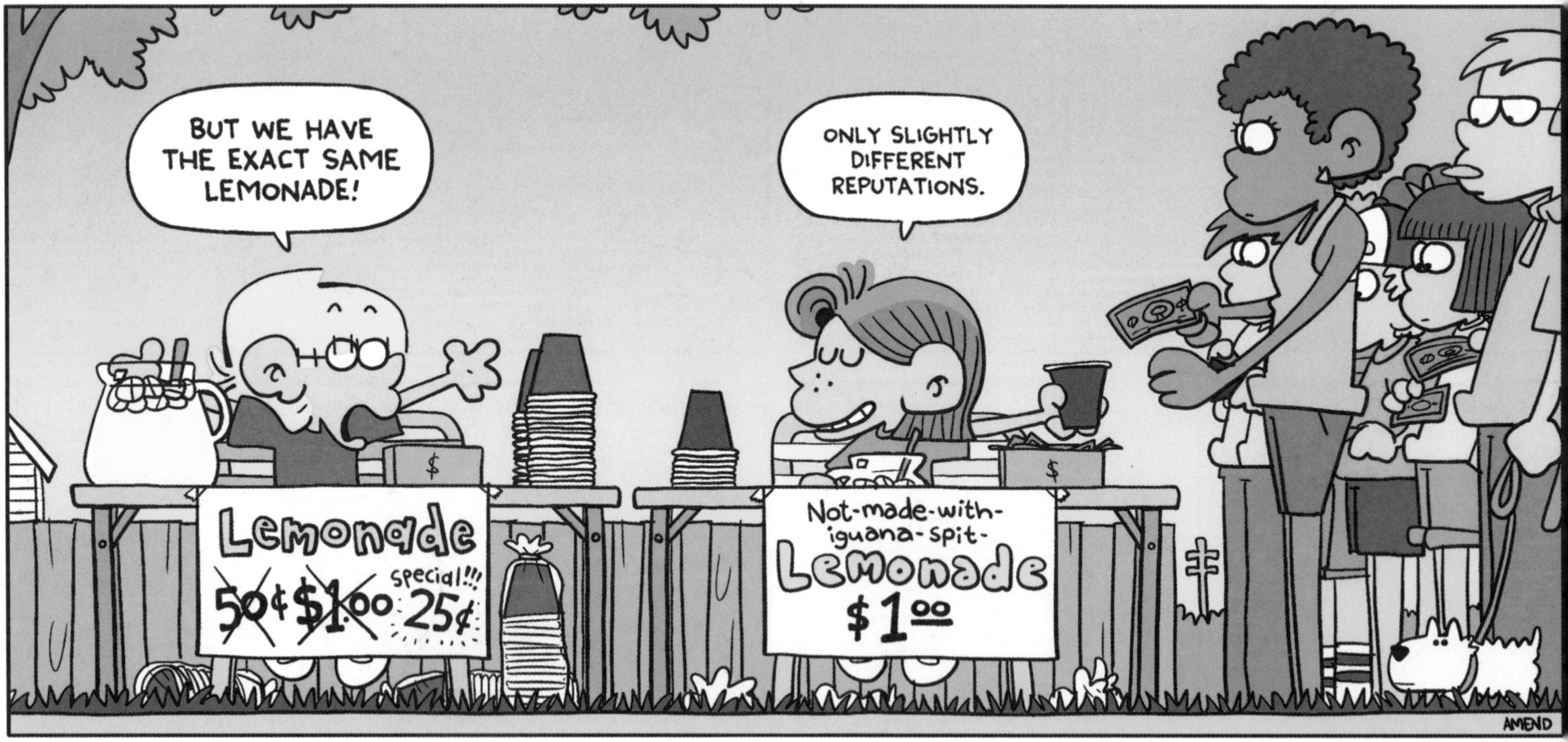
BUT WE HAVE THE EXACT SAME LEMONADE!
ONLY SLIGHTLY DIFFERENT REPUTATIONS.
Lemonade
50¢ $1.00 special!!! 25¢
$
$
Not-made-with-iguana-spit-Lemonade
$1.00
AMEND

Instagrammar

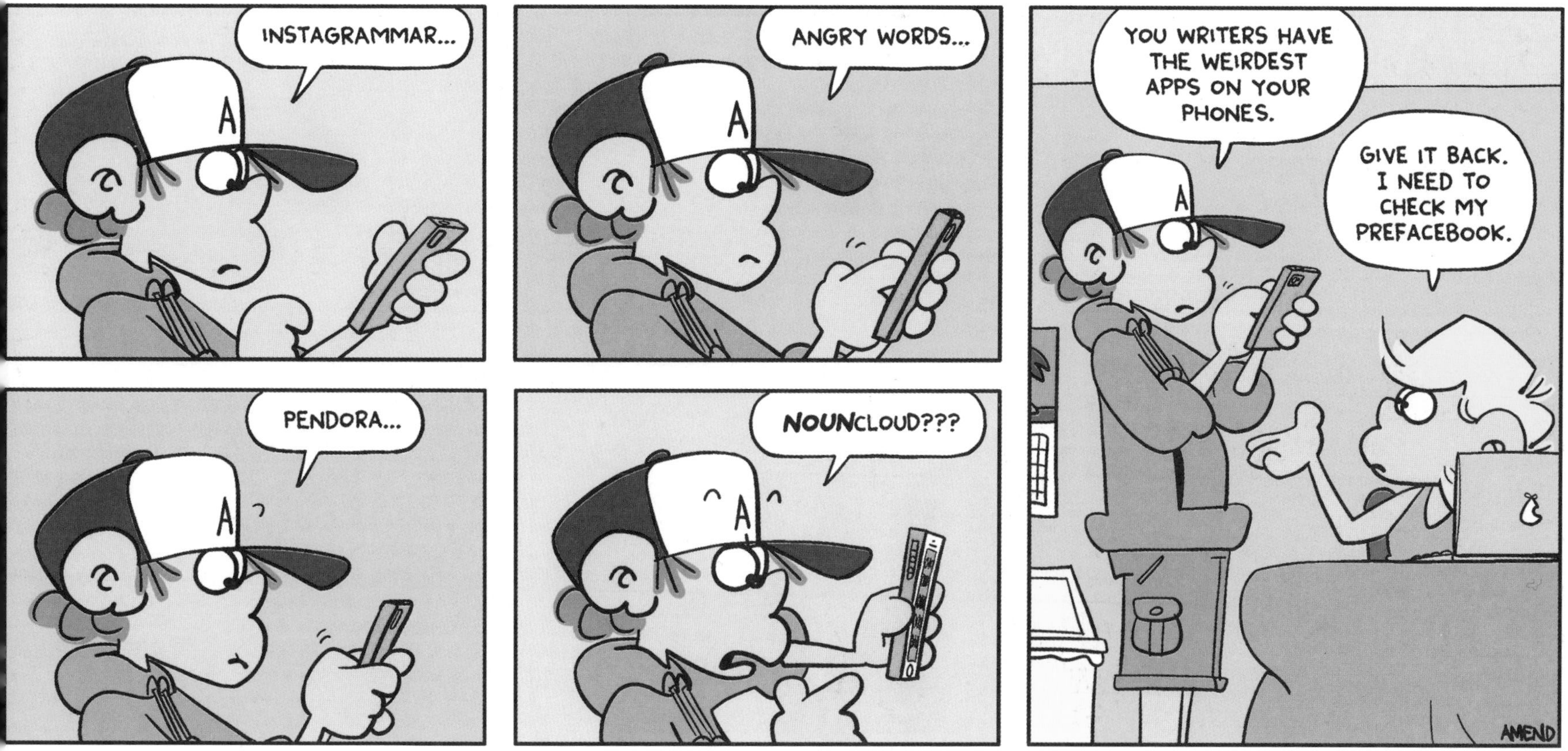
INSTAGRAMMAR...
ANGRY WORDS...
PENDORA...
NOUNCLOUD???
YOU WRITERS HAVE THE WEIRDEST APPS ON YOUR PHONES.
GIVE IT BACK. I NEED TO CHECK MY PREFACEBOOK.
AMEND

Photo Enhancement

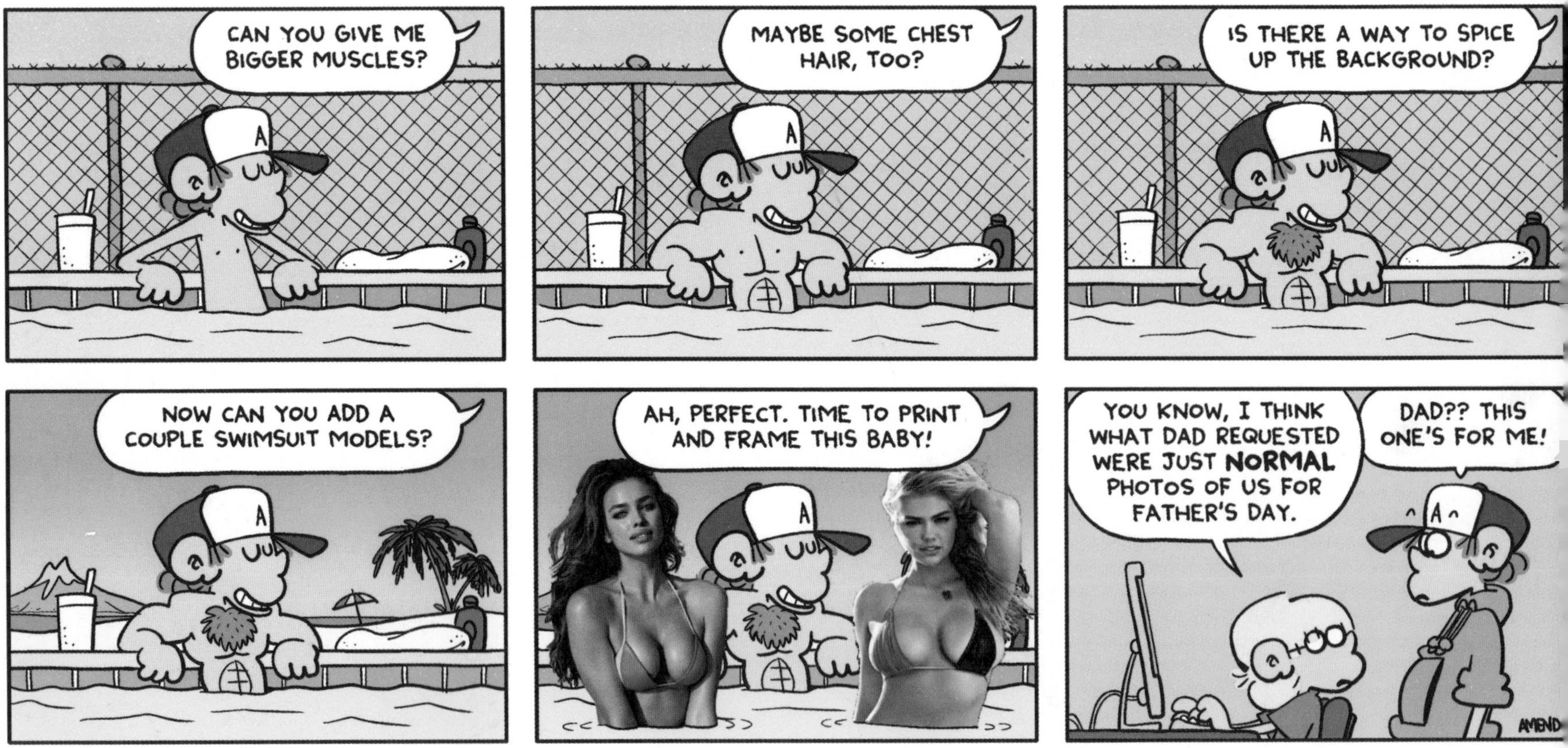
CAN YOU GIVE ME BIGGER MUSCLES?
MAYBE SOME CHEST HAIR, TOO?
IS THERE A WAY TO SPICE UP THE BACKGROUND?
NOW CAN YOU ADD A COUPLE SWIMSUIT MODELS?
AH, PERFECT. TIME TO PRINT AND FRAME THIS BABY!
YOU KNOW, I THINK WHAT DAD REQUESTED WERE JUST NORMAL PHOTOS OF US FOR FATHER'S DAY.
DAD?? THIS ONE'S FOR ME!
AMEND

Rainbow Sherbet

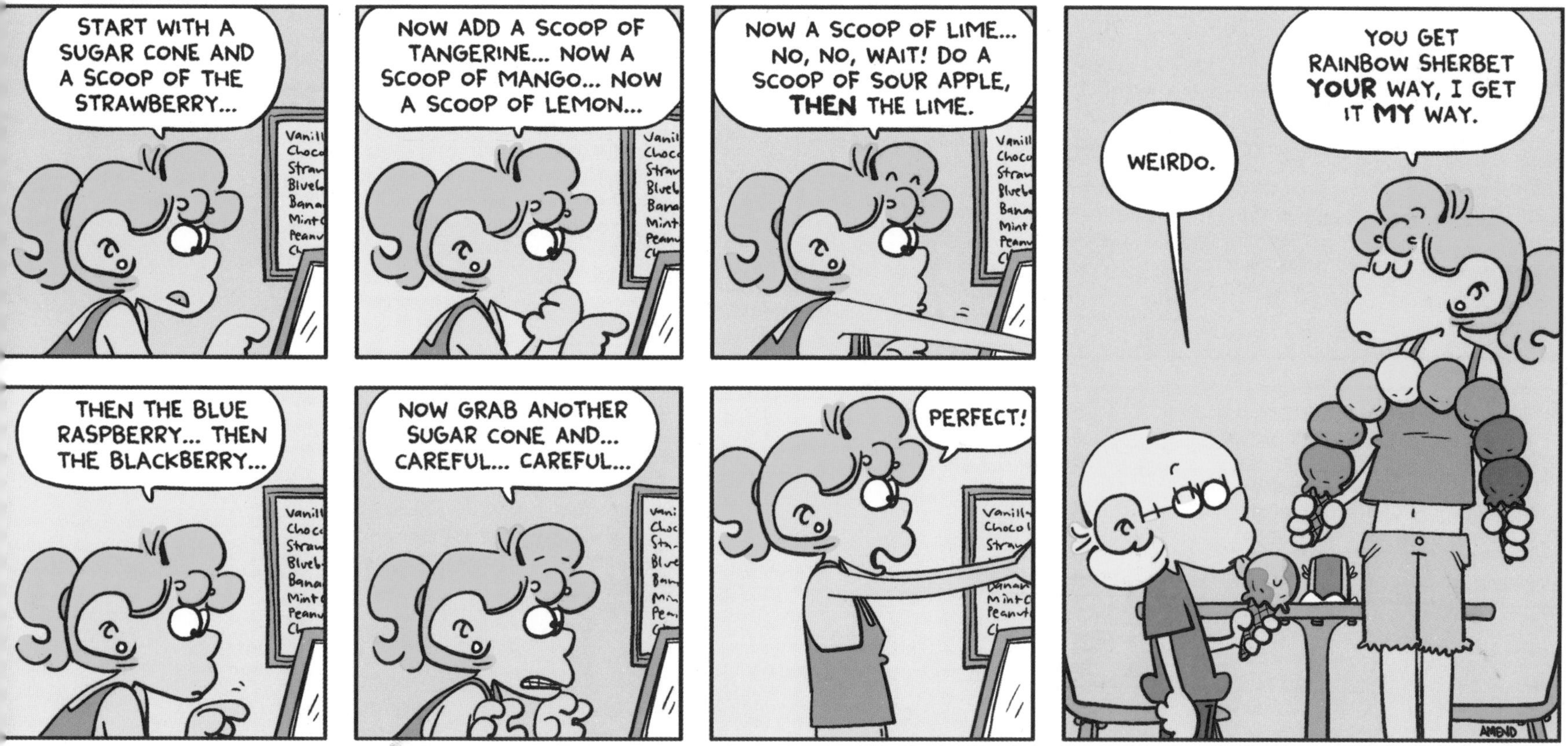

START WITH A SUGAR CONE AND A SCOOP OF THE STRAWBERRY...
NOW ADD A SCOOP OF TANGERINE... NOW A SCOOP OF MANGO... NOW A SCOOP OF LEMON...
NOW A SCOOP OF LIME... NO, NO, WAIT! DO A SCOOP OF SOUR APPLE, **THEN** THE LIME.
THEN THE BLUE RASPBERRY... THEN THE BLACKBERRY...
NOW GRAB ANOTHER SUGAR CONE AND... CAREFUL... CAREFUL...
PERFECT!
YOU GET RAINBOW SHERBET **YOUR** WAY, I GET IT **MY** WAY.
WEIRDO.
AMEND

Backdoor Bonanza

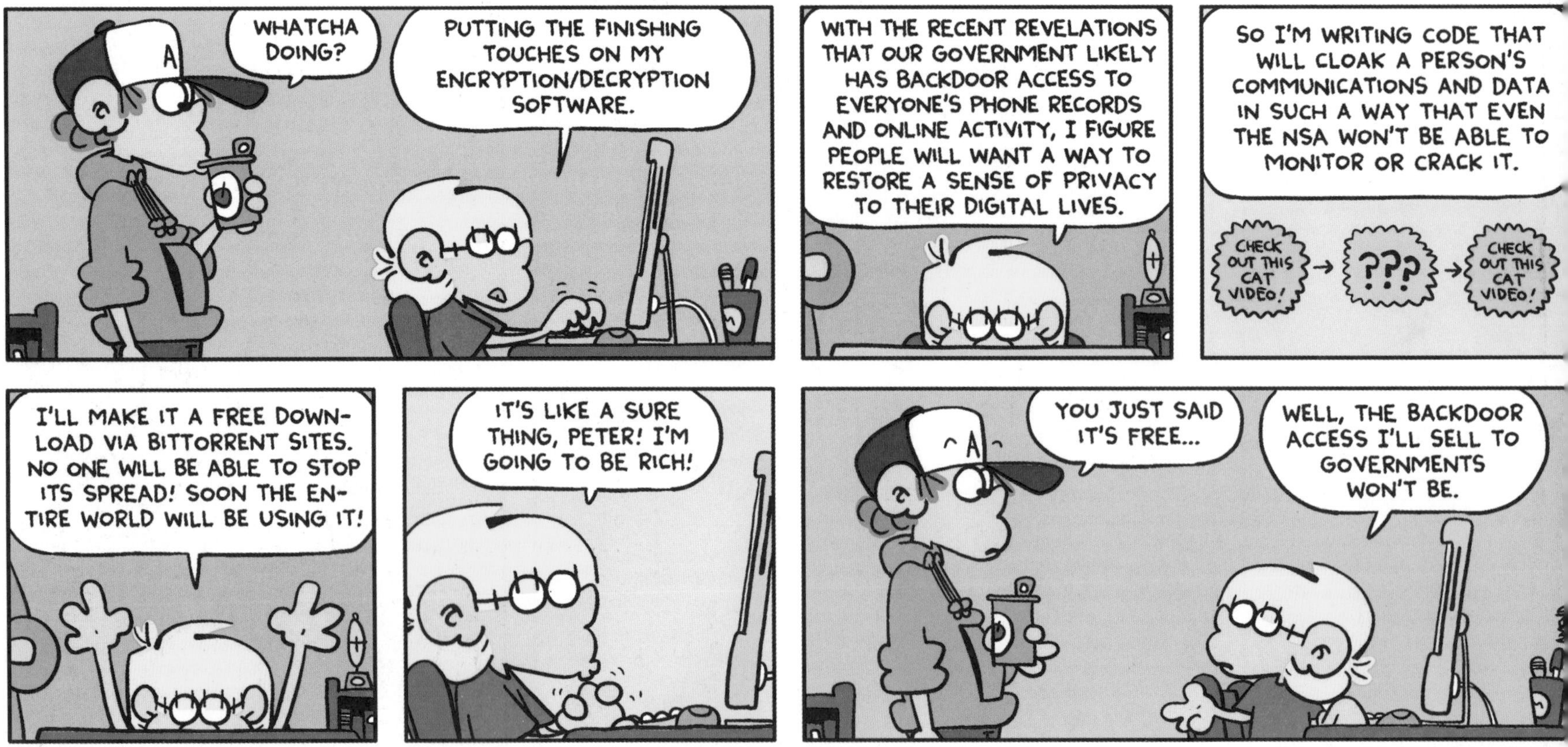

WHATCHA DOING?
PUTTING THE FINISHING TOUCHES ON MY ENCRYPTION/DECRYPTION SOFTWARE.
WITH THE RECENT REVELATIONS THAT OUR GOVERNMENT LIKELY HAS BACKDOOR ACCESS TO EVERYONE'S PHONE RECORDS AND ONLINE ACTIVITY, I FIGURE PEOPLE WILL WANT A WAY TO RESTORE A SENSE OF PRIVACY TO THEIR DIGITAL LIVES.
SO I'M WRITING CODE THAT WILL CLOAK A PERSON'S COMMUNICATIONS AND DATA IN SUCH A WAY THAT EVEN THE NSA WON'T BE ABLE TO MONITOR OR CRACK IT.
CHECK OUT THIS CAT VIDEO!
???
CHECK OUT THIS CAT VIDEO!
I'LL MAKE IT A FREE DOWNLOAD VIA BITTORRENT SITES. NO ONE WILL BE ABLE TO STOP ITS SPREAD! SOON THE ENTIRE WORLD WILL BE USING IT!
IT'S LIKE A SURE THING, PETER! I'M GOING TO BE RICH!
YOU JUST SAID IT'S FREE...
WELL, THE BACKDOOR ACCESS I'LL SELL TO GOVERNMENTS WON'T BE.

I'm Counting on You, Son

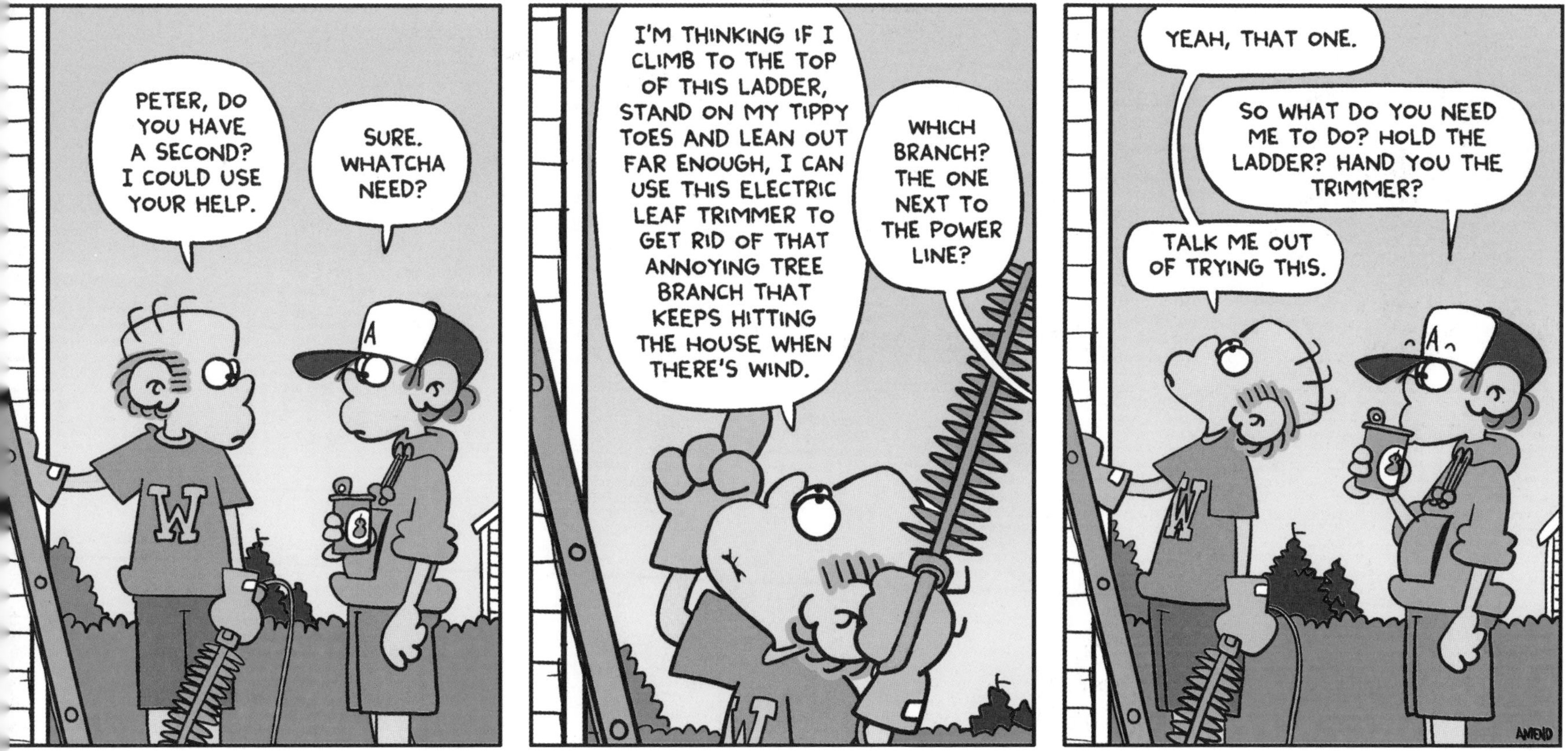

PETER, DO YOU HAVE A SECOND? I COULD USE YOUR HELP.
SURE. WHATCHA NEED?
I'M THINKING IF I CLIMB TO THE TOP OF THIS LADDER, STAND ON MY TIPPY TOES AND LEAN OUT FAR ENOUGH, I CAN USE THIS ELECTRIC LEAF TRIMMER TO GET RID OF THAT ANNOYING TREE BRANCH THAT KEEPS HITTING THE HOUSE WHEN THERE'S WIND.
WHICH BRANCH? THE ONE NEXT TO THE POWER LINE?
YEAH, THAT ONE.
SO WHAT DO YOU NEED ME TO DO? HOLD THE LADDER? HAND YOU THE TRIMMER?
TALK ME OUT OF TRYING THIS.
AMEND

Mr. Not-So-Fantastic

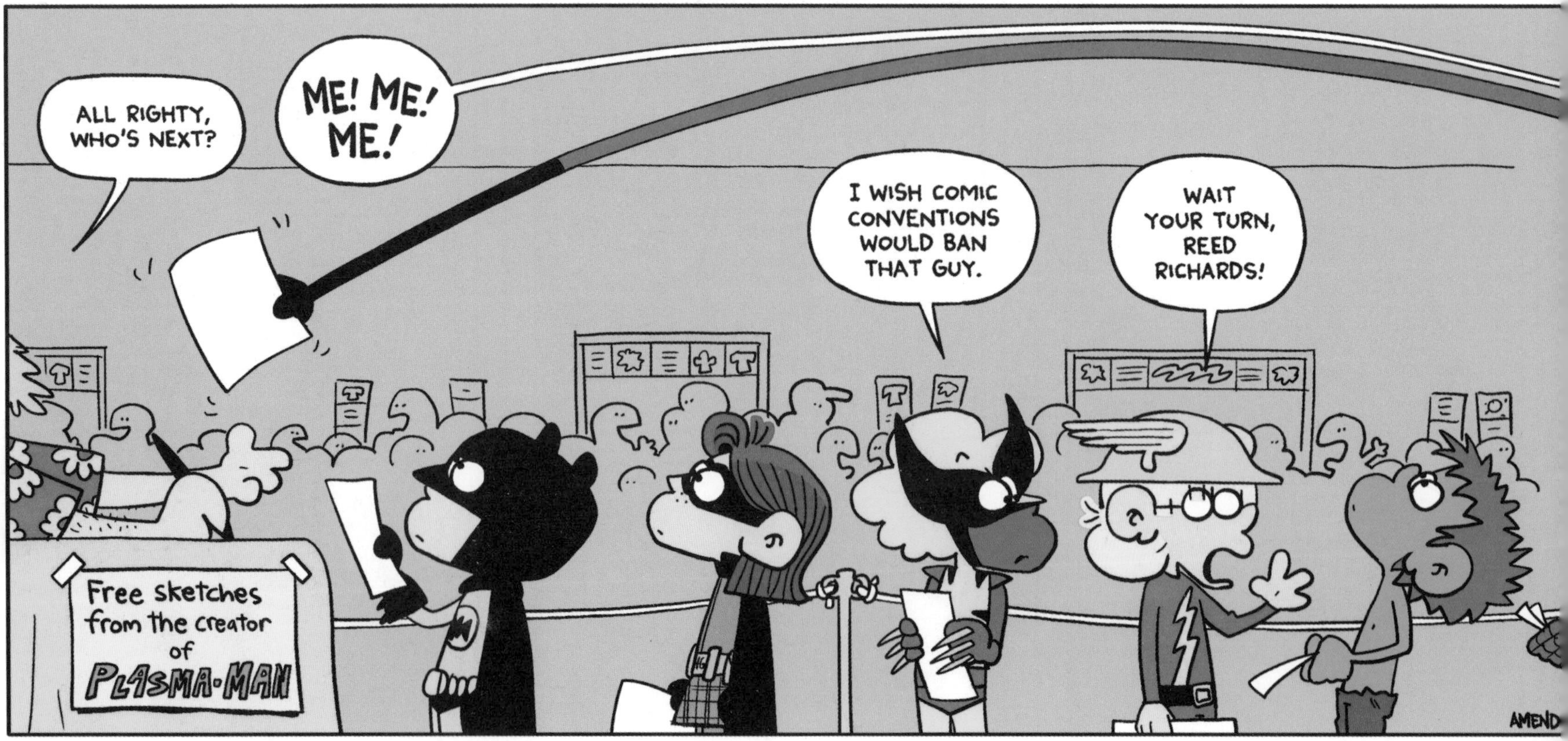
ALL RIGHTY, WHO'S NEXT?
ME! ME! ME!
I WISH COMIC CONVENTIONS WOULD BAN THAT GUY.
WAIT YOUR TURN, REED RICHARDS!
Free sketches from the creator of PLASMA-MAN
AMEND

Don't Look Down!

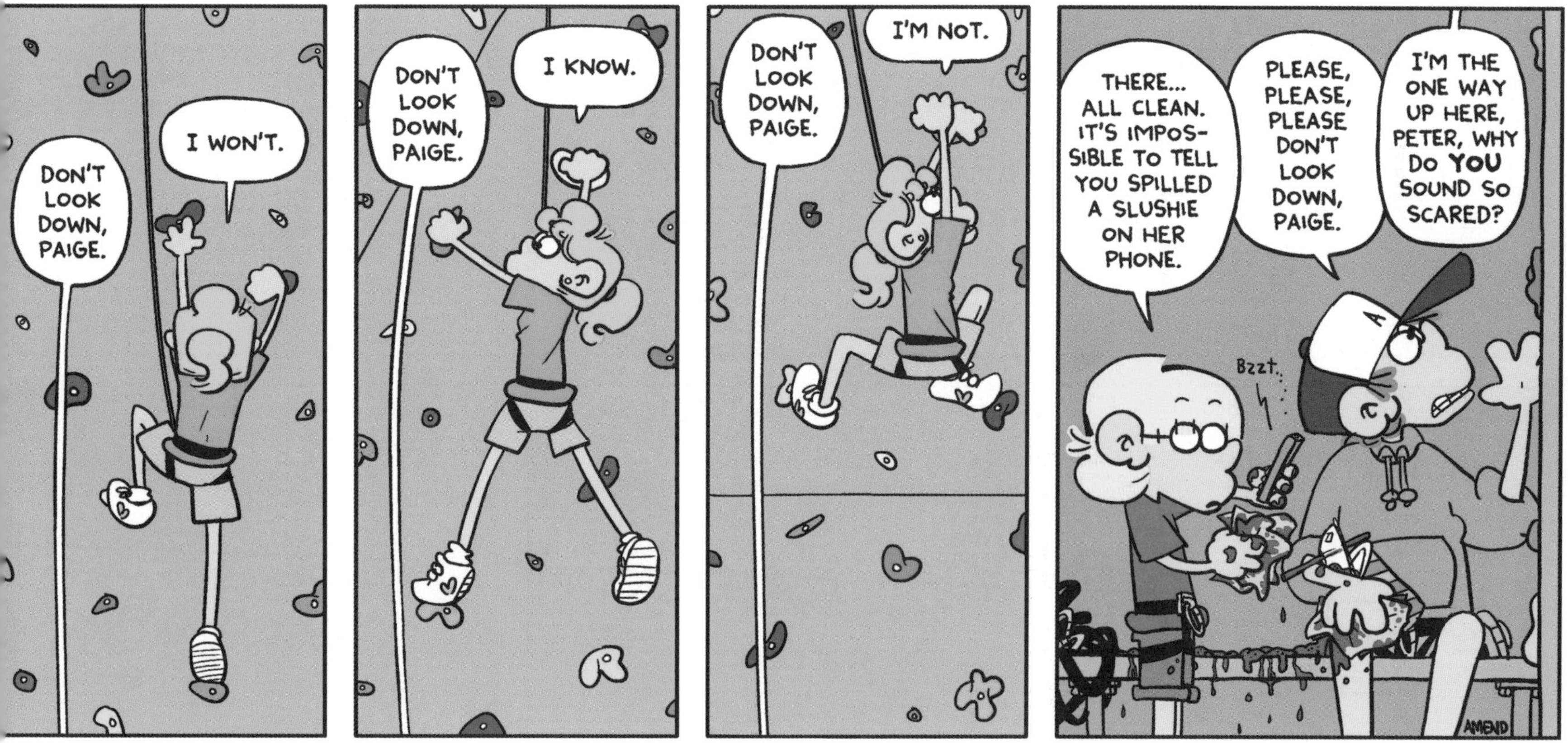
DON'T LOOK DOWN, PAIGE.
I WON'T.
DON'T LOOK DOWN, PAIGE.
I KNOW.
DON'T LOOK DOWN, PAIGE.
I'M NOT.
THERE... ALL CLEAN. IT'S IMPOSSIBLE TO TELL YOU SPILLED A SLUSHIE ON HER PHONE.
PLEASE, PLEASE, PLEASE DON'T LOOK DOWN, PAIGE.
I'M THE ONE WAY UP HERE, PETER, WHY DO **YOU** SOUND SO SCARED?
Bzzt.
AMEND

Piece-love and Misunderstanding

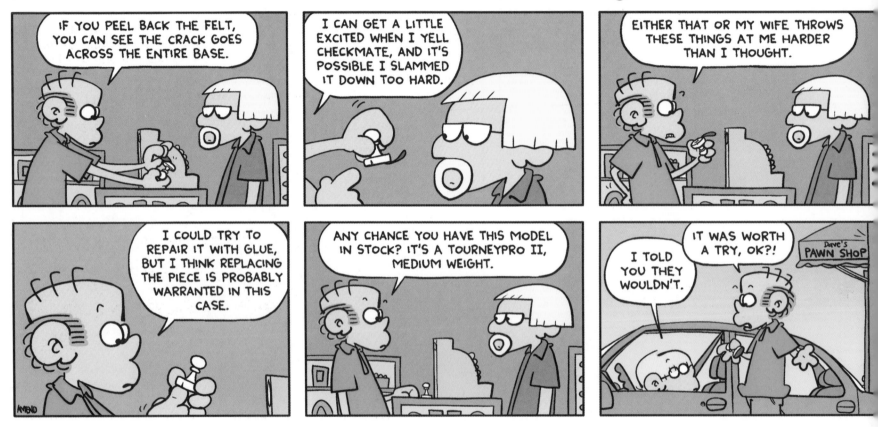

Aping Around

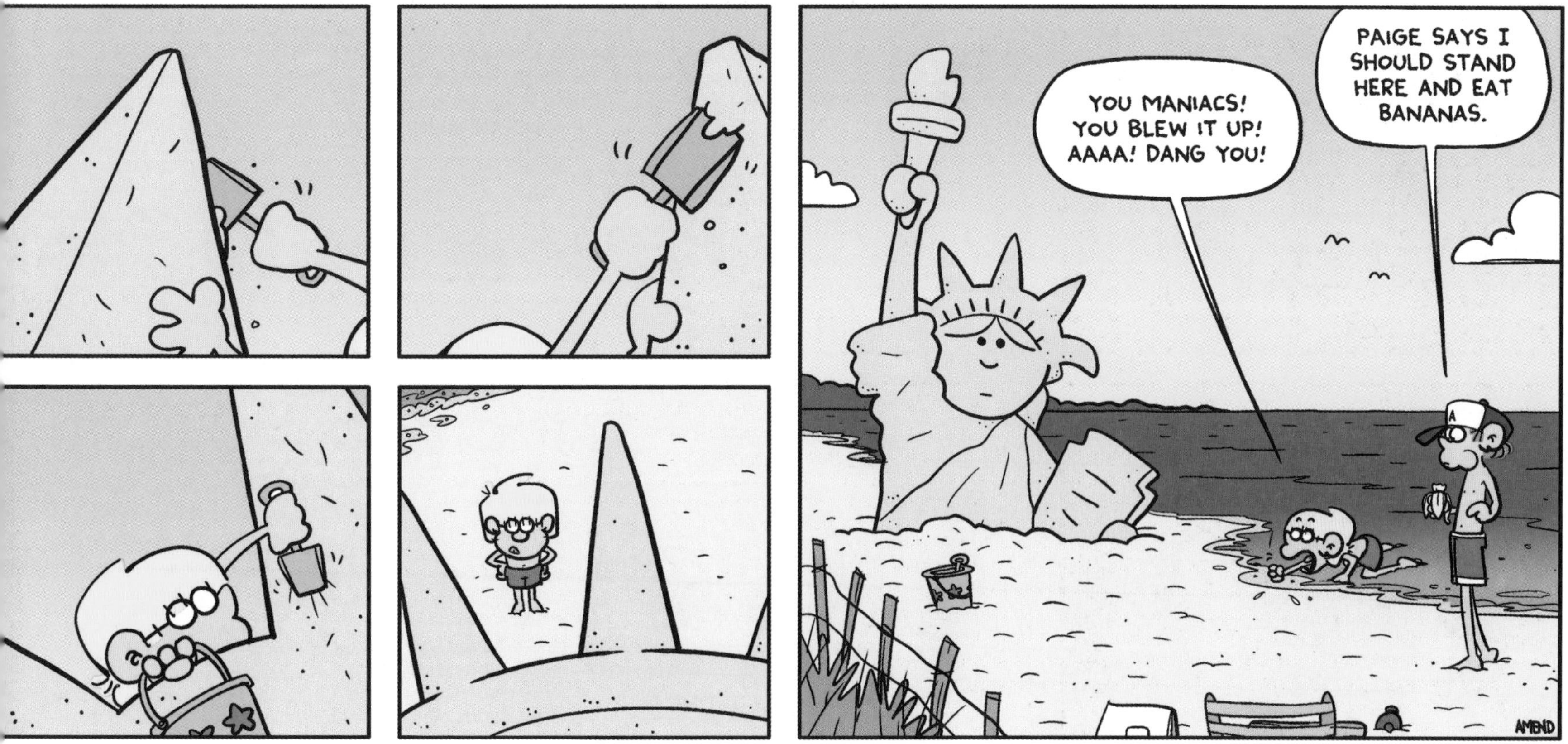
YOU MANIACS! YOU BLEW IT UP! AAAA! DANG YOU!
PAIGE SAYS I SHOULD STAND HERE AND EAT BANANAS.
AMEND

Thinking Big

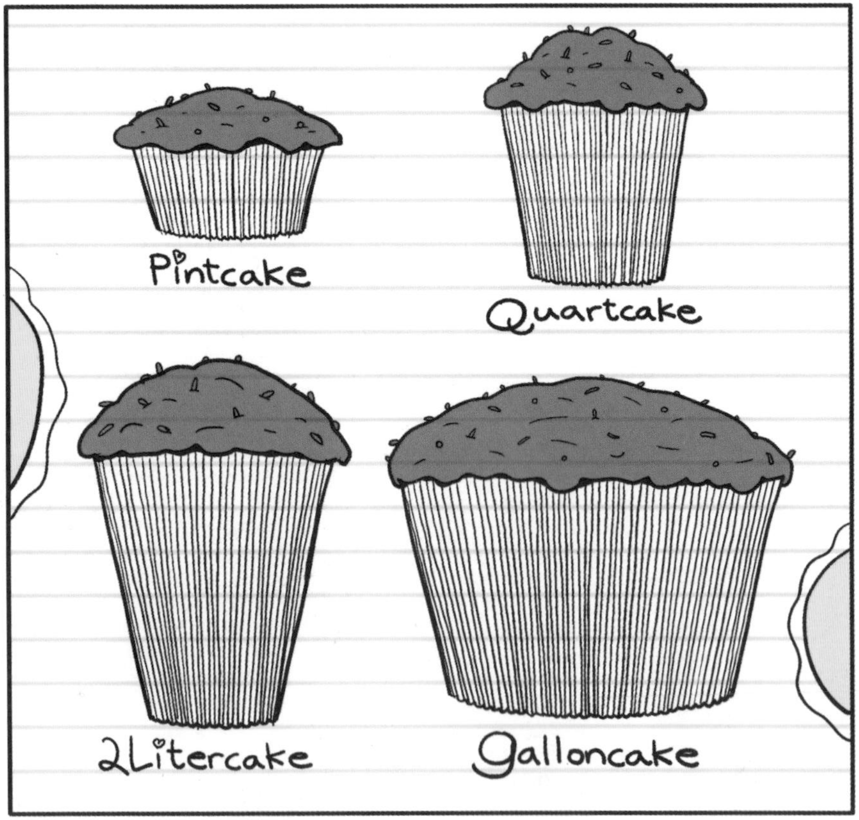
Pintcake
Quartcake
2Litercake
Galloncake

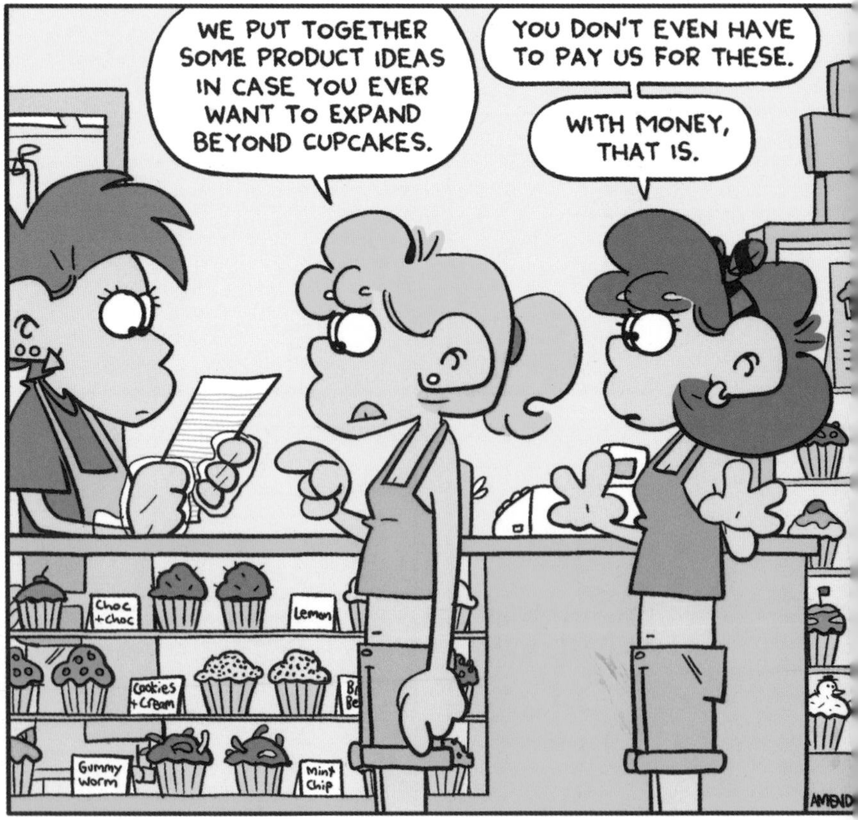
WE PUT TOGETHER SOME PRODUCT IDEAS IN CASE YOU EVER WANT TO EXPAND BEYOND CUPCAKES.
YOU DON'T EVEN HAVE TO PAY US FOR THESE.
WITH MONEY, THAT IS.
Choc +Choc
Lemon
Cookies +Cream
Gummy Worm
Mint Chip
AMEND

Pencil Test

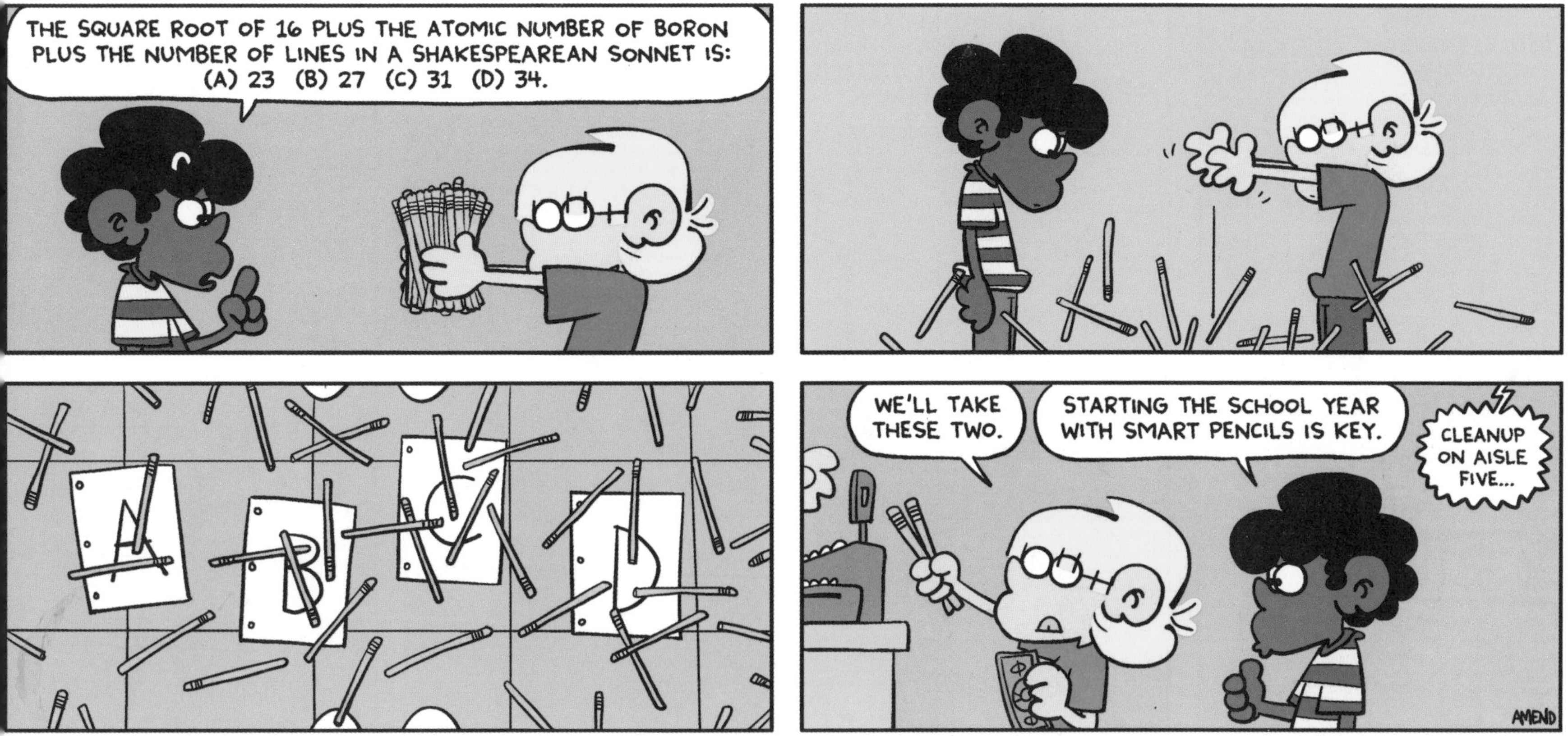
THE SQUARE ROOT OF 16 PLUS THE ATOMIC NUMBER OF BORON PLUS THE NUMBER OF LINES IN A SHAKESPEAREAN SONNET IS: (A) 23 (B) 27 (C) 31 (D) 34.
A
B
C
D
WE'LL TAKE THESE TWO.
STARTING THE SCHOOL YEAR WITH SMART PENCILS IS KEY.
CLEANUP ON AISLE FIVE...
AMEND

Anxiety Dreamer

Panel 1:
CLEAR YOUR DESKS, EVERYONE. WE'RE HAVING A QUIZ ON THE ASSIGNED SUMMER READING.

NOT THIS AGAIN!

Panel 2:
EXCUSE ME?

I HAD THIS EXACT SAME ANXIETY DREAM WHEN SCHOOL STARTED **LAST** YEAR!

Panel 3:
I SAY "WHAT SUMMER READING?!?" AND YOU SAY "DIDN'T YOU SIGN UP FOR THE ENGLISH DEPARTMENT E-MAILS?"

Panel 4:
THEN YOU SAY I WAS SUPPOSED TO READ SOME HUGE BOOK LIKE "MOBY DICK" AND THEN I FREAK OUT AND SCREAM AND WAKE UP.

Panel 5:
ACTUALLY THE ASSIGNED BOOK WAS "ANIMAL FARM." IT'S FAIRLY SHORT.

OK, SO THIS YEAR'S VERSION IS **SLIGHTLY** DIFFERENT.

Panel 8:
FIVE MINUTES LEFT, PEOPLE.

ALSO LAST YEAR I WOULD'VE WOKEN UP BY NOW. THAT'S DIFFERENT, TOO.

AMEND

Reality TV

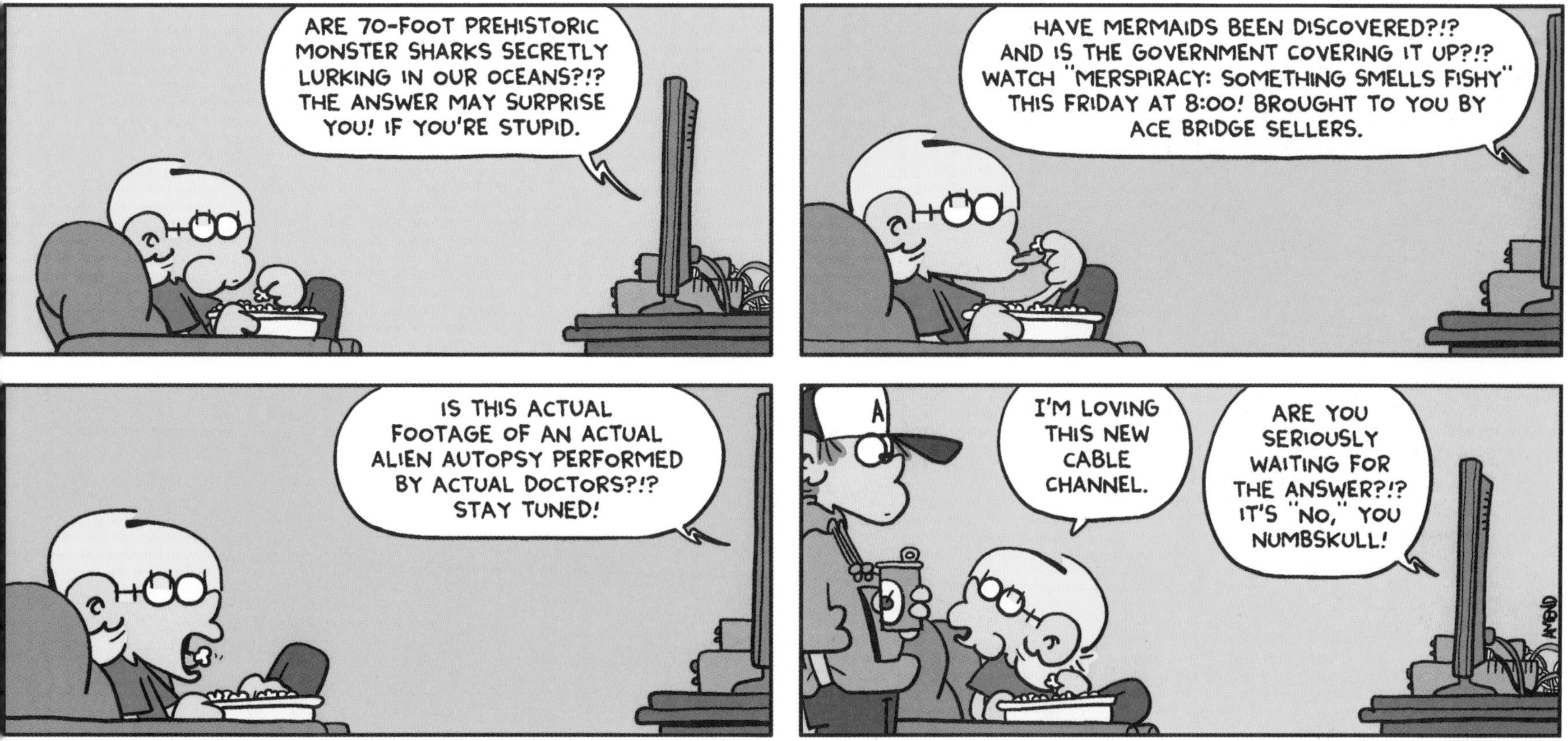

ARE 70-FOOT PREHISTORIC MONSTER SHARKS SECRETLY LURKING IN OUR OCEANS?!? THE ANSWER MAY SURPRISE YOU! IF YOU'RE STUPID.
HAVE MERMAIDS BEEN DISCOVERED?!? AND IS THE GOVERNMENT COVERING IT UP?!? WATCH "MERSPIRACY: SOMETHING SMELLS FISHY" THIS FRIDAY AT 8:00! BROUGHT TO YOU BY ACE BRIDGE SELLERS.
IS THIS ACTUAL FOOTAGE OF AN ACTUAL ALIEN AUTOPSY PERFORMED BY ACTUAL DOCTORS?!? STAY TUNED!
A
I'M LOVING THIS NEW CABLE CHANNEL.
ARE YOU SERIOUSLY WAITING FOR THE ANSWER?!? IT'S "NO," YOU NUMBSKULL!

Test Scheduling

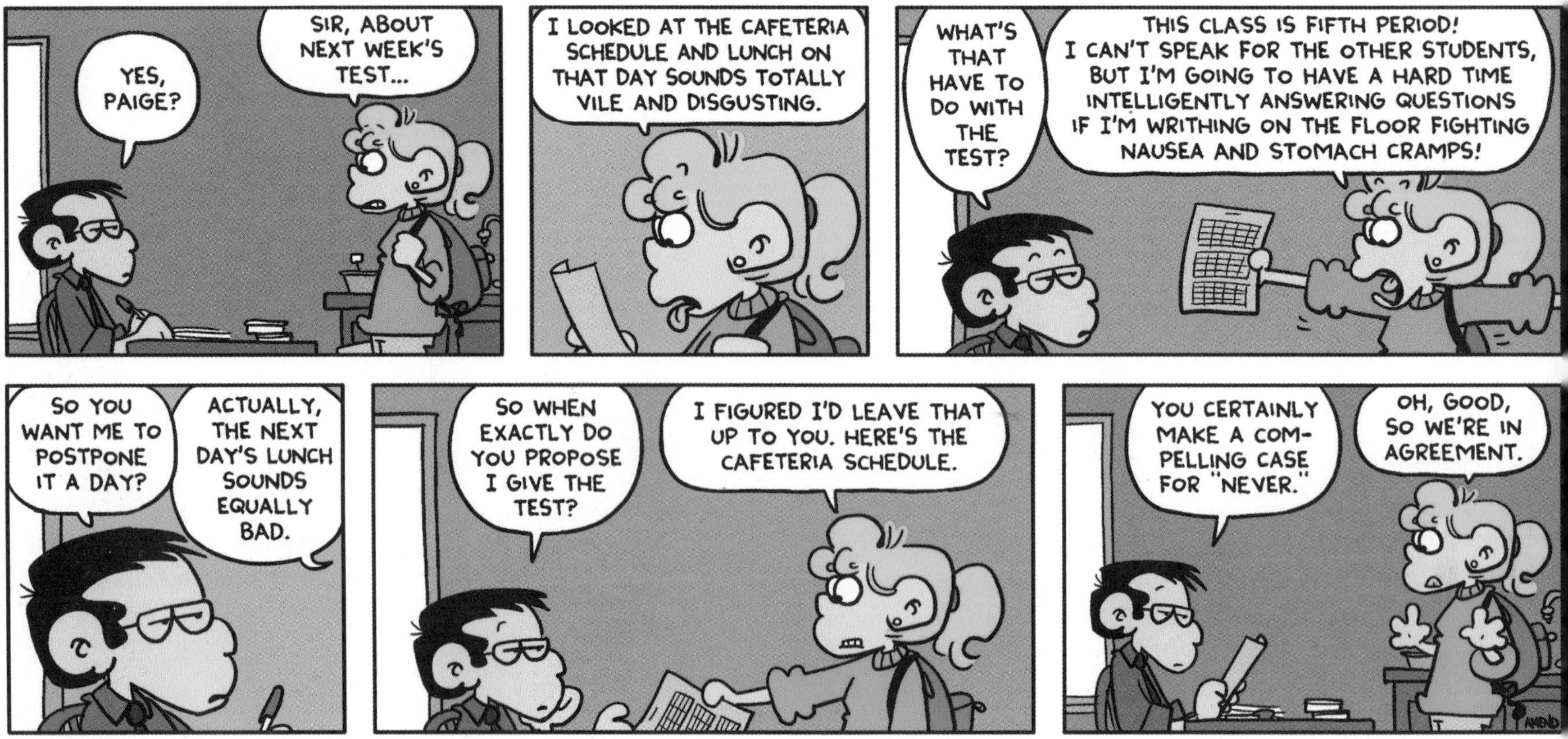

SIR, ABOUT NEXT WEEK'S TEST...
YES, PAIGE?
I LOOKED AT THE CAFETERIA SCHEDULE AND LUNCH ON THAT DAY SOUNDS TOTALLY VILE AND DISGUSTING.
WHAT'S THAT HAVE TO DO WITH THE TEST?
THIS CLASS IS FIFTH PERIOD! I CAN'T SPEAK FOR THE OTHER STUDENTS, BUT I'M GOING TO HAVE A HARD TIME INTELLIGENTLY ANSWERING QUESTIONS IF I'M WRITHING ON THE FLOOR FIGHTING NAUSEA AND STOMACH CRAMPS!
SO YOU WANT ME TO POSTPONE IT A DAY?
ACTUALLY, THE NEXT DAY'S LUNCH SOUNDS EQUALLY BAD.
SO WHEN EXACTLY DO YOU PROPOSE I GIVE THE TEST?
I FIGURED I'D LEAVE THAT UP TO YOU. HERE'S THE CAFETERIA SCHEDULE.
YOU CERTAINLY MAKE A COM-PELLING CASE FOR "NEVER."
OH, GOOD, SO WE'RE IN AGREEMENT.
AMEND

Way to Chuck It!

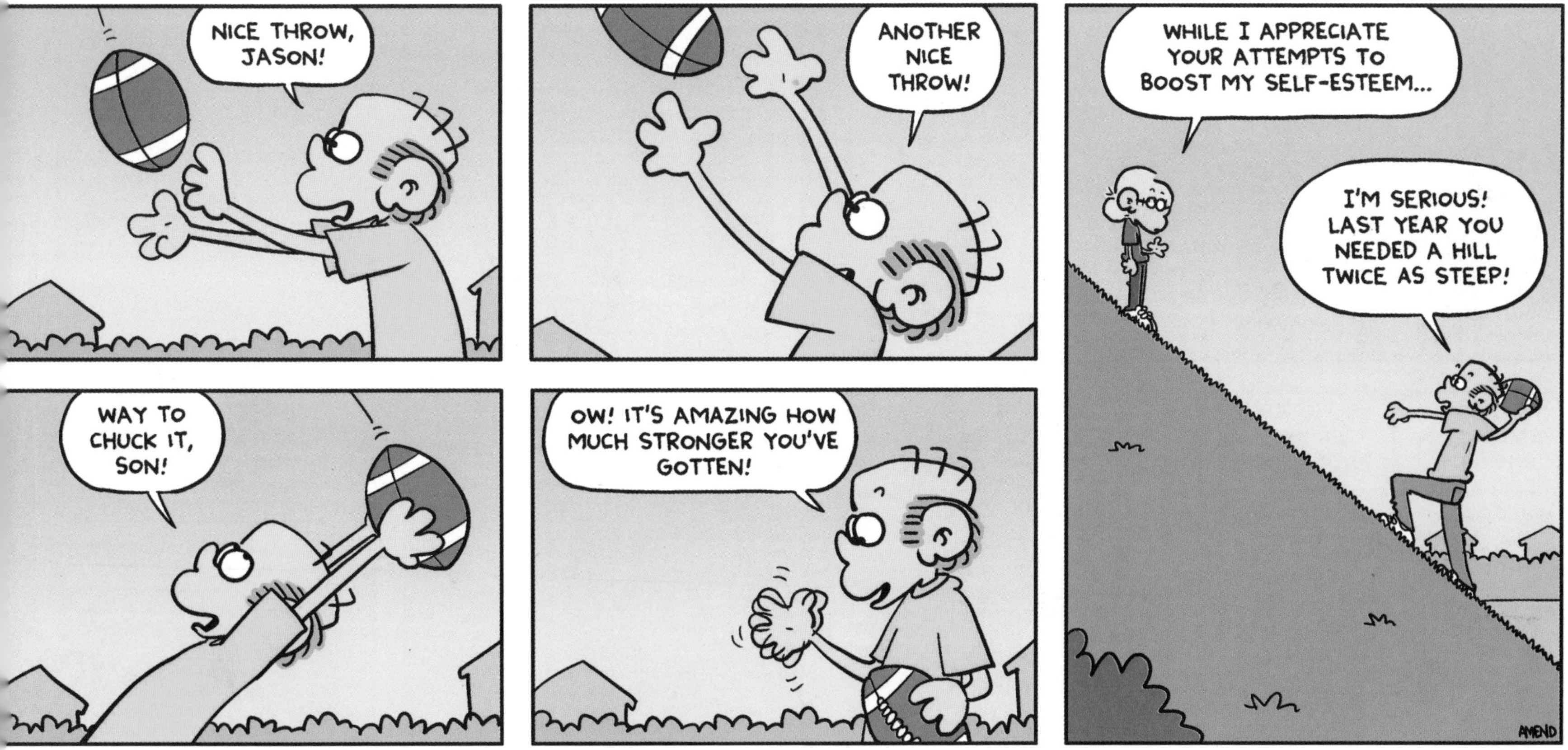
NICE THROW, JASON!
ANOTHER NICE THROW!
WAY TO CHUCK IT, SON!
OW! IT'S AMAZING HOW MUCH STRONGER YOU'VE GOTTEN!
WHILE I APPRECIATE YOUR ATTEMPTS TO BOOST MY SELF-ESTEEM...
I'M SERIOUS! LAST YEAR YOU NEEDED A HILL TWICE AS STEEP!
AMEND

Hobbit Day

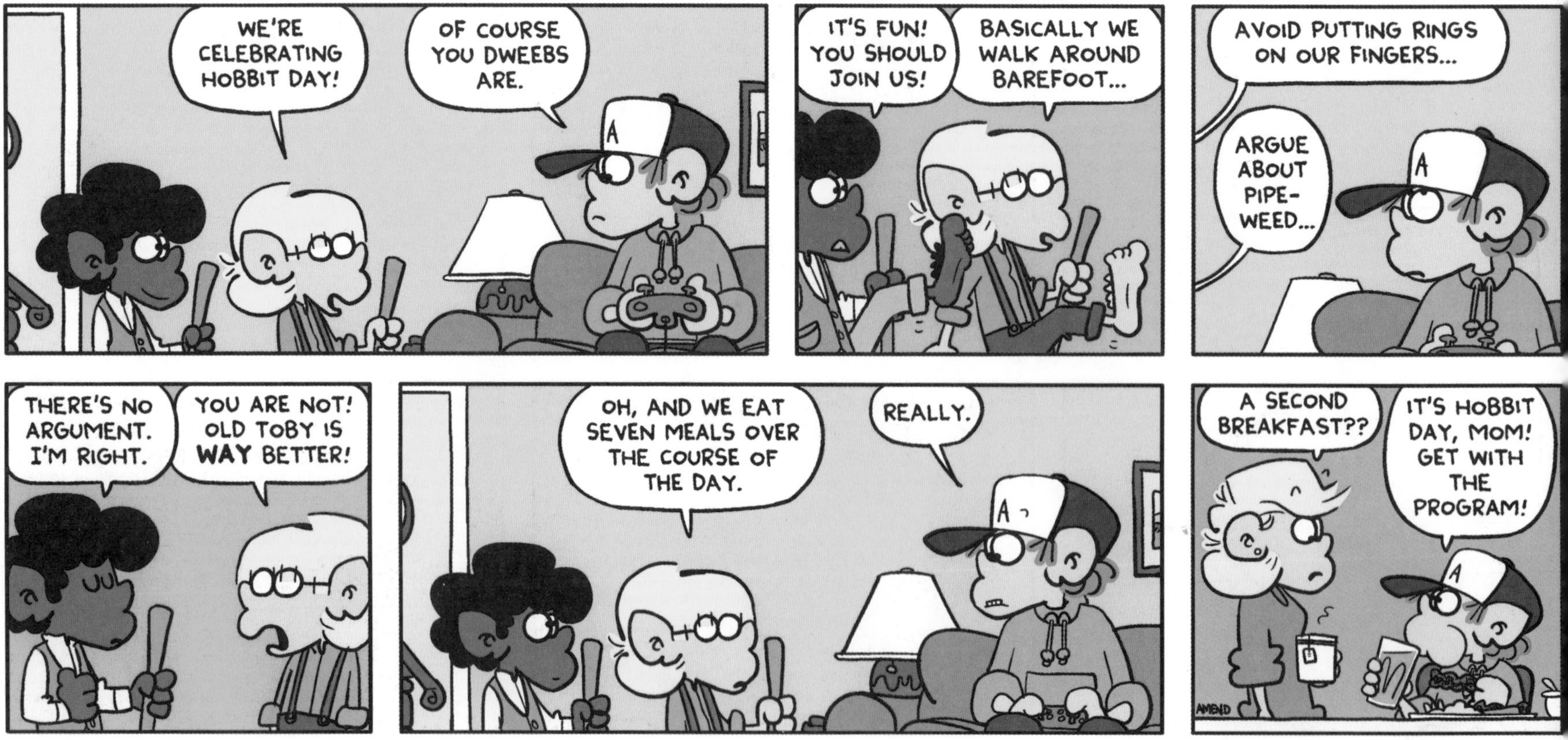
WE'RE CELEBRATING HOBBIT DAY!
OF COURSE YOU DWEEBS ARE.
IT'S FUN! YOU SHOULD JOIN US!
BASICALLY WE WALK AROUND BAREFOOT...
AVOID PUTTING RINGS ON OUR FINGERS...
ARGUE ABOUT PIPE-WEED...
THERE'S NO ARGUMENT. I'M RIGHT.
YOU ARE NOT! OLD TOBY IS WAY BETTER!
OH, AND WE EAT SEVEN MEALS OVER THE COURSE OF THE DAY.
REALLY.
A SECOND BREAKFAST??
IT'S HOBBIT DAY, MOM! GET WITH THE PROGRAM!
AMEND

American-ish Government

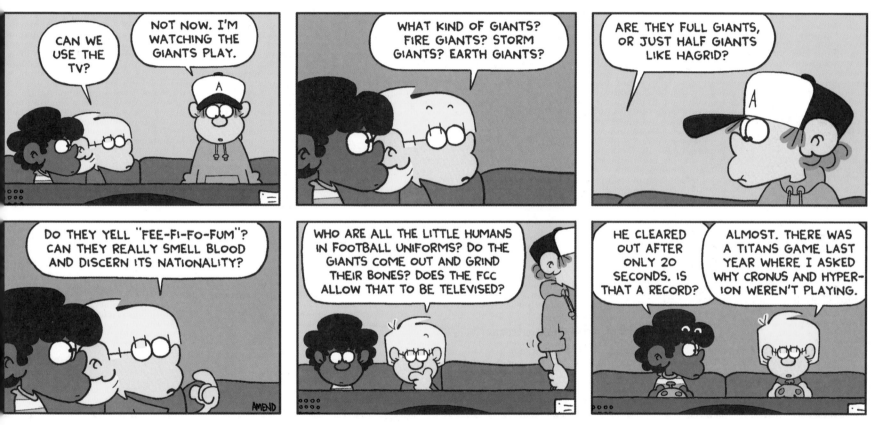

Slowhandy

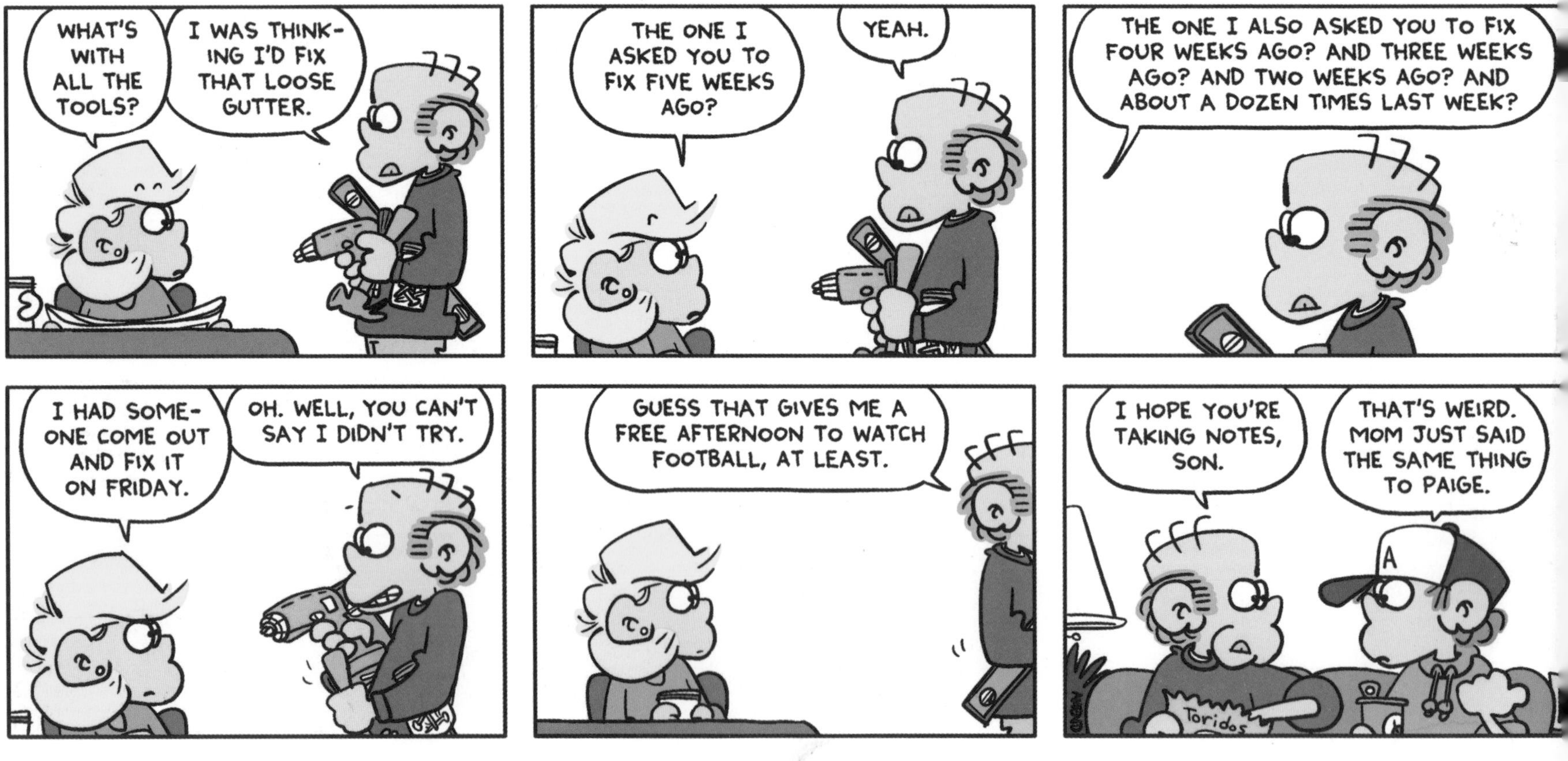
WHAT'S WITH ALL THE TOOLS?
I WAS THINKING I'D FIX THAT LOOSE GUTTER.
THE ONE I ASKED YOU TO FIX FIVE WEEKS AGO?
YEAH.
THE ONE I ALSO ASKED YOU TO FIX FOUR WEEKS AGO? AND THREE WEEKS AGO? AND TWO WEEKS AGO? AND ABOUT A DOZEN TIMES LAST WEEK?
I HAD SOMEONE COME OUT AND FIX IT ON FRIDAY.
OH. WELL, YOU CAN'T SAY I DIDN'T TRY.
GUESS THAT GIVES ME A FREE AFTERNOON TO WATCH FOOTBALL, AT LEAST.
I HOPE YOU'RE TAKING NOTES, SON.
THAT'S WEIRD. MOM JUST SAID THE SAME THING TO PAIGE.
A
Toridos

Les Physz

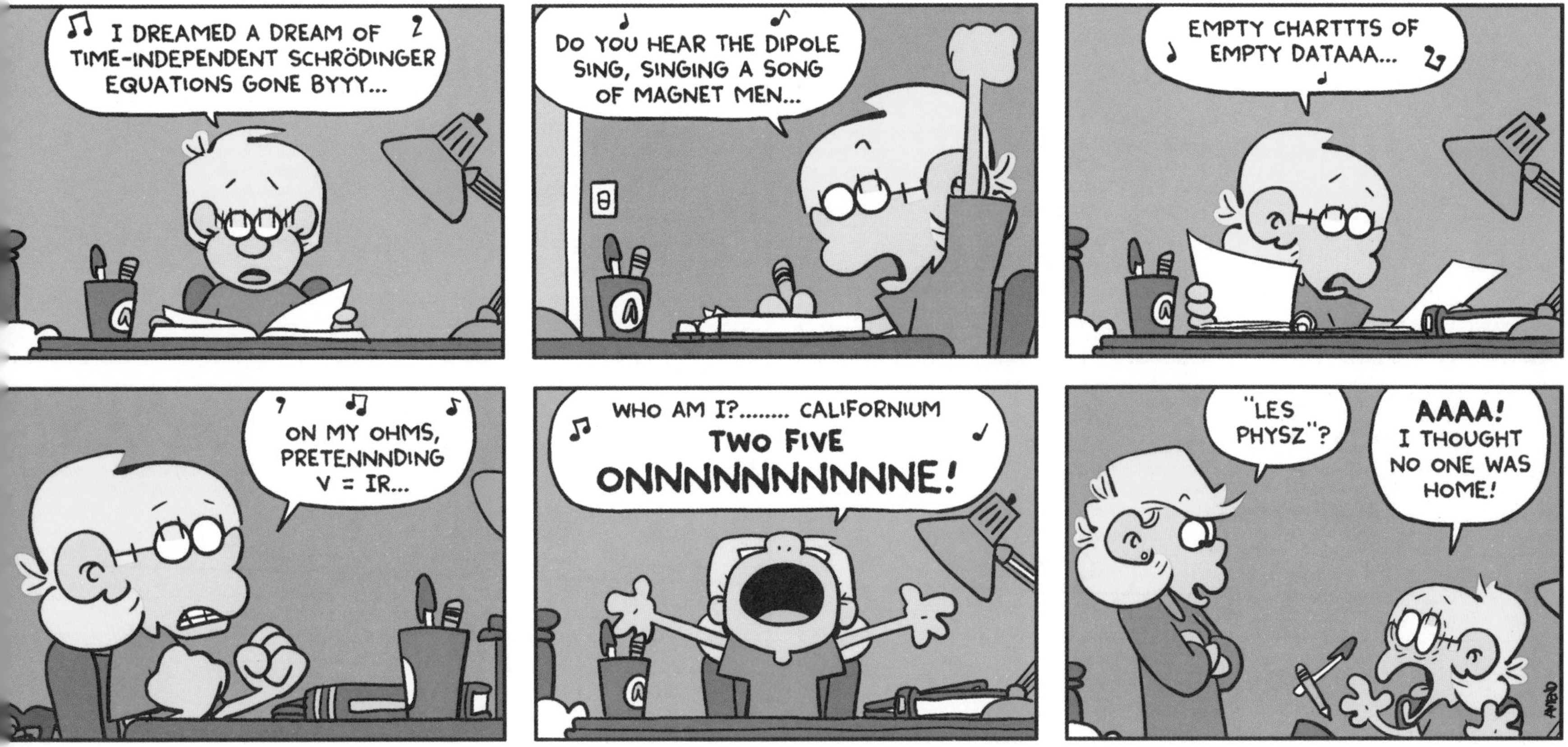

I DREAMED A DREAM OF TIME-INDEPENDENT SCHRÖDINGER EQUATIONS GONE BYYY...
DO YOU HEAR THE DIPOLE SING, SINGING A SONG OF MAGNET MEN...
EMPTY CHARTTTS OF EMPTY DATAAA...
ON MY OHMS, PRETENNNDING V = IR...
WHO AM I?........ CALIFORNIUM TWO FIVE ONNNNNNNNNNE!
"LES PHYSZ"?
AAAA! I THOUGHT NO ONE WAS HOME!

Scare Different

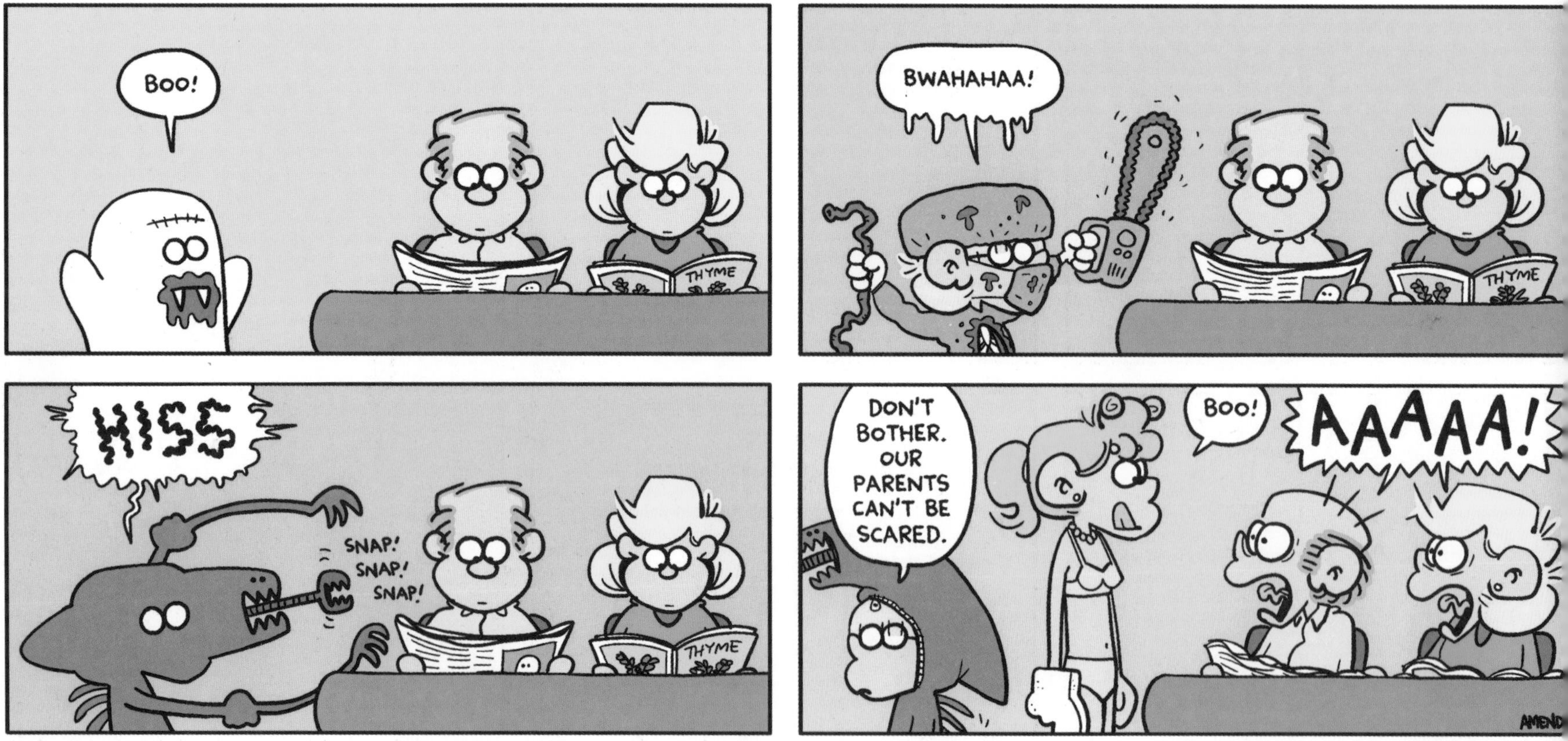

BOO!
BWAHAHAA!
HISS
SNAP! SNAP! SNAP!
THYME
DON'T BOTHER. OUR PARENTS CAN'T BE SCARED.
BOO!
AAAAA!
AMEND

Super Safe

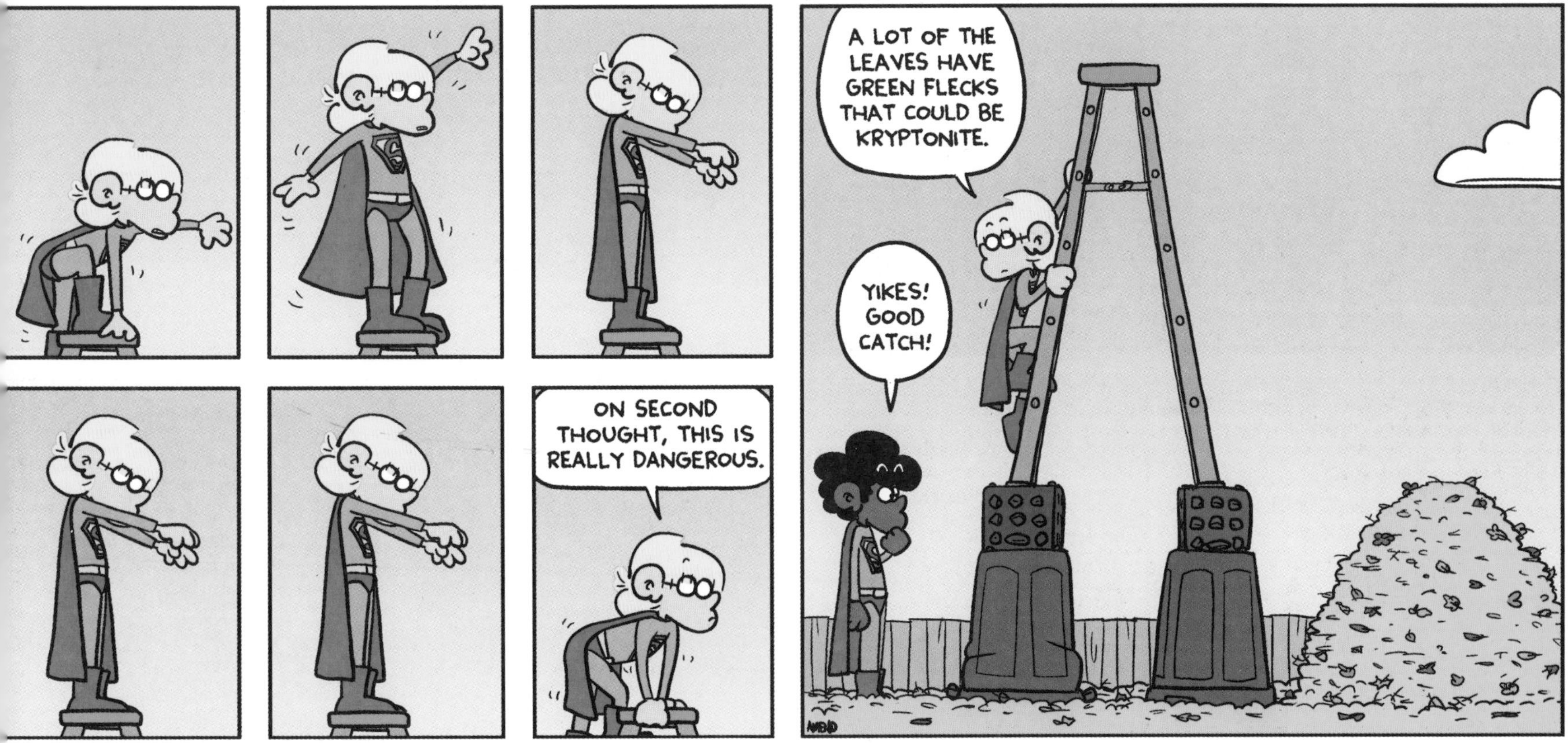
ON SECOND THOUGHT, THIS IS REALLY DANGEROUS.
A LOT OF THE LEAVES HAVE GREEN FLECKS THAT COULD BE KRYPTONITE.
YIKES! GOOD CATCH!

Hide and Go "Eek!"

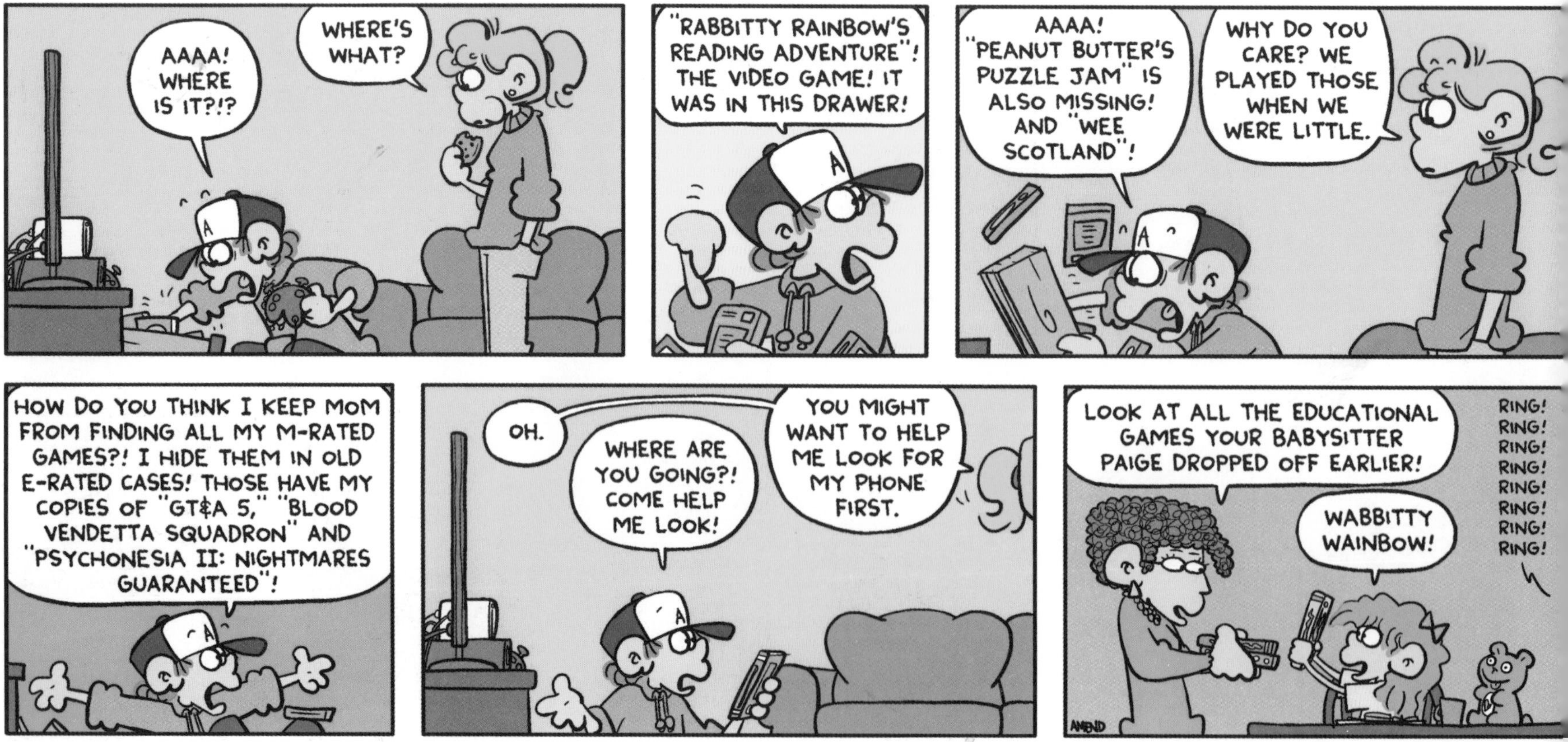
AAAA! WHERE IS IT?!?
WHERE'S WHAT?
"RABBITTY RAINBOW'S READING ADVENTURE"! THE VIDEO GAME! IT WAS IN THIS DRAWER!
AAAA! "PEANUT BUTTER'S PUZZLE JAM" IS ALSO MISSING! AND "WEE SCOTLAND"!
WHY DO YOU CARE? WE PLAYED THOSE WHEN WE WERE LITTLE.
HOW DO YOU THINK I KEEP MOM FROM FINDING ALL MY M-RATED GAMES?! I HIDE THEM IN OLD E-RATED CASES! THOSE HAVE MY COPIES OF "GT&A 5," "BLOOD VENDETTA SQUADRON" AND "PSYCHONESIA II: NIGHTMARES GUARANTEED"!
OH.
WHERE ARE YOU GOING?! COME HELP ME LOOK!
YOU MIGHT WANT TO HELP ME LOOK FOR MY PHONE FIRST.
LOOK AT ALL THE EDUCATIONAL GAMES YOUR BABYSITTER PAIGE DROPPED OFF EARLIER!
WABBITTY WAINBOW!
RING! RING! RING! RING! RING! RING! RING! RING!
AMEND

Clever Title

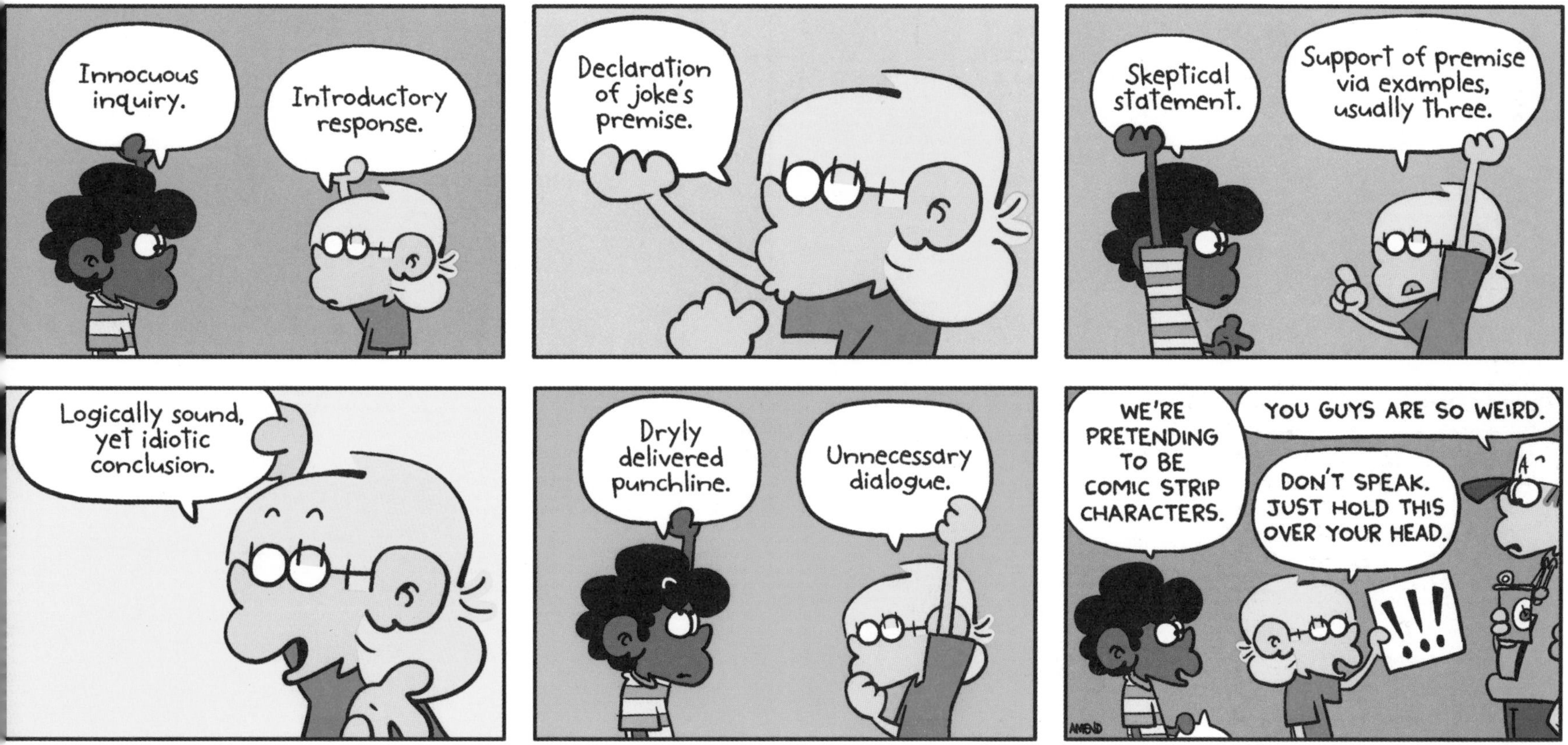
Innocuous inquiry.
Introductory response.
Declaration of joke's premise.
Skeptical statement.
Support of premise via examples, usually three.
Logically sound, yet idiotic conclusion.
Dryly delivered punchline.
Unnecessary dialogue.
WE'RE PRETENDING TO BE COMIC STRIP CHARACTERS.
YOU GUYS ARE SO WEIRD.
DON'T SPEAK. JUST HOLD THIS OVER YOUR HEAD.
!!!
AMEND

Mall of Duty

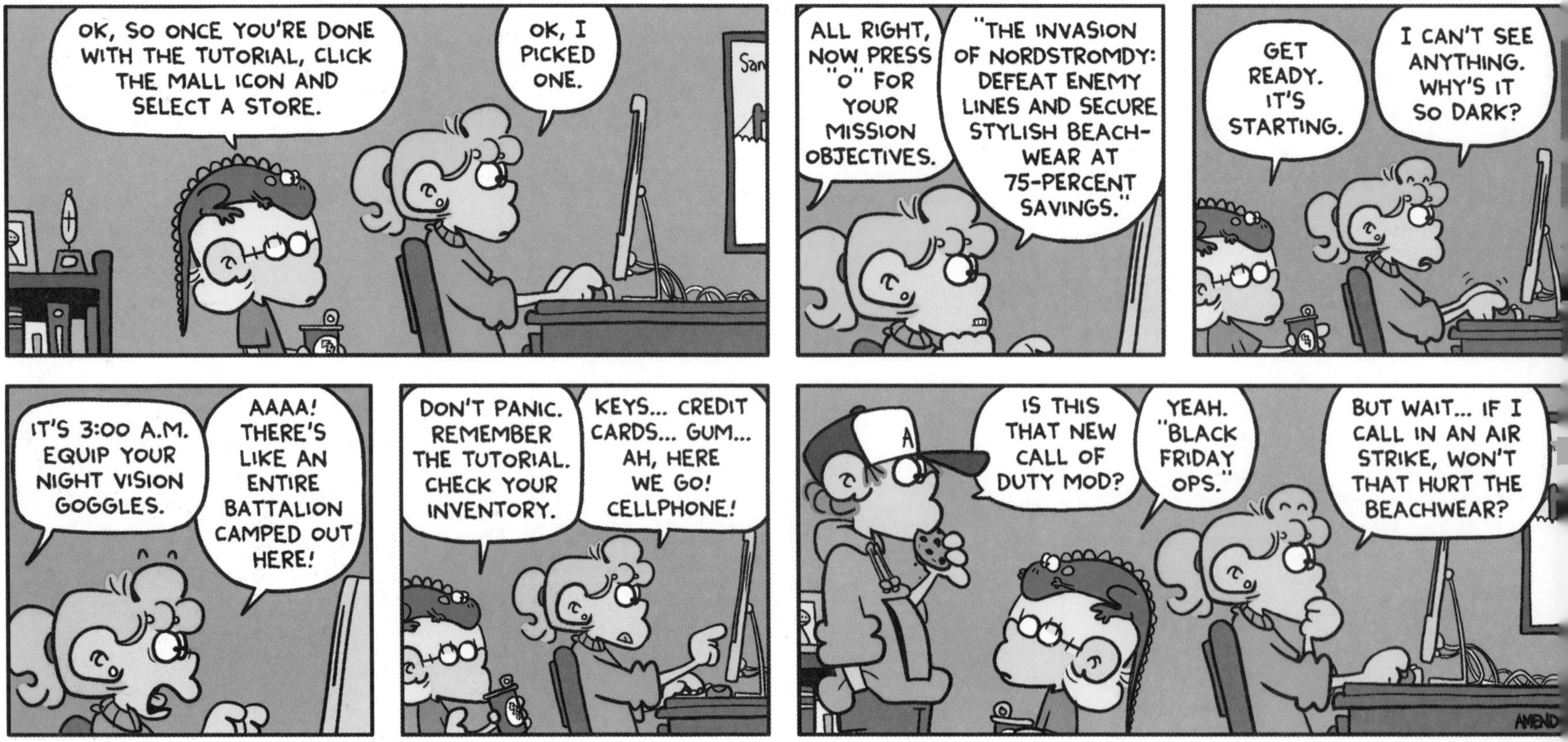

OK, SO ONCE YOU'RE DONE WITH THE TUTORIAL, CLICK THE MALL ICON AND SELECT A STORE.
OK, I PICKED ONE.
ALL RIGHT, NOW PRESS "O" FOR YOUR MISSION OBJECTIVES.
"THE INVASION OF NORDSTROMDY: DEFEAT ENEMY LINES AND SECURE STYLISH BEACH-WEAR AT 75-PERCENT SAVINGS."
GET READY. IT'S STARTING.
I CAN'T SEE ANYTHING. WHY'S IT SO DARK?
IT'S 3:00 A.M. EQUIP YOUR NIGHT VISION GOGGLES.
AAAA! THERE'S LIKE AN ENTIRE BATTALION CAMPED OUT HERE!
DON'T PANIC. REMEMBER THE TUTORIAL. CHECK YOUR INVENTORY.
KEYS... CREDIT CARDS... GUM... AH, HERE WE GO! CELLPHONE!
IS THIS THAT NEW CALL OF DUTY MOD?
YEAH. "BLACK FRIDAY OPS."
BUT WAIT... IF I CALL IN AN AIR STRIKE, WON'T THAT HURT THE BEACHWEAR?
AMEND

Laundrigami

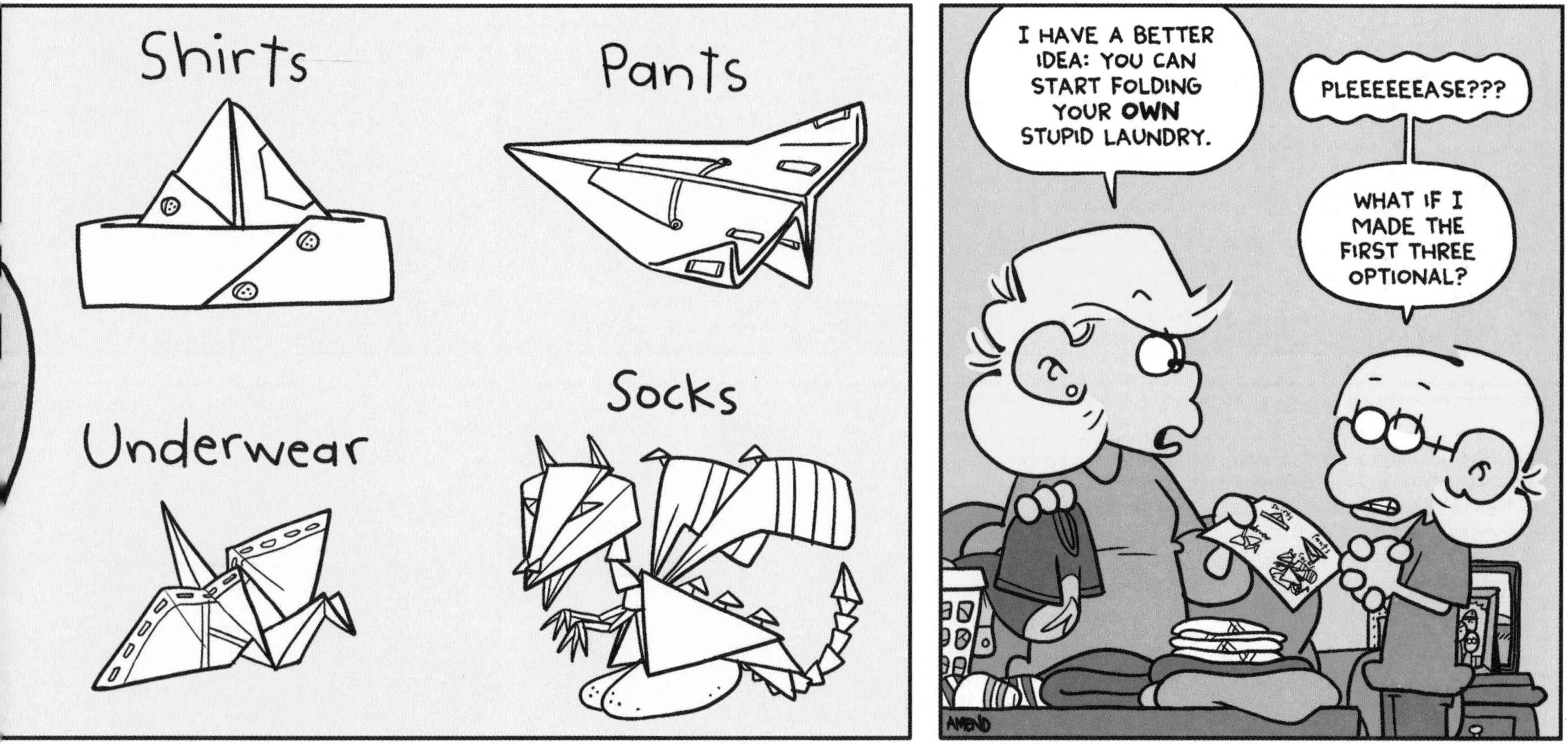
Shirts
Pants
Underwear
Socks
I HAVE A BETTER IDEA: YOU CAN START FOLDING YOUR **OWN** STUPID LAUNDRY.
PLEEEEEEEASE???
WHAT IF I MADE THE FIRST THREE OPTIONAL?
AMEND

Gullibility Research

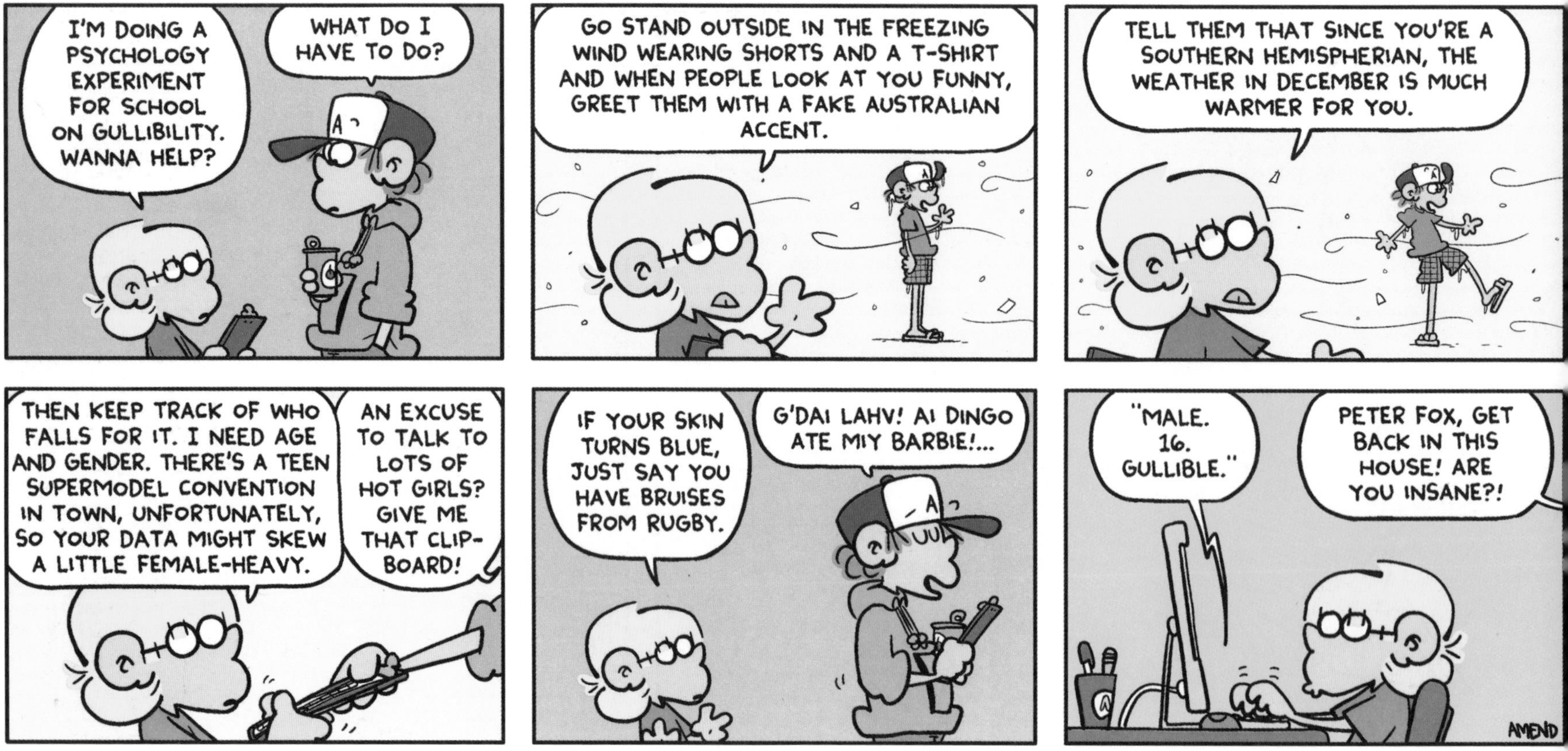

I'M DOING A PSYCHOLOGY EXPERIMENT FOR SCHOOL ON GULLIBILITY. WANNA HELP?
WHAT DO I HAVE TO DO?
A
GO STAND OUTSIDE IN THE FREEZING WIND WEARING SHORTS AND A T-SHIRT AND WHEN PEOPLE LOOK AT YOU FUNNY, GREET THEM WITH A FAKE AUSTRALIAN ACCENT.
TELL THEM THAT SINCE YOU'RE A SOUTHERN HEMISPHERIAN, THE WEATHER IN DECEMBER IS MUCH WARMER FOR YOU.
THEN KEEP TRACK OF WHO FALLS FOR IT. I NEED AGE AND GENDER. THERE'S A TEEN SUPERMODEL CONVENTION IN TOWN, UNFORTUNATELY, SO YOUR DATA MIGHT SKEW A LITTLE FEMALE-HEAVY.
AN EXCUSE TO TALK TO LOTS OF HOT GIRLS? GIVE ME THAT CLIP-BOARD!
IF YOUR SKIN TURNS BLUE, JUST SAY YOU HAVE BRUISES FROM RUGBY.
G'DAI LAHV! AI DINGO ATE MIY BARBIE!...
"MALE. 16. GULLIBLE."
PETER FOX, GET BACK IN THIS HOUSE! ARE YOU INSANE?!
AMEND

An Iguana on Mars?

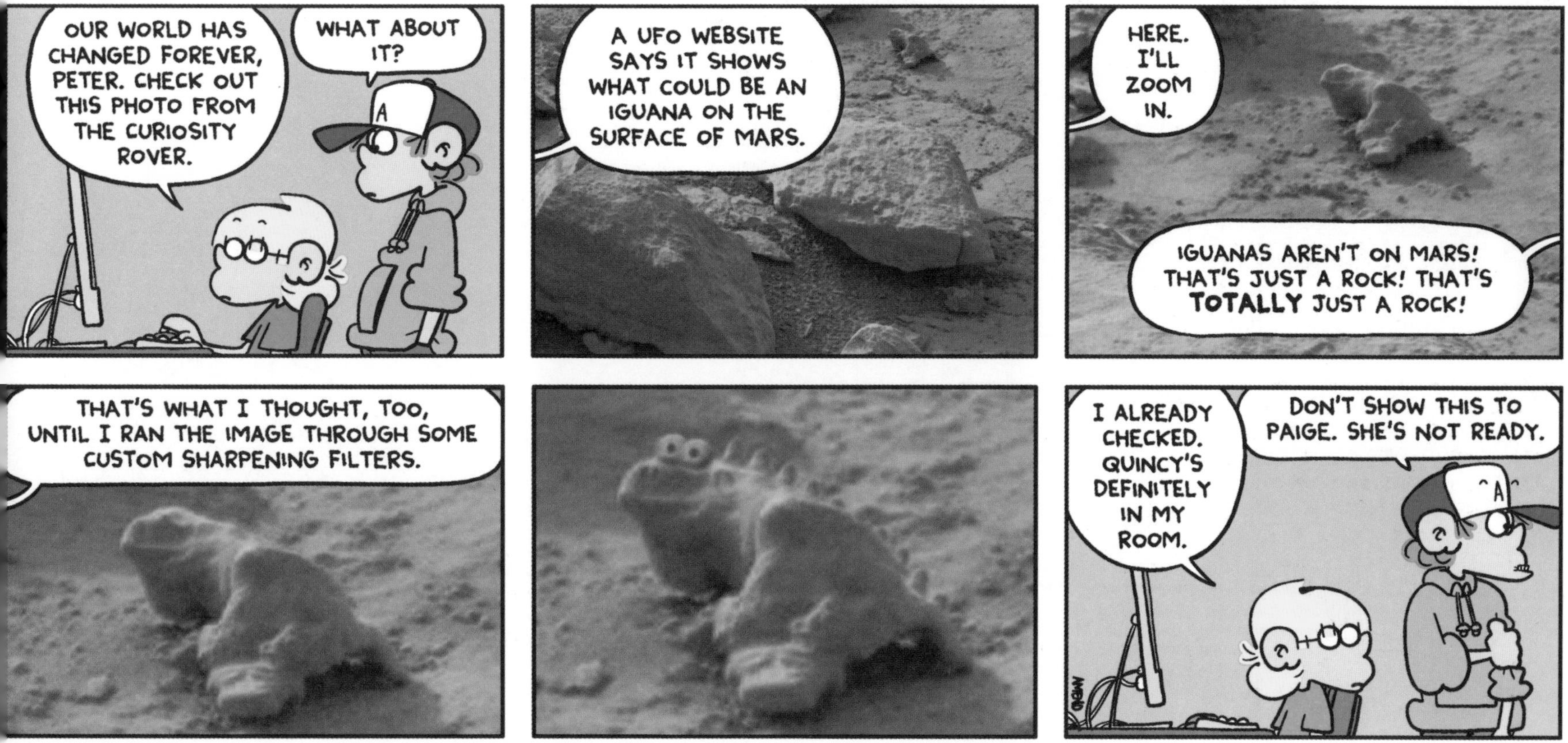

OUR WORLD HAS CHANGED FOREVER, PETER. CHECK OUT THIS PHOTO FROM THE CURIOSITY ROVER.
WHAT ABOUT IT?
A UFO WEBSITE SAYS IT SHOWS WHAT COULD BE AN IGUANA ON THE SURFACE OF MARS.
HERE. I'LL ZOOM IN.
IGUANAS AREN'T ON MARS! THAT'S JUST A ROCK! THAT'S **TOTALLY** JUST A ROCK!
THAT'S WHAT I THOUGHT, TOO, UNTIL I RAN THE IMAGE THROUGH SOME CUSTOM SHARPENING FILTERS.
I ALREADY CHECKED. QUINCY'S DEFINITELY IN MY ROOM.
DON'T SHOW THIS TO PAIGE. SHE'S NOT READY.

Some Assembly Desired

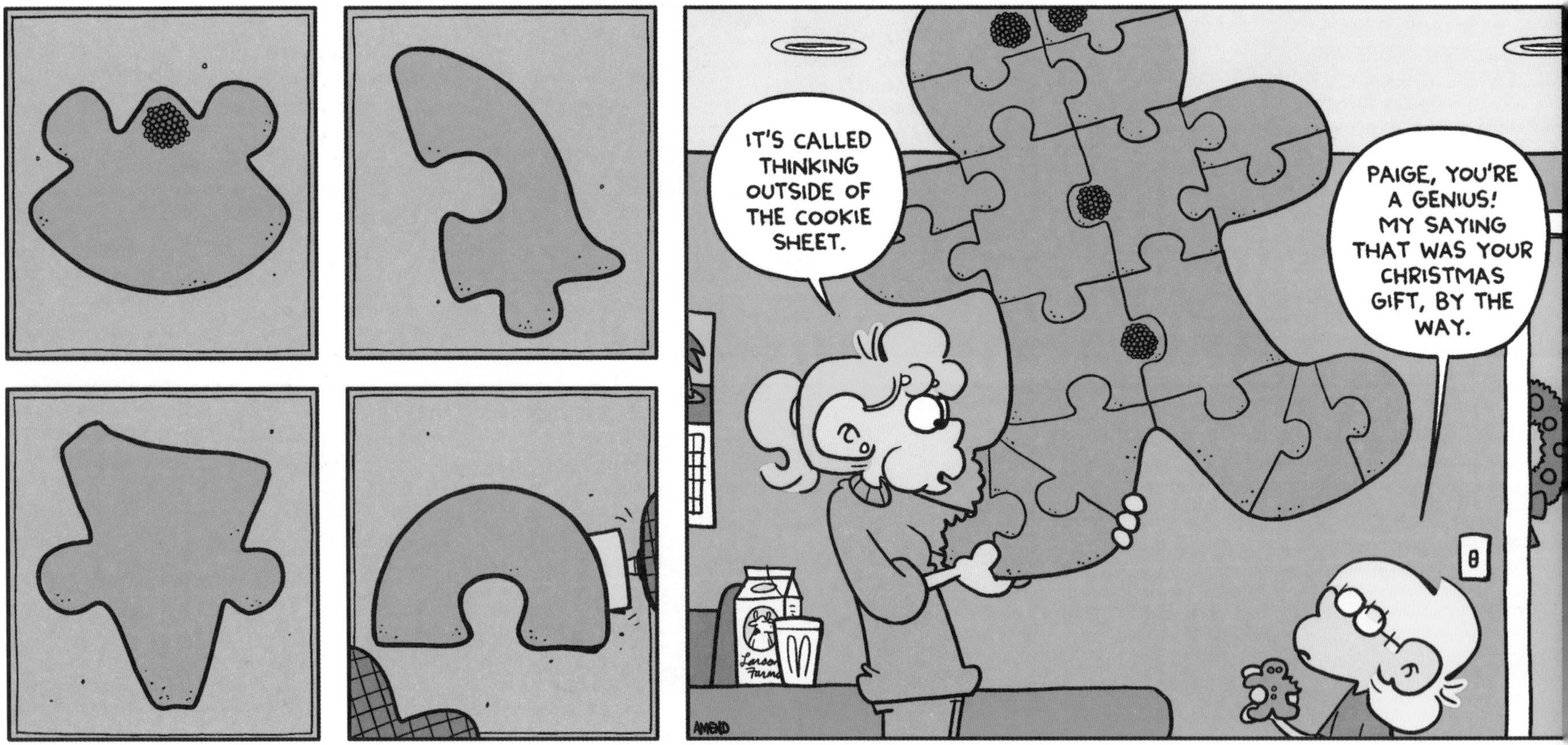

IT'S CALLED THINKING OUTSIDE OF THE COOKIE SHEET.
PAIGE, YOU'RE A GENIUS! MY SAYING THAT WAS YOUR CHRISTMAS GIFT, BY THE WAY.
AMEND

Weight Up!

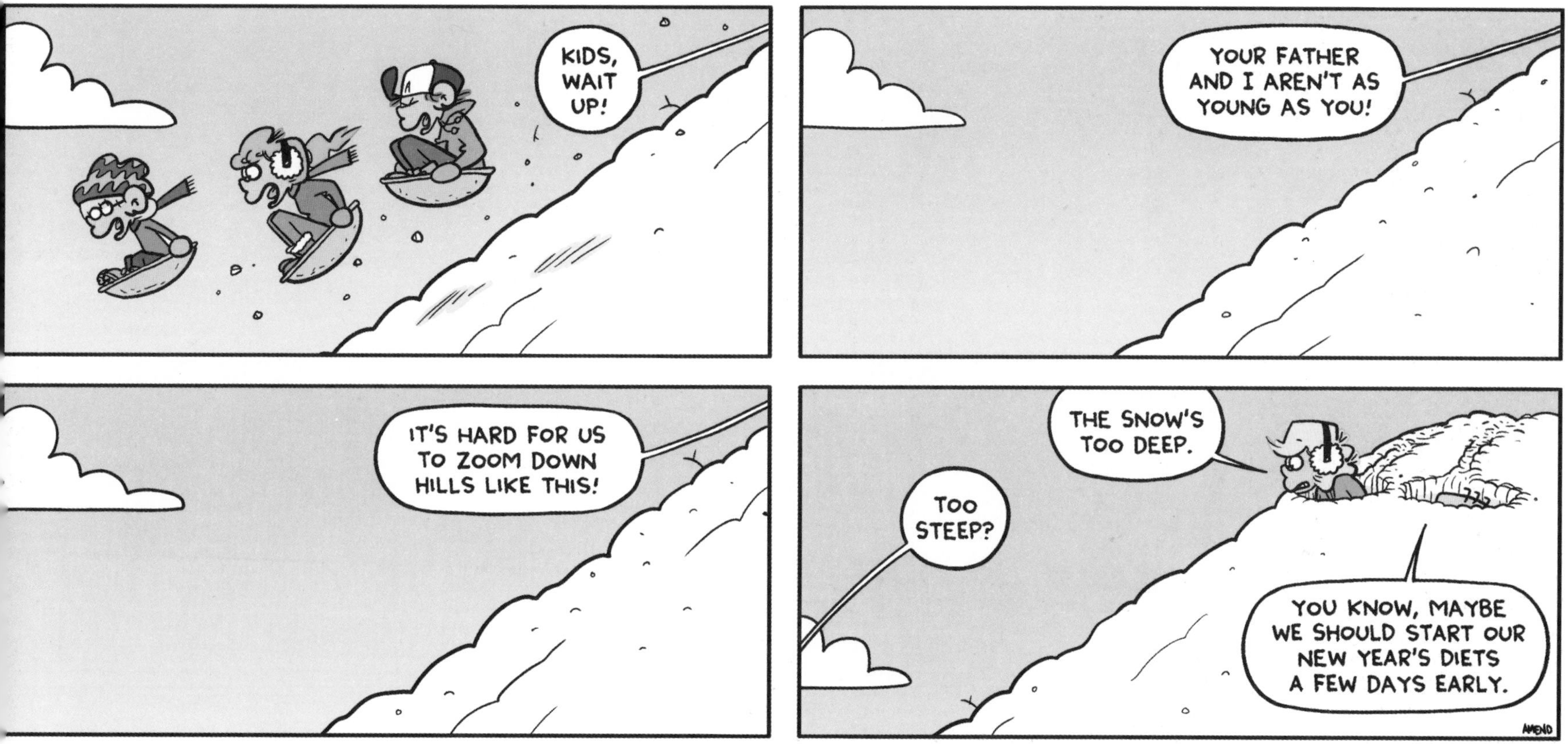
KIDS, WAIT UP!
YOUR FATHER AND I AREN'T AS YOUNG AS YOU!
IT'S HARD FOR US TO ZOOM DOWN HILLS LIKE THIS!
TOO STEEP?
THE SNOW'S TOO DEEP.
YOU KNOW, MAYBE WE SHOULD START OUR NEW YEAR'S DIETS A FEW DAYS EARLY.
AMEND

Parthenotquite

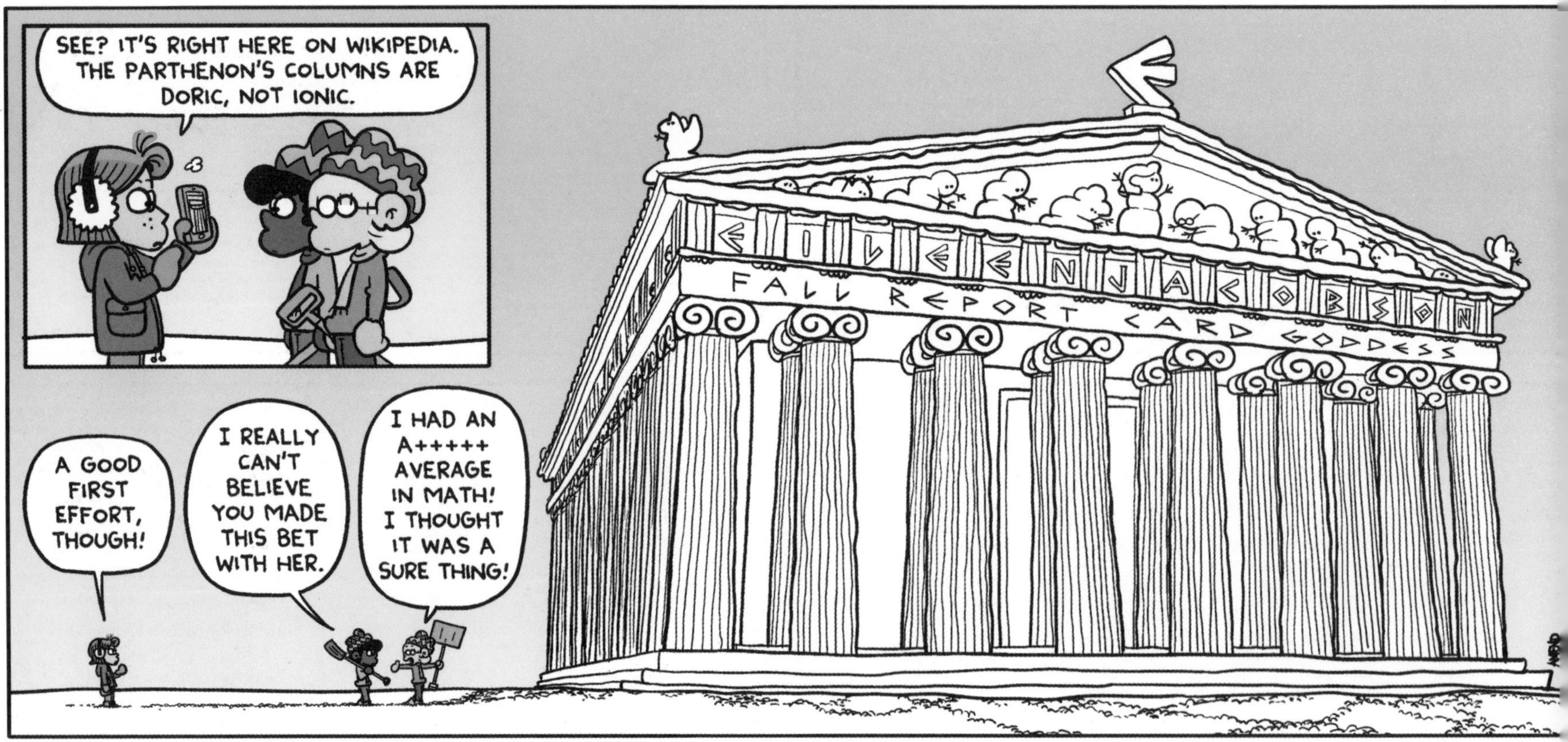

SEE? IT'S RIGHT HERE ON WIKIPEDIA. THE PARTHENON'S COLUMNS ARE DORIC, NOT IONIC.
A GOOD FIRST EFFORT, THOUGH!
I REALLY CAN'T BELIEVE YOU MADE THIS BET WITH HER.
I HAD AN A+++++ AVERAGE IN MATH! I THOUGHT IT WAS A SURE THING!
FALL REPORT CARD GODDESS

Vacation Memories

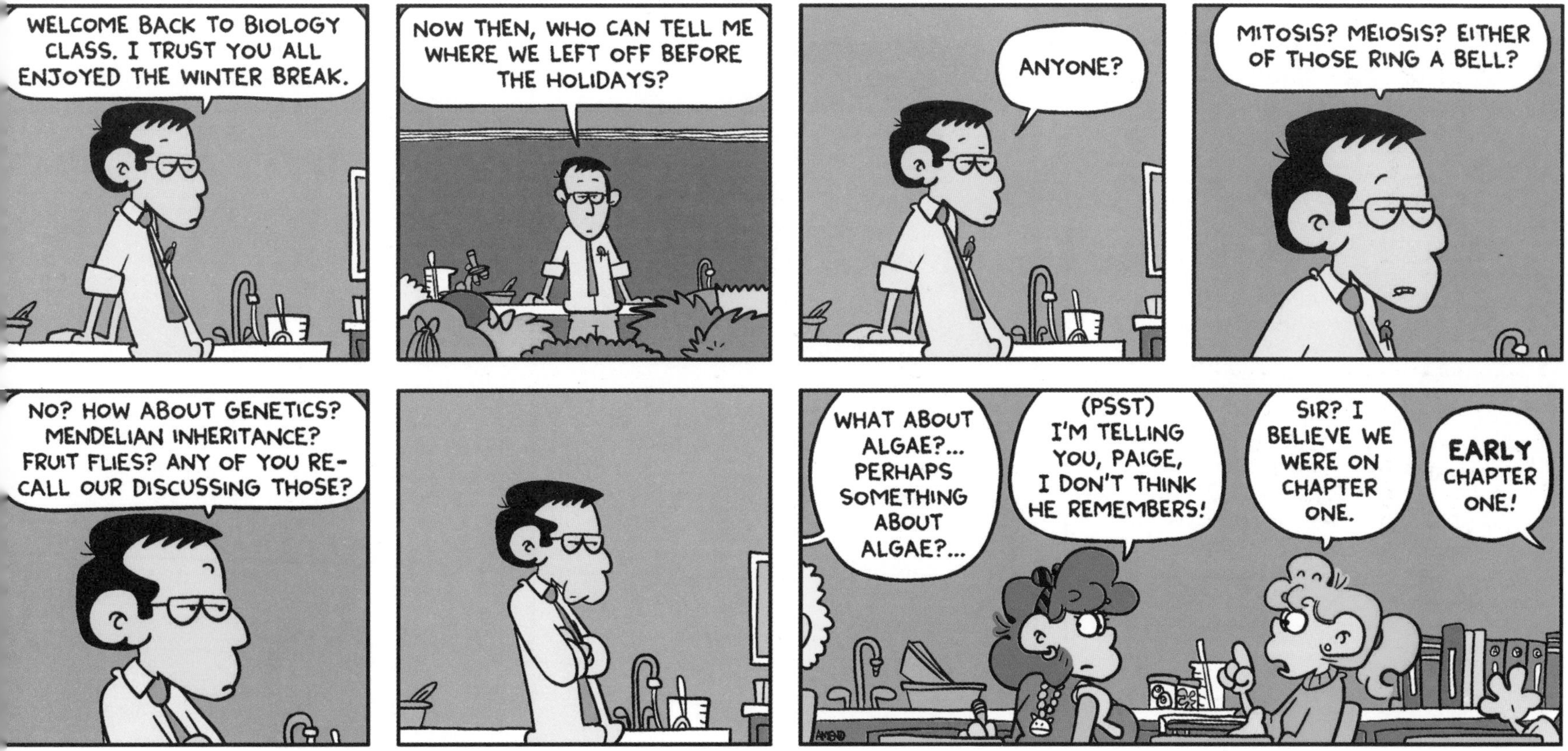
WELCOME BACK TO BIOLOGY CLASS. I TRUST YOU ALL ENJOYED THE WINTER BREAK.
NOW THEN, WHO CAN TELL ME WHERE WE LEFT OFF BEFORE THE HOLIDAYS?
ANYONE?
MITOSIS? MEIOSIS? EITHER OF THOSE RING A BELL?
NO? HOW ABOUT GENETICS? MENDELIAN INHERITANCE? FRUIT FLIES? ANY OF YOU RE-CALL OUR DISCUSSING THOSE?
WHAT ABOUT ALGAE?... PERHAPS SOMETHING ABOUT ALGAE?...
(PSST) I'M TELLING YOU, PAIGE, I DON'T THINK HE REMEMBERS!
SIR? I BELIEVE WE WERE ON CHAPTER ONE.
EARLY CHAPTER ONE!

Napchat

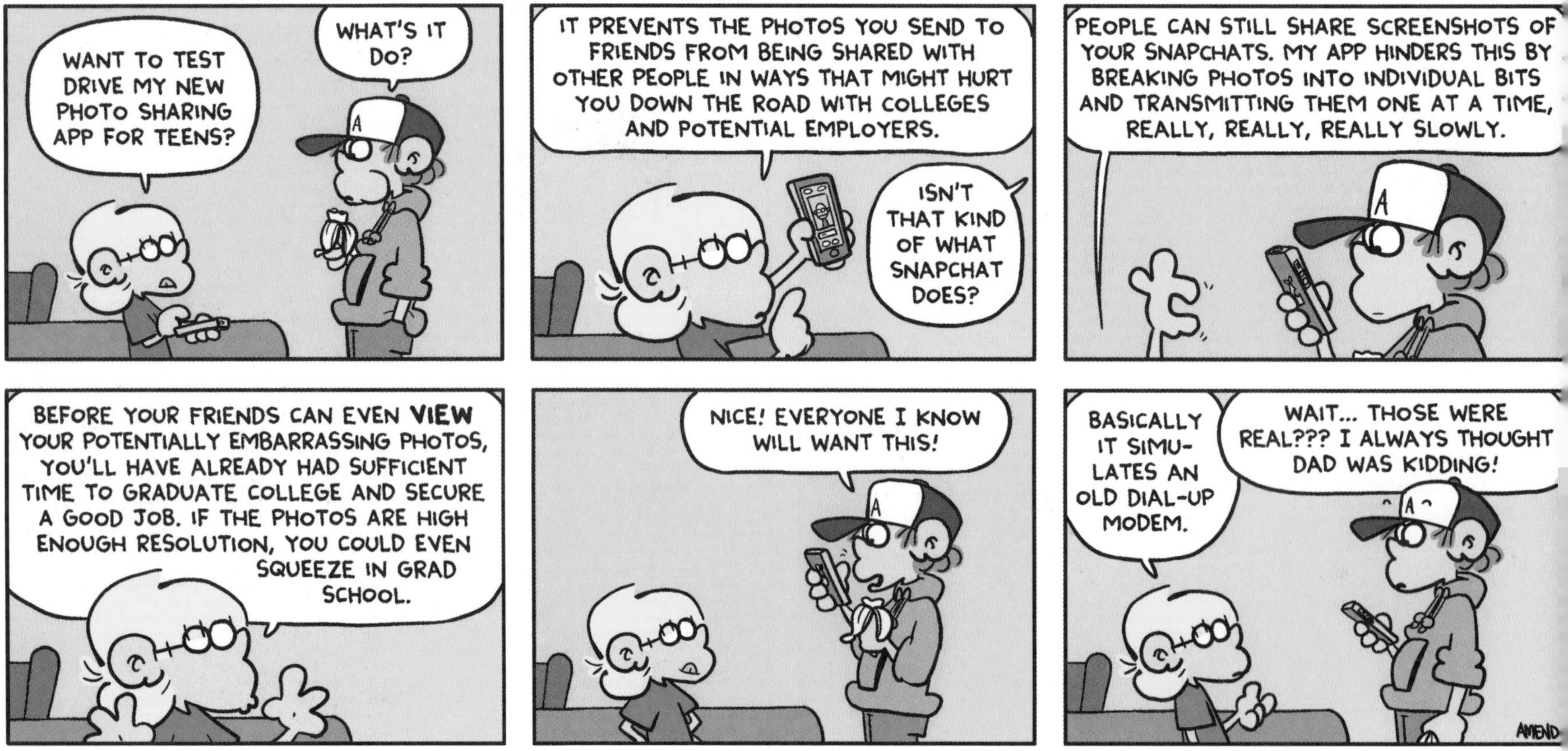

WANT TO TEST DRIVE MY NEW PHOTO SHARING APP FOR TEENS?
WHAT'S IT DO?
IT PREVENTS THE PHOTOS YOU SEND TO FRIENDS FROM BEING SHARED WITH OTHER PEOPLE IN WAYS THAT MIGHT HURT YOU DOWN THE ROAD WITH COLLEGES AND POTENTIAL EMPLOYERS.
ISN'T THAT KIND OF WHAT SNAPCHAT DOES?
PEOPLE CAN STILL SHARE SCREENSHOTS OF YOUR SNAPCHATS. MY APP HINDERS THIS BY BREAKING PHOTOS INTO INDIVIDUAL BITS AND TRANSMITTING THEM ONE AT A TIME, REALLY, REALLY, REALLY SLOWLY.
BEFORE YOUR FRIENDS CAN EVEN **VIEW** YOUR POTENTIALLY EMBARRASSING PHOTOS, YOU'LL HAVE ALREADY HAD SUFFICIENT TIME TO GRADUATE COLLEGE AND SECURE A GOOD JOB. IF THE PHOTOS ARE HIGH ENOUGH RESOLUTION, YOU COULD EVEN SQUEEZE IN GRAD SCHOOL.
NICE! EVERYONE I KNOW WILL WANT THIS!
BASICALLY IT SIMU-LATES AN OLD DIAL-UP MODEM.
WAIT... THOSE WERE REAL??? I ALWAYS THOUGHT DAD WAS KIDDING!
AMEND

Deniably Plausible

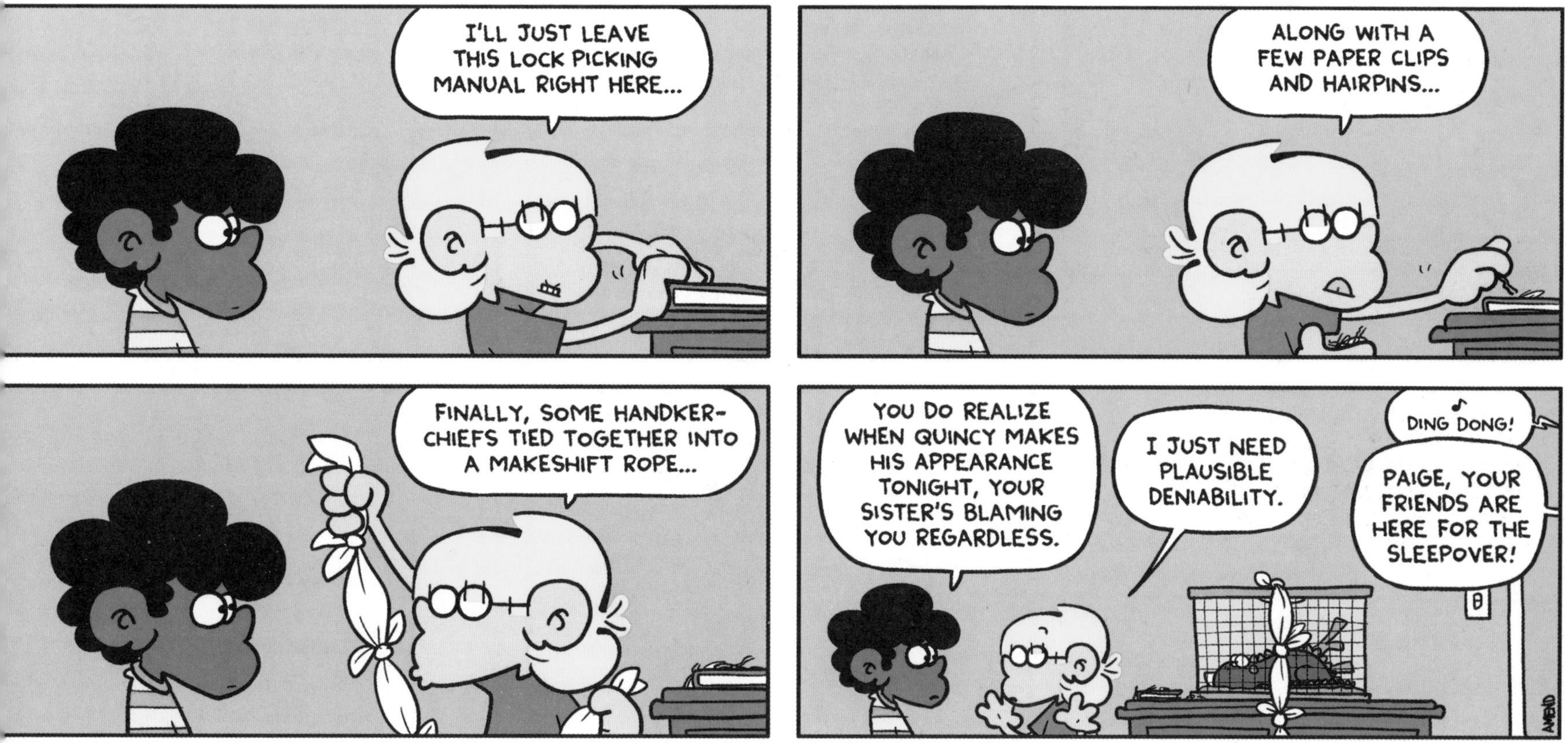
I'LL JUST LEAVE THIS LOCK PICKING MANUAL RIGHT HERE...
ALONG WITH A FEW PAPER CLIPS AND HAIRPINS...
FINALLY, SOME HANDKERCHIEFS TIED TOGETHER INTO A MAKESHIFT ROPE...
YOU DO REALIZE WHEN QUINCY MAKES HIS APPEARANCE TONIGHT, YOUR SISTER'S BLAMING YOU REGARDLESS.
I JUST NEED PLAUSIBLE DENIABILITY.
DING DONG!
PAIGE, YOUR FRIENDS ARE HERE FOR THE SLEEPOVER!
AMEND

Fourth Downton and Goal

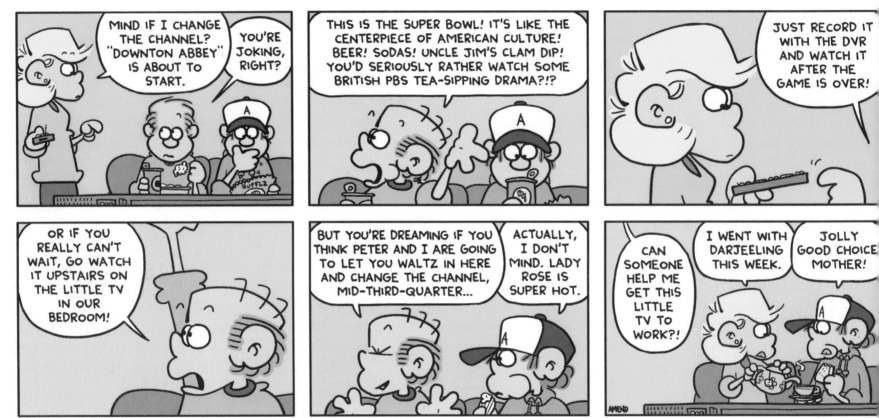

Special Valentines

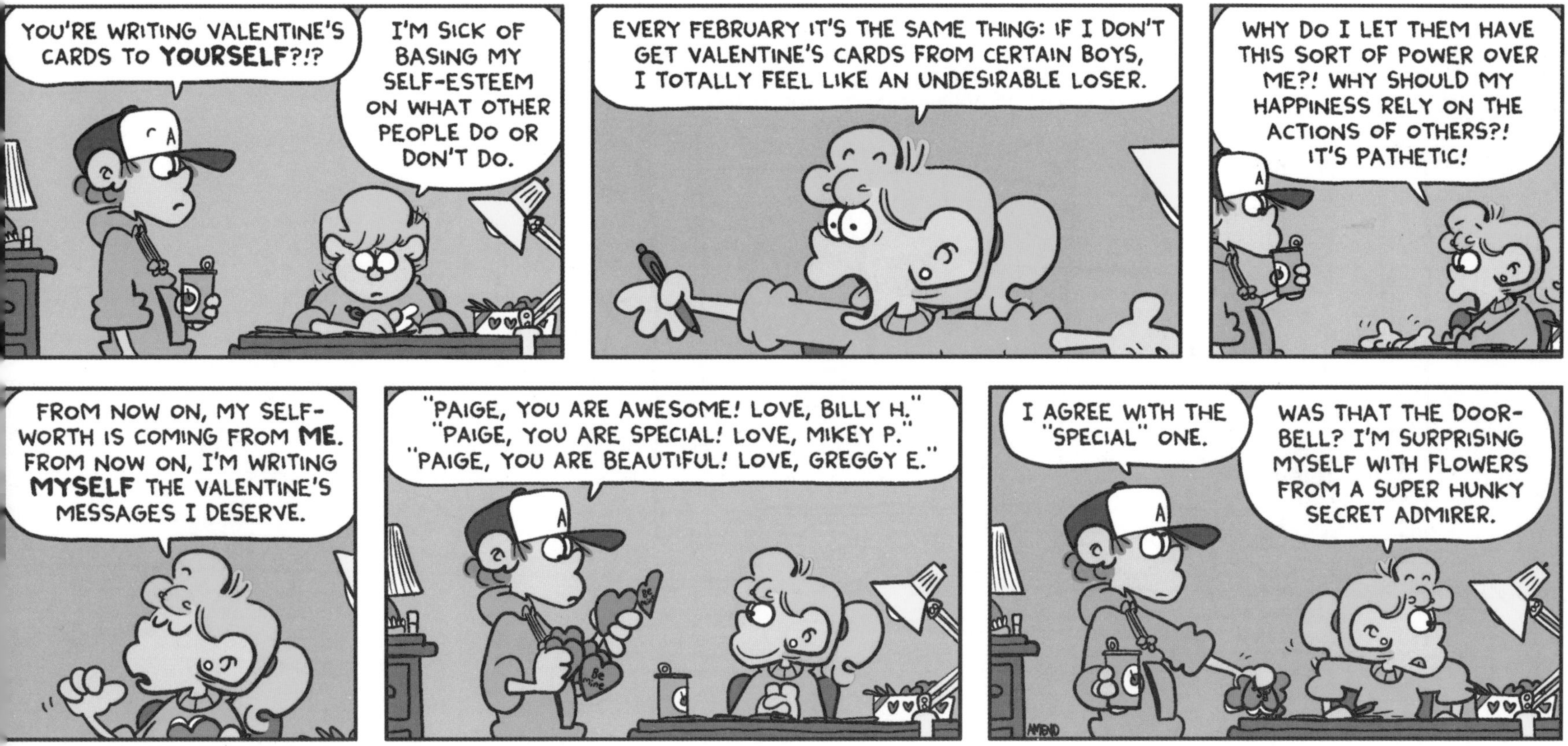

YOU'RE WRITING VALENTINE'S CARDS TO **YOURSELF**?!?
I'M SICK OF BASING MY SELF-ESTEEM ON WHAT OTHER PEOPLE DO OR DON'T DO.
EVERY FEBRUARY IT'S THE SAME THING: IF I DON'T GET VALENTINE'S CARDS FROM CERTAIN BOYS, I TOTALLY FEEL LIKE AN UNDESIRABLE LOSER.
WHY DO I LET THEM HAVE THIS SORT OF POWER OVER ME?! WHY SHOULD MY HAPPINESS RELY ON THE ACTIONS OF OTHERS?! IT'S PATHETIC!
FROM NOW ON, MY SELF-WORTH IS COMING FROM **ME**. FROM NOW ON, I'M WRITING **MYSELF** THE VALENTINE'S MESSAGES I DESERVE.
"PAIGE, YOU ARE AWESOME! LOVE, BILLY H." "PAIGE, YOU ARE SPECIAL! LOVE, MIKEY P." "PAIGE, YOU ARE BEAUTIFUL! LOVE, GREGGY E."
I AGREE WITH THE "SPECIAL" ONE.
WAS THAT THE DOORBELL? I'M SURPRISING MYSELF WITH FLOWERS FROM A SUPER HUNKY SECRET ADMIRER.

Minecrafty

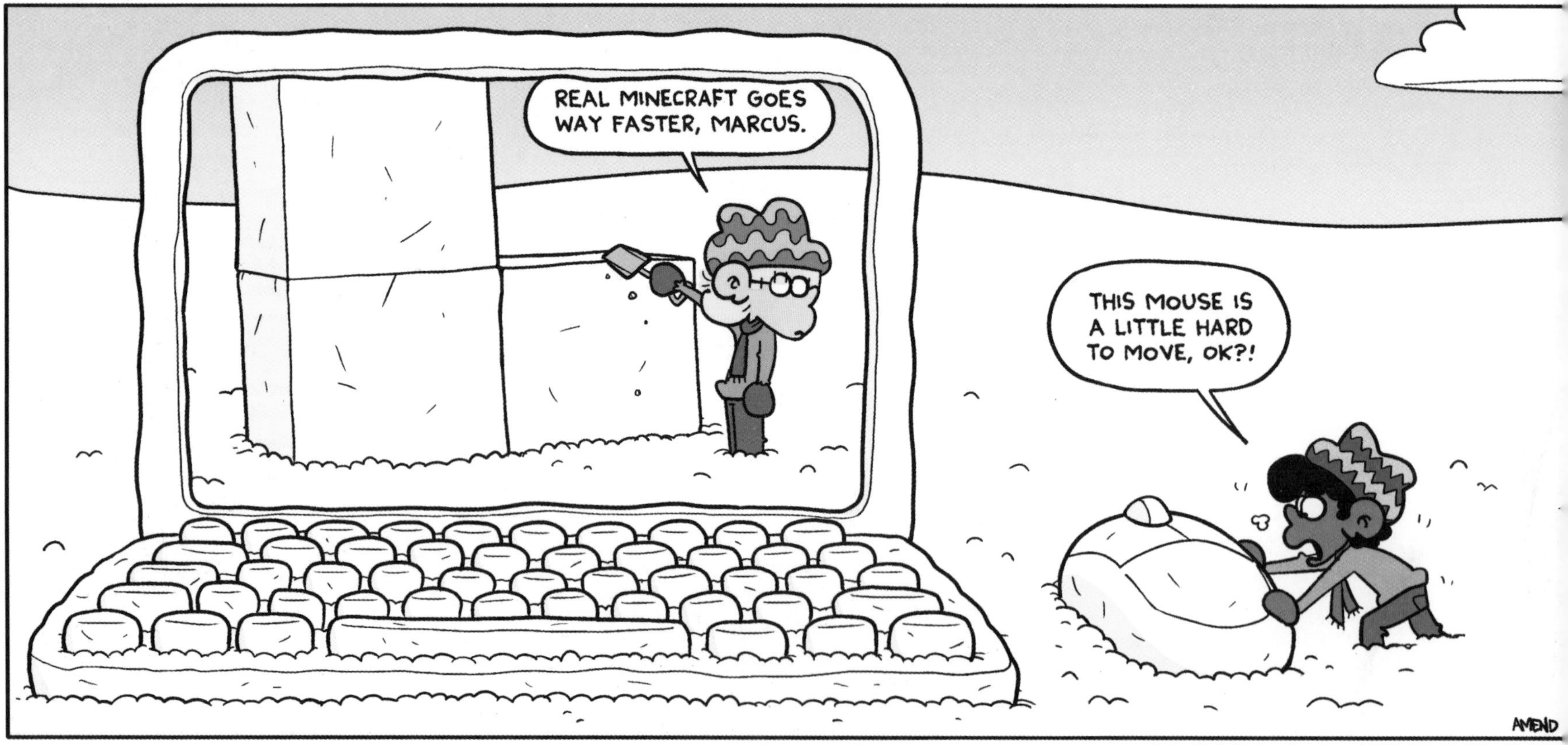
REAL MINECRAFT GOES WAY FASTER, MARCUS.
THIS MOUSE IS A LITTLE HARD TO MOVE, OK?!
AMEND

Ice Blocked

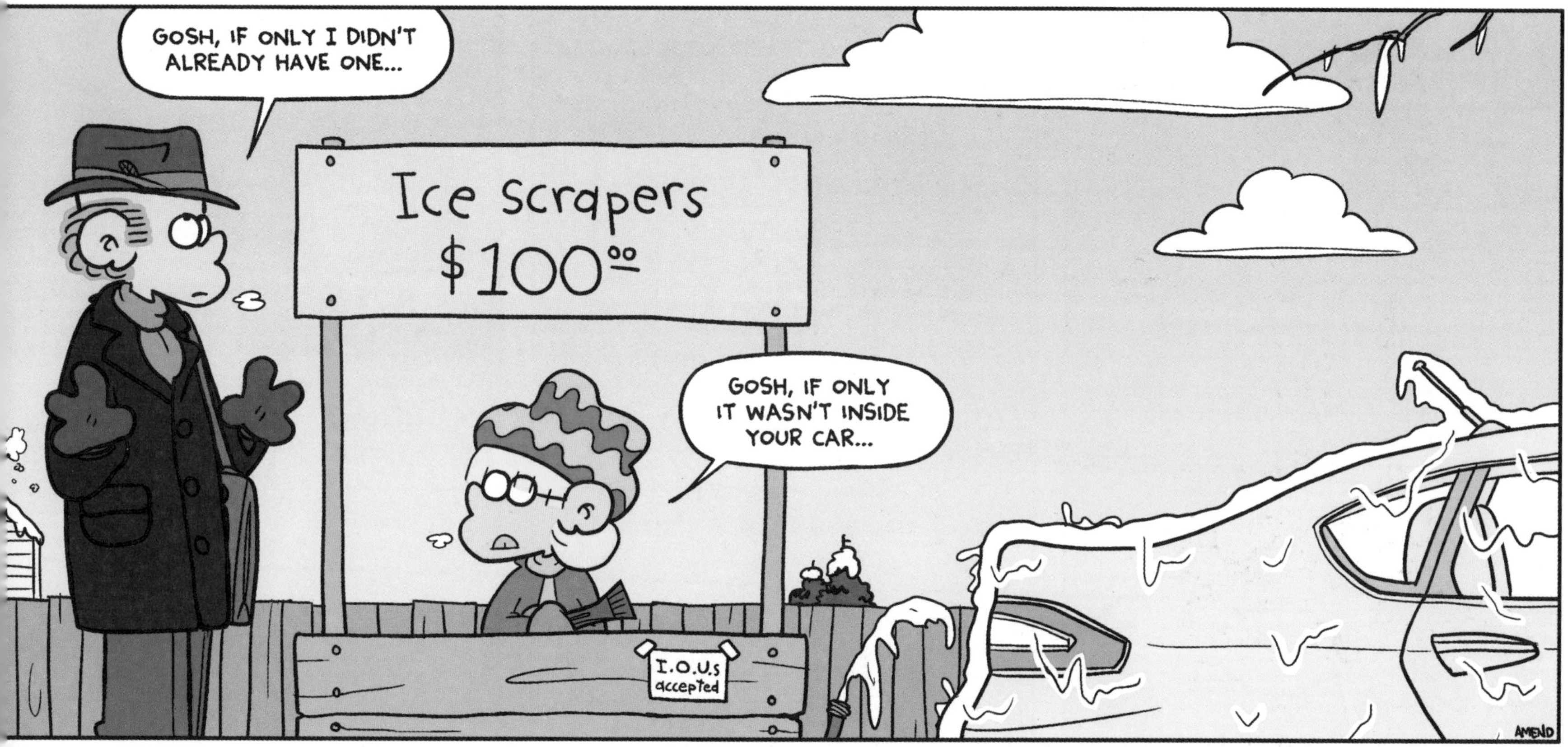

GOSH, IF ONLY I DIDN'T ALREADY HAVE ONE...
Ice scrapers $100.00
GOSH, IF ONLY IT WASN'T INSIDE YOUR CAR...
I.O.U.s accepted
AMEND

Good Muse, Bad Muse

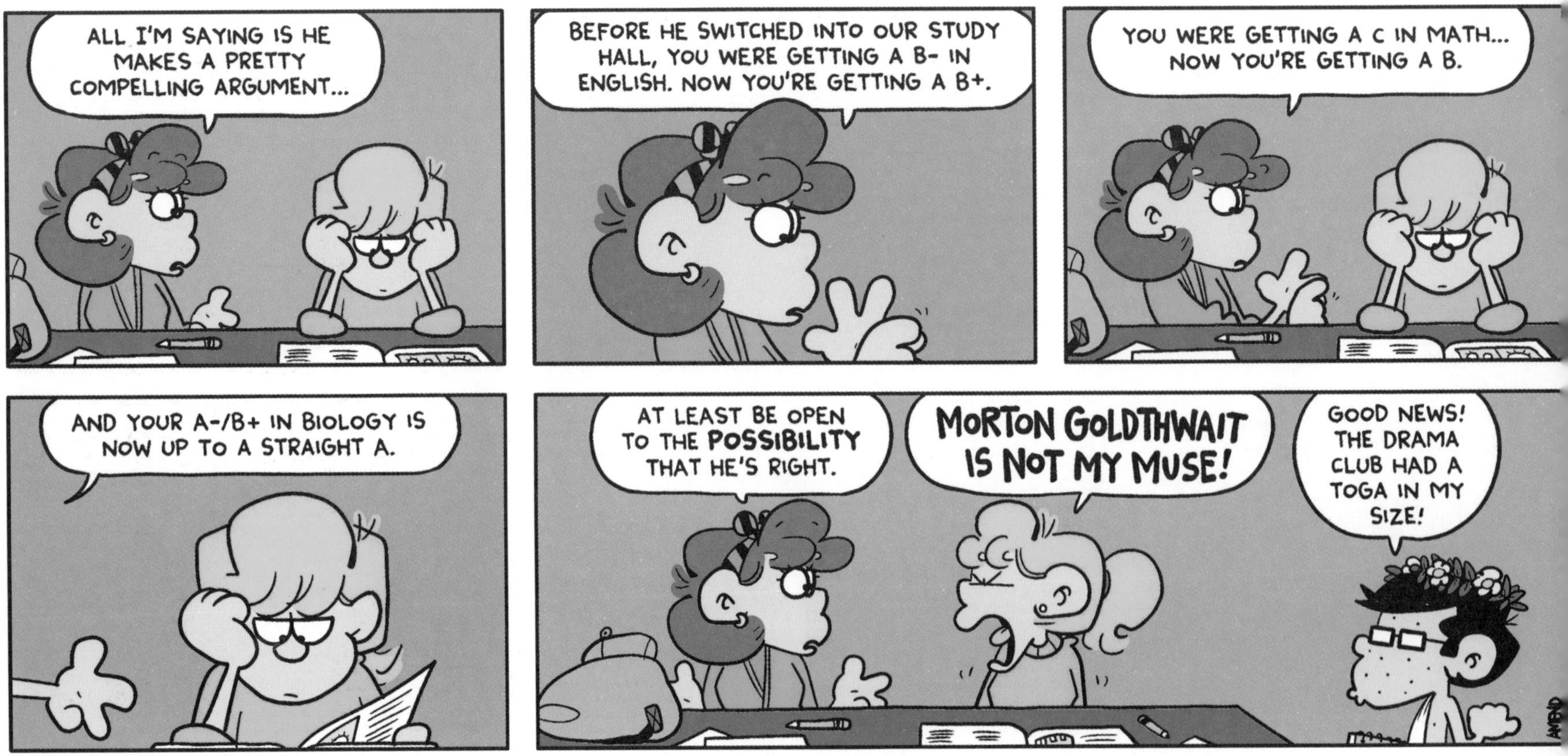
ALL I'M SAYING IS HE MAKES A PRETTY COMPELLING ARGUMENT...
BEFORE HE SWITCHED INTO OUR STUDY HALL, YOU WERE GETTING A B- IN ENGLISH. NOW YOU'RE GETTING A B+.
YOU WERE GETTING A C IN MATH... NOW YOU'RE GETTING A B.
AND YOUR A-/B+ IN BIOLOGY IS NOW UP TO A STRAIGHT A.
AT LEAST BE OPEN TO THE POSSIBILITY THAT HE'S RIGHT.
MORTON GOLDTHWAIT IS NOT MY MUSE!
GOOD NEWS! THE DRAMA CLUB HAD A TOGA IN MY SIZE!
AMEND

Spring Forwarder

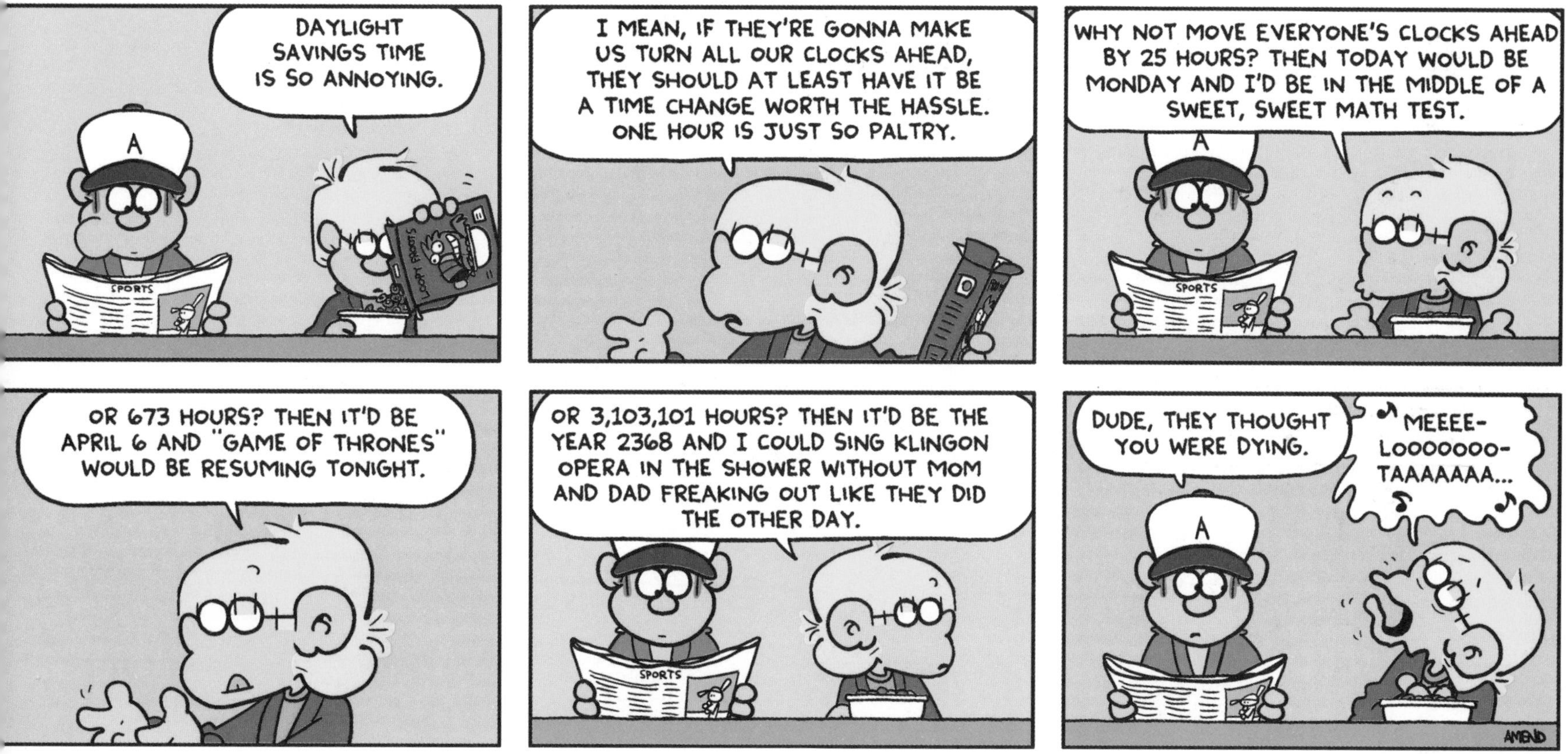
DAYLIGHT SAVINGS TIME IS SO ANNOYING.
LOOPY FROSTS
I MEAN, IF THEY'RE GONNA MAKE US TURN ALL OUR CLOCKS AHEAD, THEY SHOULD AT LEAST HAVE IT BE A TIME CHANGE WORTH THE HASSLE. ONE HOUR IS JUST SO PALTRY.
WHY NOT MOVE EVERYONE'S CLOCKS AHEAD BY 25 HOURS? THEN TODAY WOULD BE MONDAY AND I'D BE IN THE MIDDLE OF A SWEET, SWEET MATH TEST.
SPORTS
OR 673 HOURS? THEN IT'D BE APRIL 6 AND "GAME OF THRONES" WOULD BE RESUMING TONIGHT.
OR 3,103,101 HOURS? THEN IT'D BE THE YEAR 2368 AND I COULD SING KLINGON OPERA IN THE SHOWER WITHOUT MOM AND DAD FREAKING OUT LIKE THEY DID THE OTHER DAY.
DUDE, THEY THOUGHT YOU WERE DYING.
MEEEE-LOOOOOOO-TAAAAAAA...
AMEND

Jabberguac

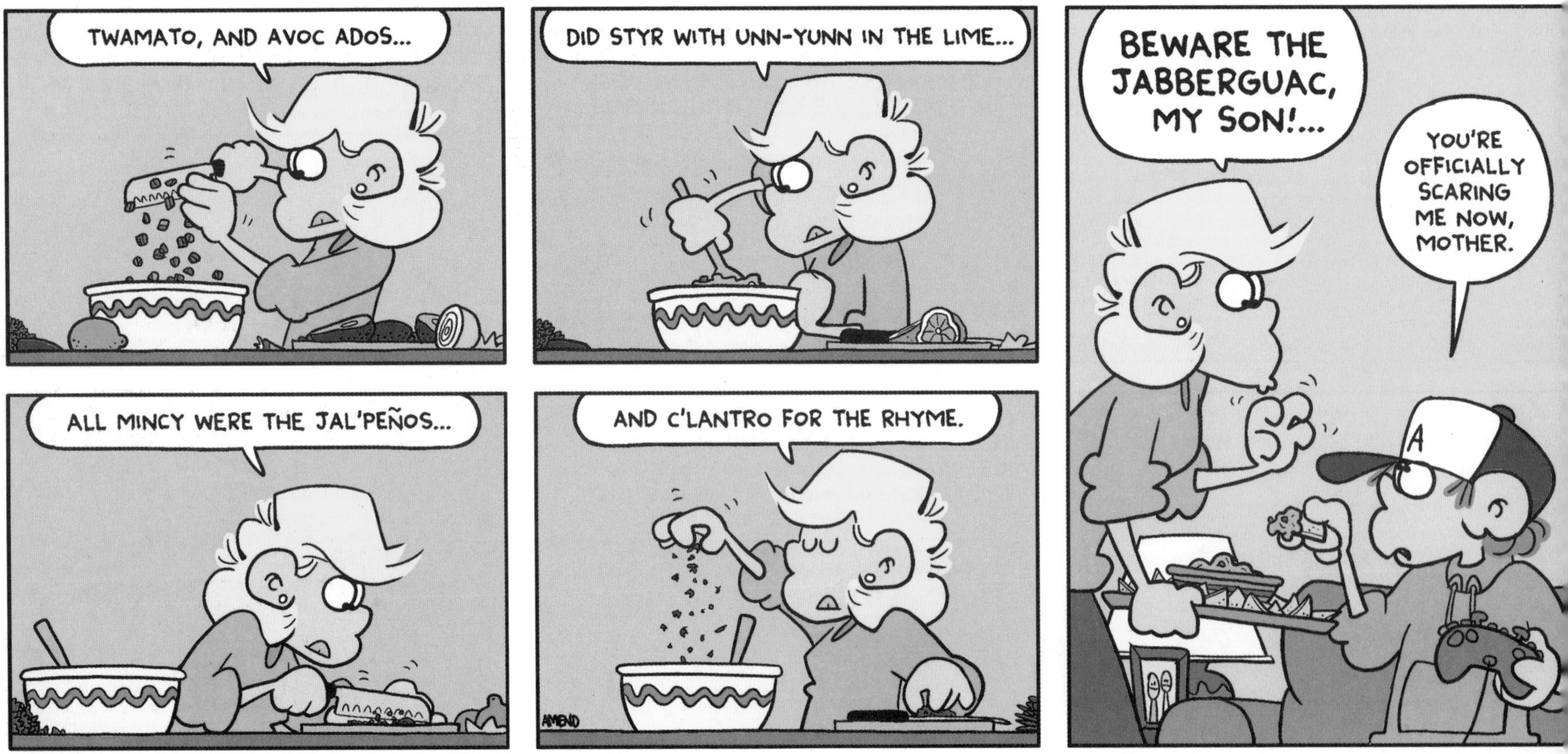
TWAMATO, AND AVOC ADOS...
DID STYR WITH UNN-YUNN IN THE LIME...
ALL MINCY WERE THE JAL'PEÑOS...
AND C'LANTRO FOR THE RHYME.
BEWARE THE JABBERGUAC, MY SON!...
YOU'RE OFFICIALLY SCARING ME NOW, MOTHER.
AMEND

Candy™Farm™Dungeon™

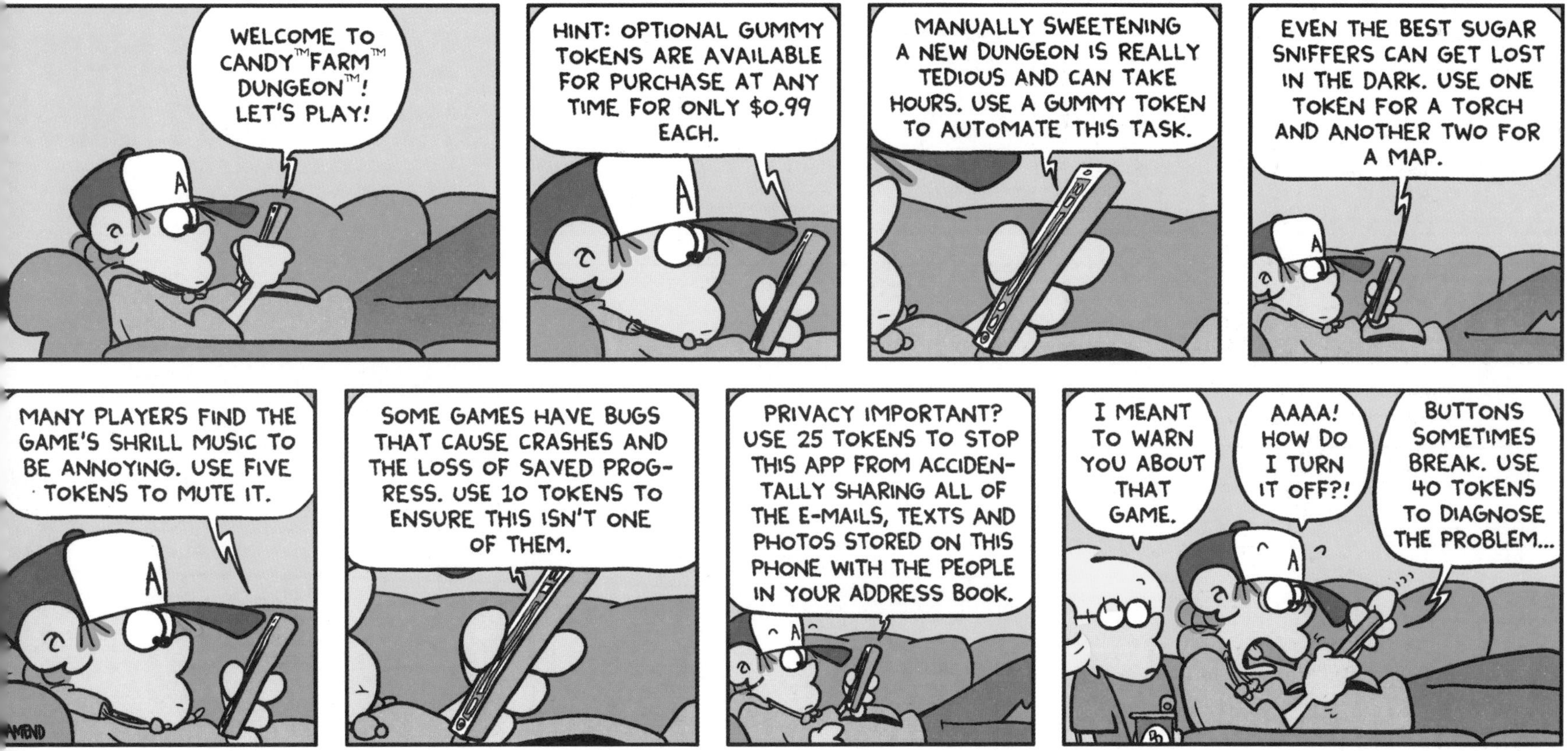

WELCOME TO CANDY™FARM™ DUNGEON™! LET'S PLAY!
HINT: OPTIONAL GUMMY TOKENS ARE AVAILABLE FOR PURCHASE AT ANY TIME FOR ONLY $0.99 EACH.
MANUALLY SWEETENING A NEW DUNGEON IS REALLY TEDIOUS AND CAN TAKE HOURS. USE A GUMMY TOKEN TO AUTOMATE THIS TASK.
EVEN THE BEST SUGAR SNIFFERS CAN GET LOST IN THE DARK. USE ONE TOKEN FOR A TORCH AND ANOTHER TWO FOR A MAP.
MANY PLAYERS FIND THE GAME'S SHRILL MUSIC TO BE ANNOYING. USE FIVE TOKENS TO MUTE IT.
AMEND
SOME GAMES HAVE BUGS THAT CAUSE CRASHES AND THE LOSS OF SAVED PROGRESS. USE 10 TOKENS TO ENSURE THIS ISN'T ONE OF THEM.
PRIVACY IMPORTANT? USE 25 TOKENS TO STOP THIS APP FROM ACCIDENTALLY SHARING ALL OF THE E-MAILS, TEXTS AND PHOTOS STORED ON THIS PHONE WITH THE PEOPLE IN YOUR ADDRESS BOOK.
I MEANT TO WARN YOU ABOUT THAT GAME.
AAAA! HOW DO I TURN IT OFF?!
BUTTONS SOMETIMES BREAK. USE 40 TOKENS TO DIAGNOSE THE PROBLEM...

Loop-de-loopholes

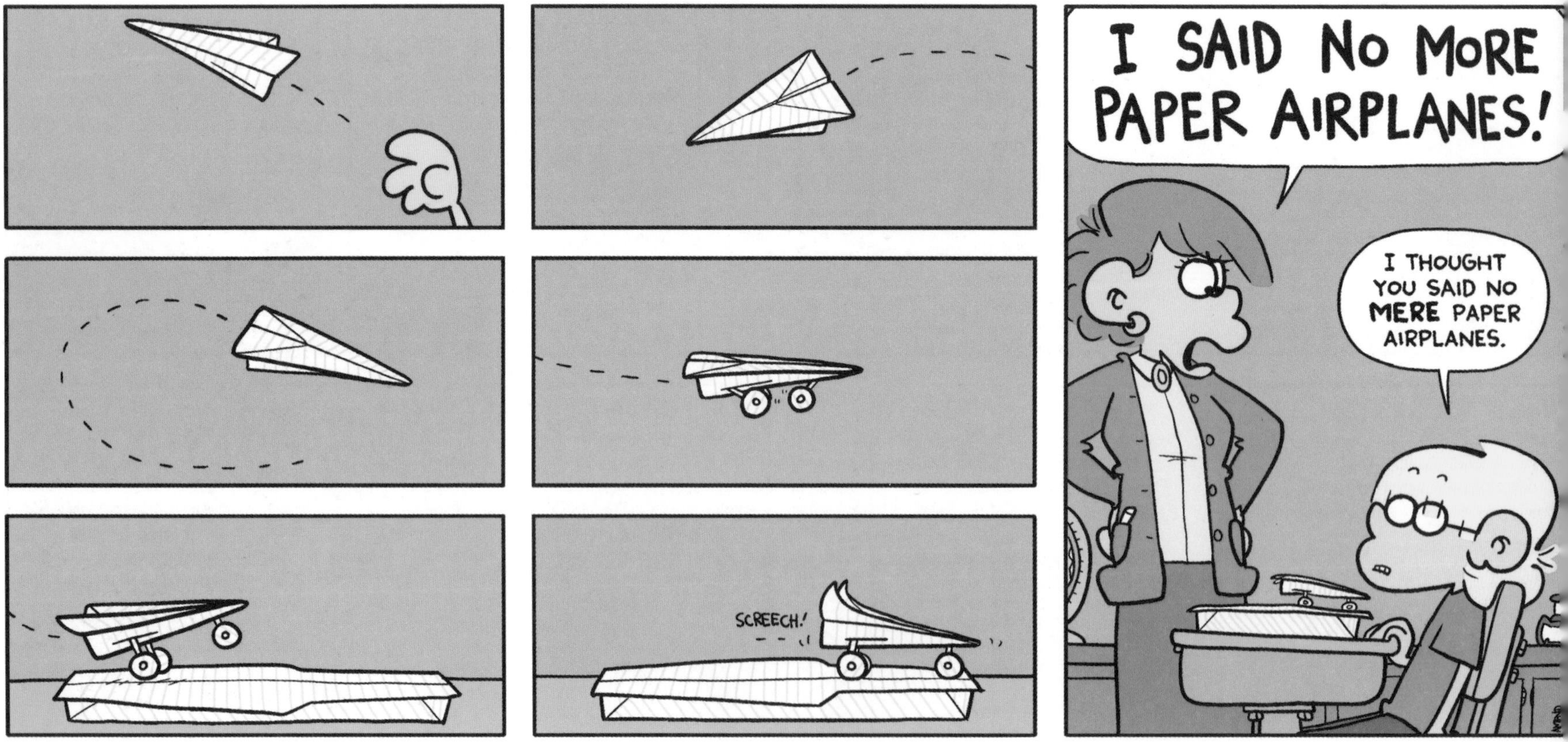

SCREECH!
I SAID NO MORE PAPER AIRPLANES!
I THOUGHT YOU SAID NO MERE PAPER AIRPLANES.

The Iron Sofa

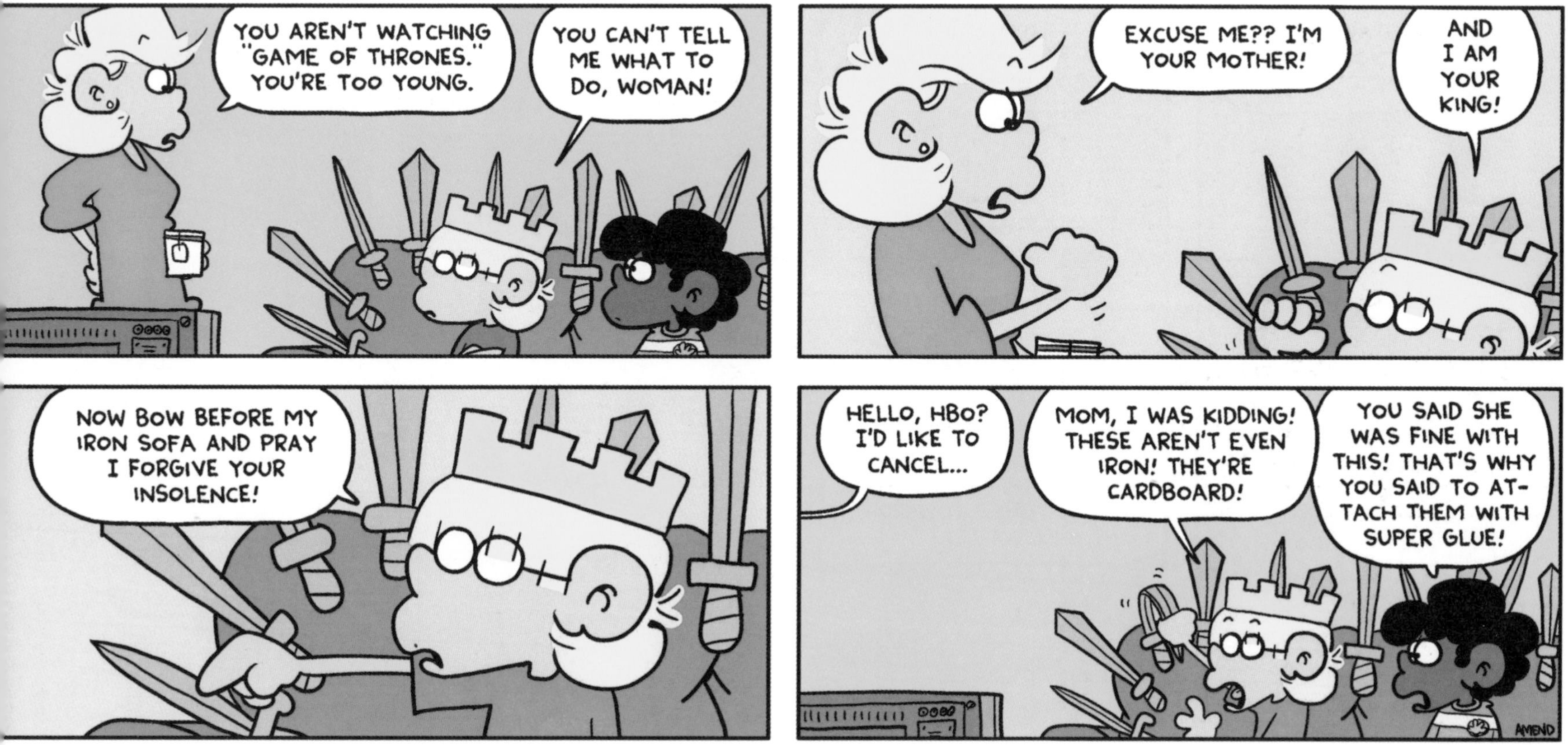
YOU AREN'T WATCHING "GAME OF THRONES." YOU'RE TOO YOUNG.
YOU CAN'T TELL ME WHAT TO DO, WOMAN!
EXCUSE ME?? I'M YOUR MOTHER!
AND I AM YOUR KING!
NOW BOW BEFORE MY IRON SOFA AND PRAY I FORGIVE YOUR INSOLENCE!
HELLO, HBO? I'D LIKE TO CANCEL...
MOM, I WAS KIDDING! THESE AREN'T EVEN IRON! THEY'RE CARDBOARD!
YOU SAID SHE WAS FINE WITH THIS! THAT'S WHY YOU SAID TO AT-TACH THEM WITH SUPER GLUE!
AMEND

Pitching Practice

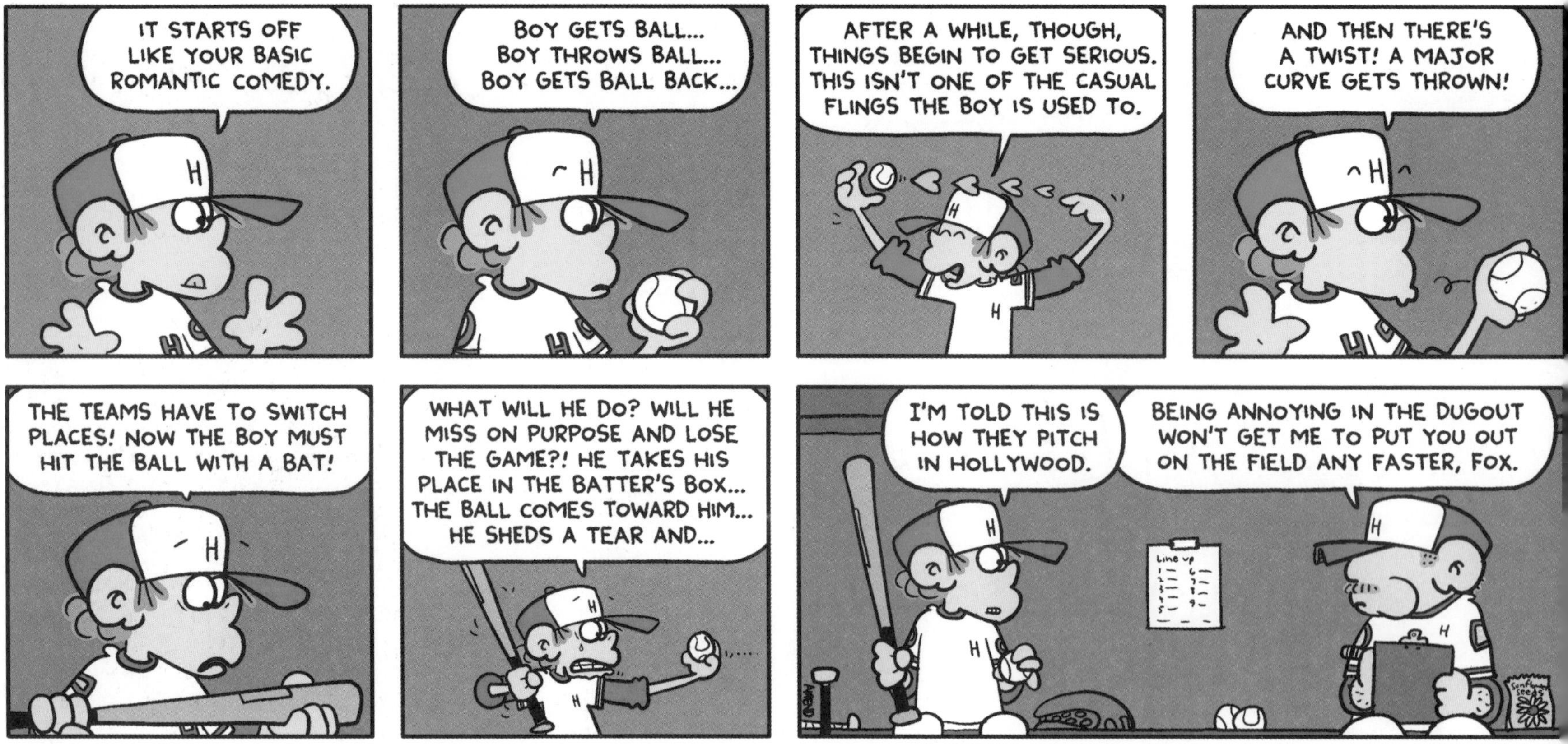
IT STARTS OFF LIKE YOUR BASIC ROMANTIC COMEDY.
BOY GETS BALL... BOY THROWS BALL... BOY GETS BALL BACK...
AFTER A WHILE, THOUGH, THINGS BEGIN TO GET SERIOUS. THIS ISN'T ONE OF THE CASUAL FLINGS THE BOY IS USED TO.
AND THEN THERE'S A TWIST! A MAJOR CURVE GETS THROWN!
THE TEAMS HAVE TO SWITCH PLACES! NOW THE BOY MUST HIT THE BALL WITH A BAT!
WHAT WILL HE DO? WILL HE MISS ON PURPOSE AND LOSE THE GAME?! HE TAKES HIS PLACE IN THE BATTER'S BOX... THE BALL COMES TOWARD HIM... HE SHEDS A TEAR AND...
I'M TOLD THIS IS HOW THEY PITCH IN HOLLYWOOD.
BEING ANNOYING IN THE DUGOUT WON'T GET ME TO PUT YOU OUT ON THE FIELD ANY FASTER, FOX.

Who'll Stop the Rain?

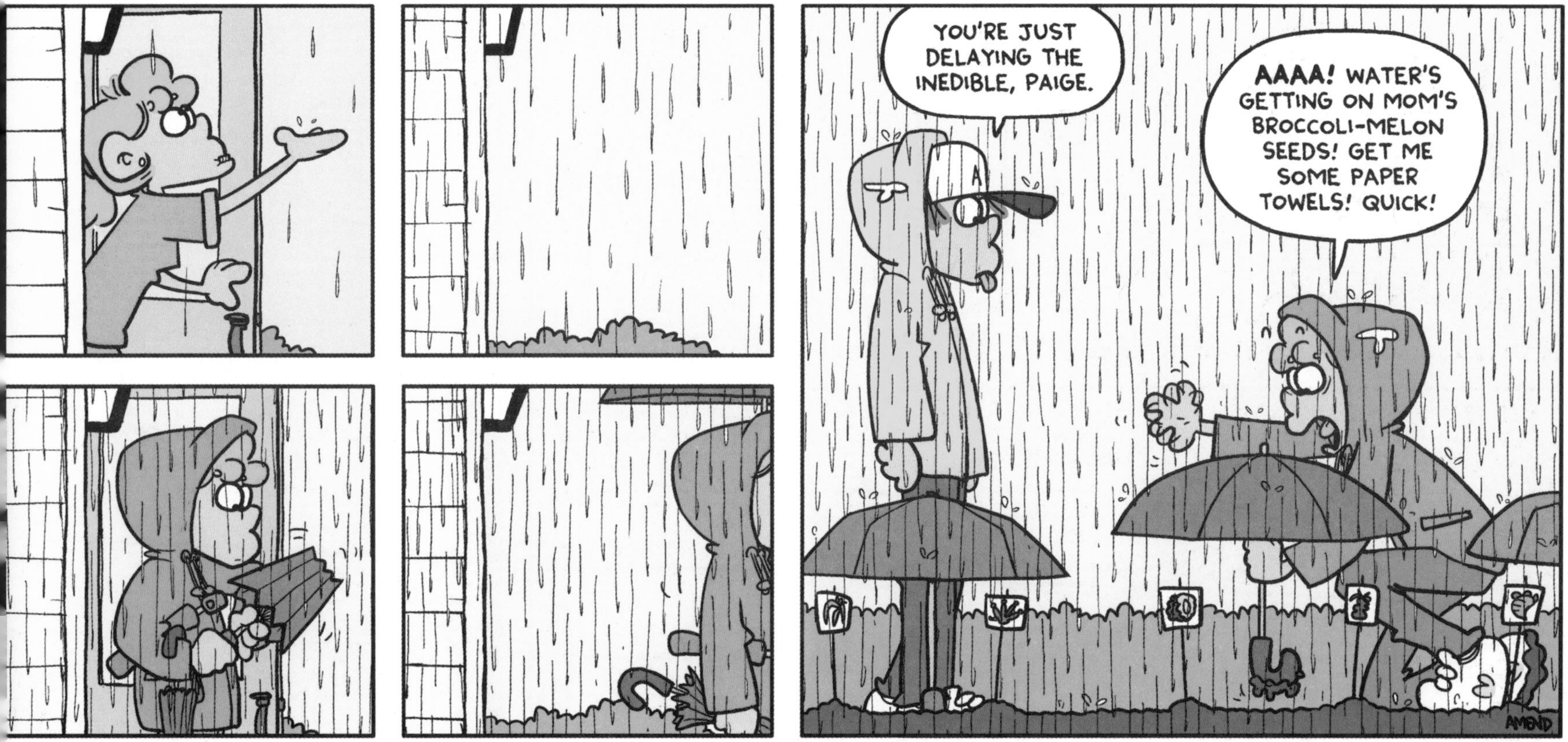
YOU'RE JUST DELAYING THE INEDIBLE, PAIGE.
AAAA! WATER'S GETTING ON MOM'S BROCCOLI-MELON SEEDS! GET ME SOME PAPER TOWELS! QUICK!
AMEND

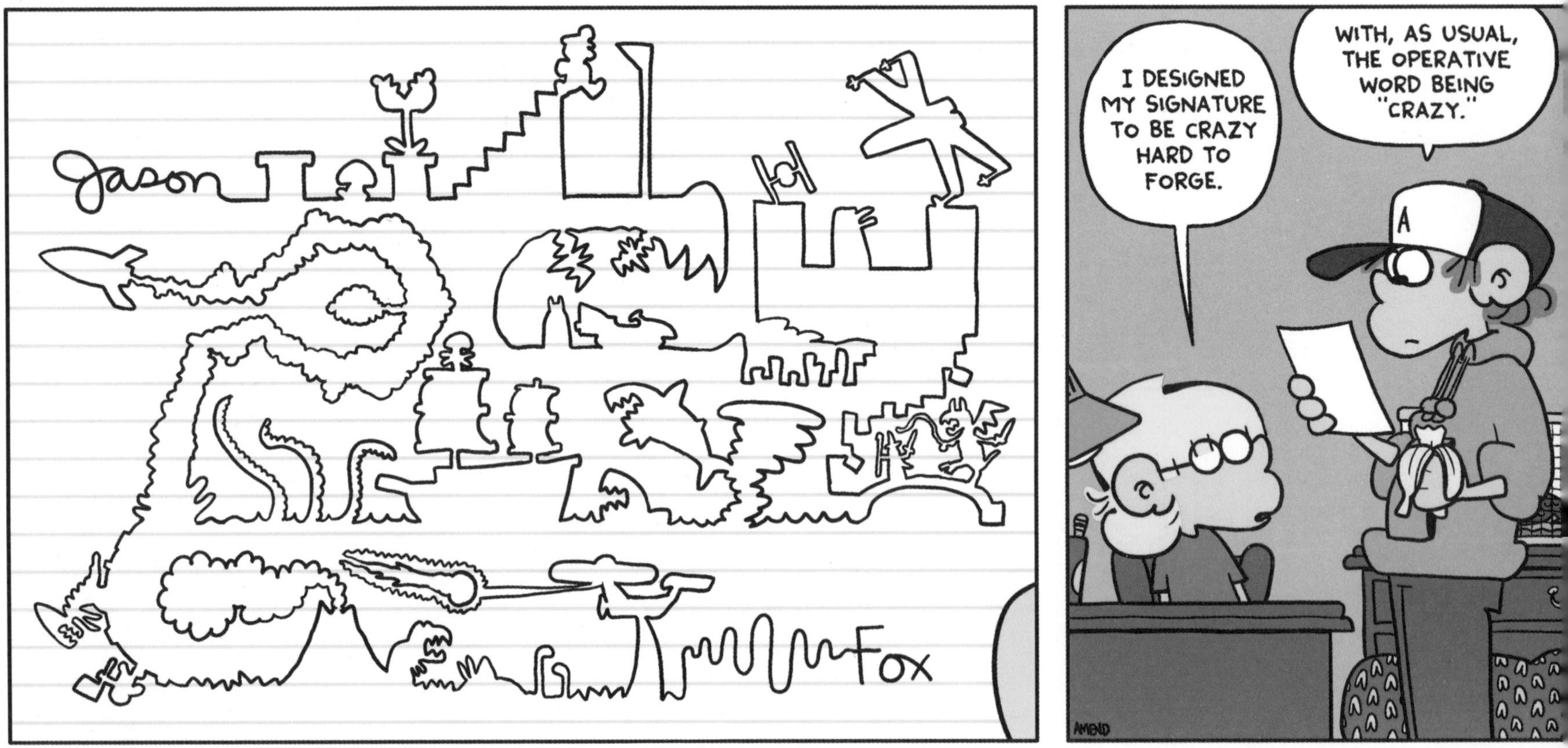
Jason
Fox
I DESIGNED MY SIGNATURE TO BE CRAZY HARD TO FORGE.
WITH, AS USUAL, THE OPERATIVE WORD BEING "CRAZY."
A
AMEND

May the Fourth

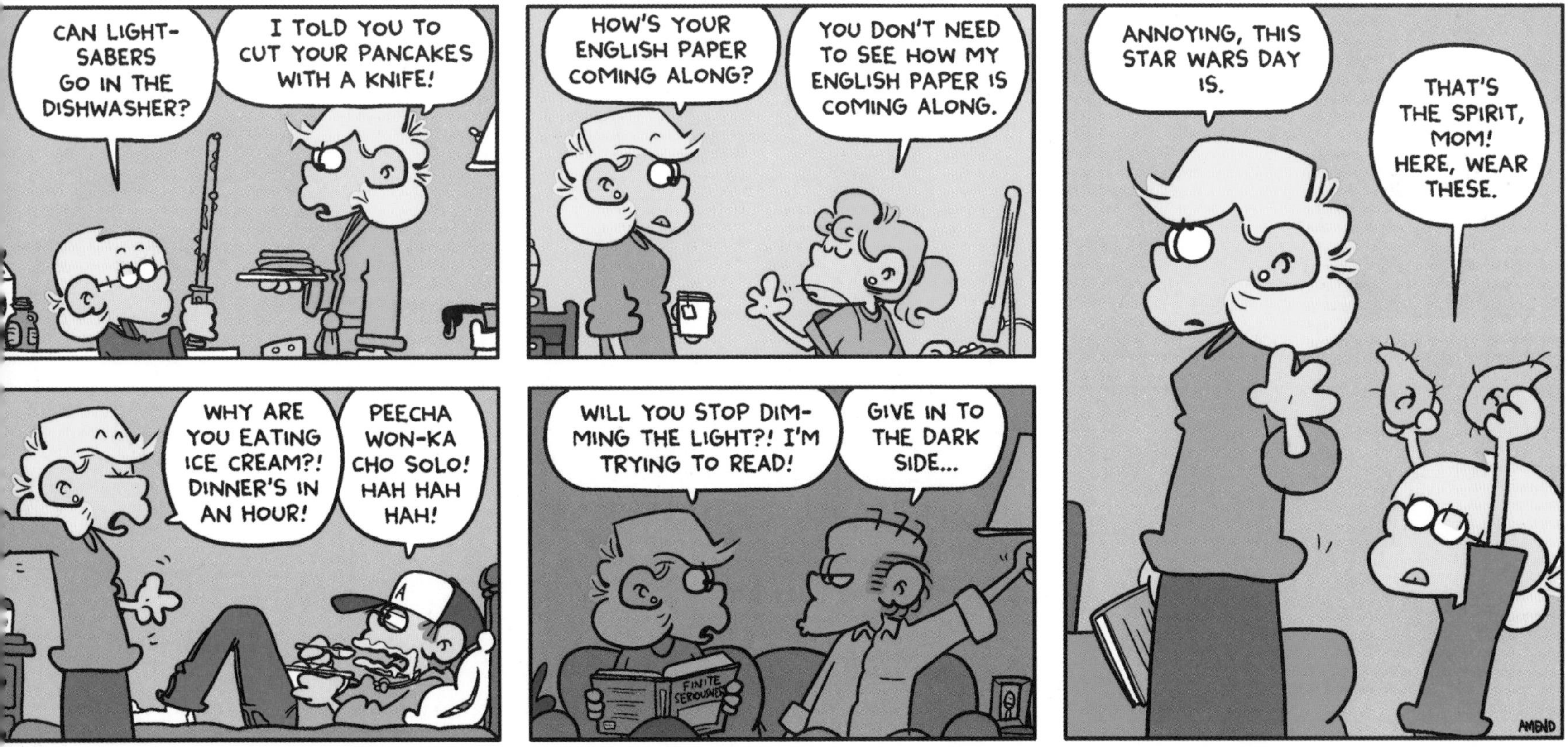
CAN LIGHT-SABERS GO IN THE DISHWASHER?
I TOLD YOU TO CUT YOUR PANCAKES WITH A KNIFE!
HOW'S YOUR ENGLISH PAPER COMING ALONG?
YOU DON'T NEED TO SEE HOW MY ENGLISH PAPER IS COMING ALONG.
WHY ARE YOU EATING ICE CREAM?! DINNER'S IN AN HOUR!
PEECHA WON-KA CHO SOLO! HAH HAH HAH!
WILL YOU STOP DIM-MING THE LIGHT?! I'M TRYING TO READ!
GIVE IN TO THE DARK SIDE...
FINITE SERIOUSNESS
ANNOYING, THIS STAR WARS DAY IS.
THAT'S THE SPIRIT, MOM! HERE, WEAR THESE.
AMEND

Biologically Speaking

Totally Calm

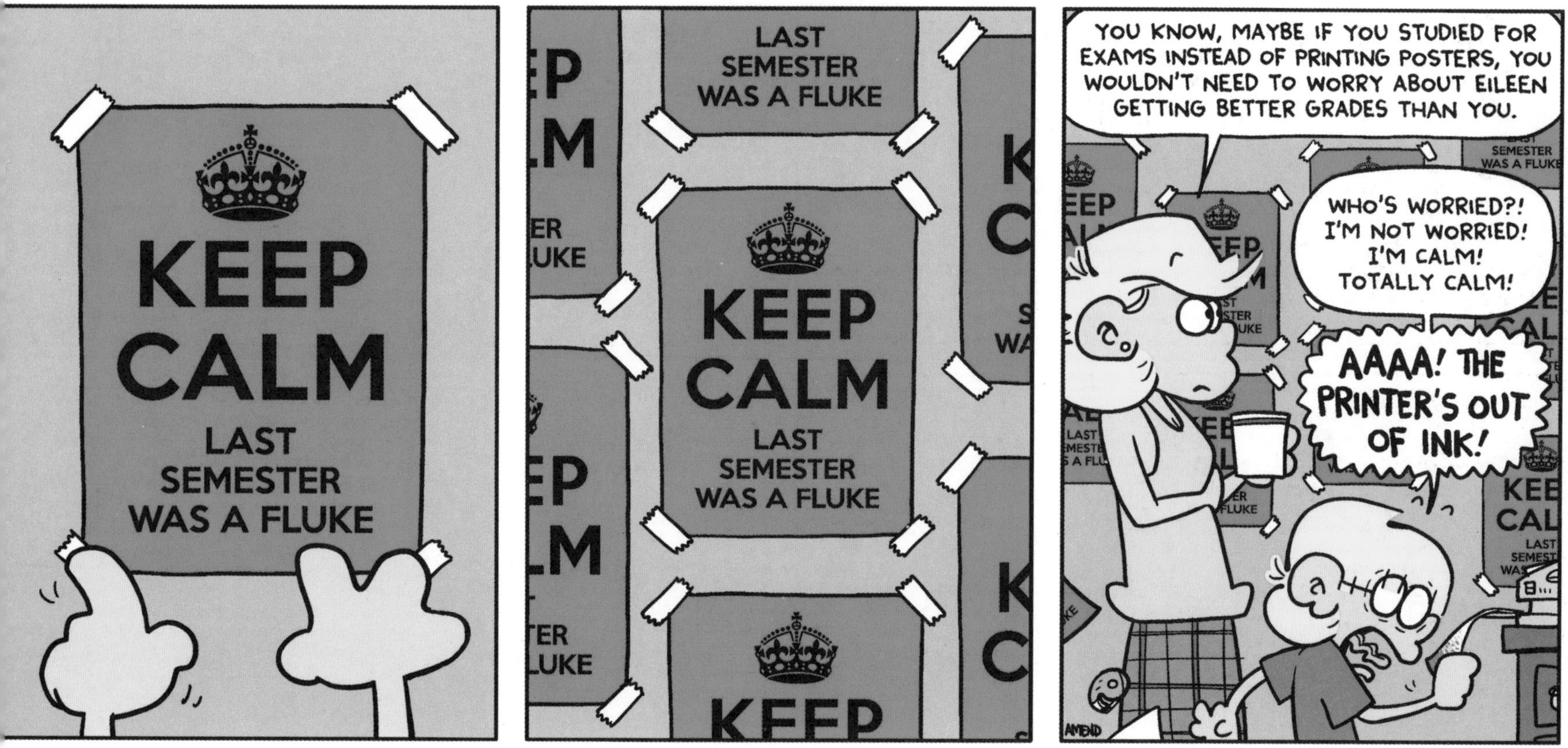
KEEP CALM
LAST SEMESTER WAS A FLUKE
LAST SEMESTER WAS A FLUKE
KEEP CALM
LAST SEMESTER WAS A FLUKE
YOU KNOW, MAYBE IF YOU STUDIED FOR EXAMS INSTEAD OF PRINTING POSTERS, YOU WOULDN'T NEED TO WORRY ABOUT EILEEN GETTING BETTER GRADES THAN YOU.
WHO'S WORRIED?! I'M NOT WORRIED! I'M CALM! TOTALLY CALM!
AAAA! THE PRINTER'S OUT OF INK!
AMEND

Stream Baby Stream

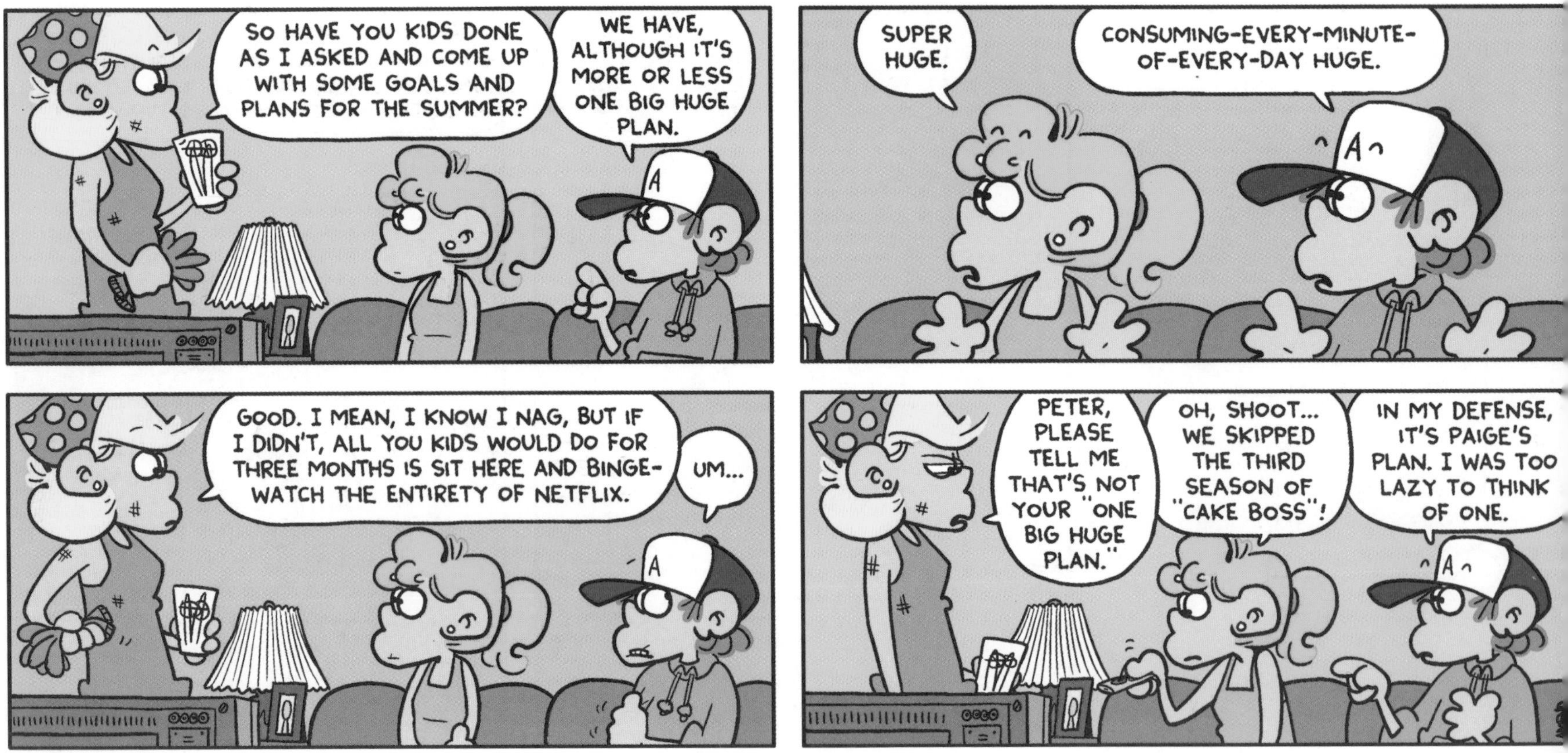
SO HAVE YOU KIDS DONE AS I ASKED AND COME UP WITH SOME GOALS AND PLANS FOR THE SUMMER?
WE HAVE, ALTHOUGH IT'S MORE OR LESS ONE BIG HUGE PLAN.
SUPER HUGE.
CONSUMING-EVERY-MINUTE-OF-EVERY-DAY HUGE.
GOOD. I MEAN, I KNOW I NAG, BUT IF I DIDN'T, ALL YOU KIDS WOULD DO FOR THREE MONTHS IS SIT HERE AND BINGE-WATCH THE ENTIRETY OF NETFLIX.
UM...
PETER, PLEASE TELL ME THAT'S NOT YOUR "ONE BIG HUGE PLAN."
OH, SHOOT... WE SKIPPED THE THIRD SEASON OF "CAKE BOSS"!
IN MY DEFENSE, IT'S PAIGE'S PLAN. I WAS TOO LAZY TO THINK OF ONE.

Nut Neutrality

IN WASHINGTON, THE FCC FINDS ITSELF KNEE-DEEP IN PUBLIC REACTION TO REPORTS IT MAY LOOSEN, IF NOT FULLY ABANDON, ITS STATED COMMITMENT TO PRESERVE NET NEUTRALITY AND AN OPEN INTERNET.

THOUSANDS AND THOUSANDS OF LETTERS, E-MAILS AND PHONE CALLS HAVE POURED IN ON A NEAR-DAILY BASIS FROM AGHAST CITIZENS, TECHNOLOGISTS, ACADEMICS, AND BUSINESS OWNERS, ASKING COMMISSION MEMBERS TO KEEP THE INTERNET'S LEVEL PLAYING FIELD AND NON-DISCRIMINATORY DATA PRACTICES INTACT.

WE ARE TOLD, HOWEVER, THAT THE FCC HAS RECEIVED A NEAR-EQUAL NUMBER OF E-MAILS DEMANDING AN **END** TO NET NEUTRALITY, ALL FROM THE SAME 14-YEAR-OLD GIRL. "MAKING IT SO PEOPLE CAN ONLY WEAR NEUTRAL COLORS LIKE BEIGE AND TAUPE IN THEIR INSTAGRAM SELFIES IS DOWNRIGHT UNAMERICAN," READS ONE.

YOU PROBABLY SHOULDN'T HAVE TOLD YOUR SISTER THAT'S WHAT IT MEANT.

I WAS KIDDING, PAIGE! I WAS KIDDING!

(CLICK) SEND.
(CLICK) SEND.
(CLICK) SEND.

Brrskin-Robbins

Panel 1: HOLD ON A SEC...

Panel 2: (no dialogue)

Panel 3: (no dialogue)

Panel 4: OK, PROCEED.

Panel 5: I LIKE TO TAKE COLD-WEATHER PRECAUTIONS WHEN JOINING YOU FOR ICE CREAM.

THIS'LL BE GONE IN 30 SECONDS, YOU WIMP.

Reply All

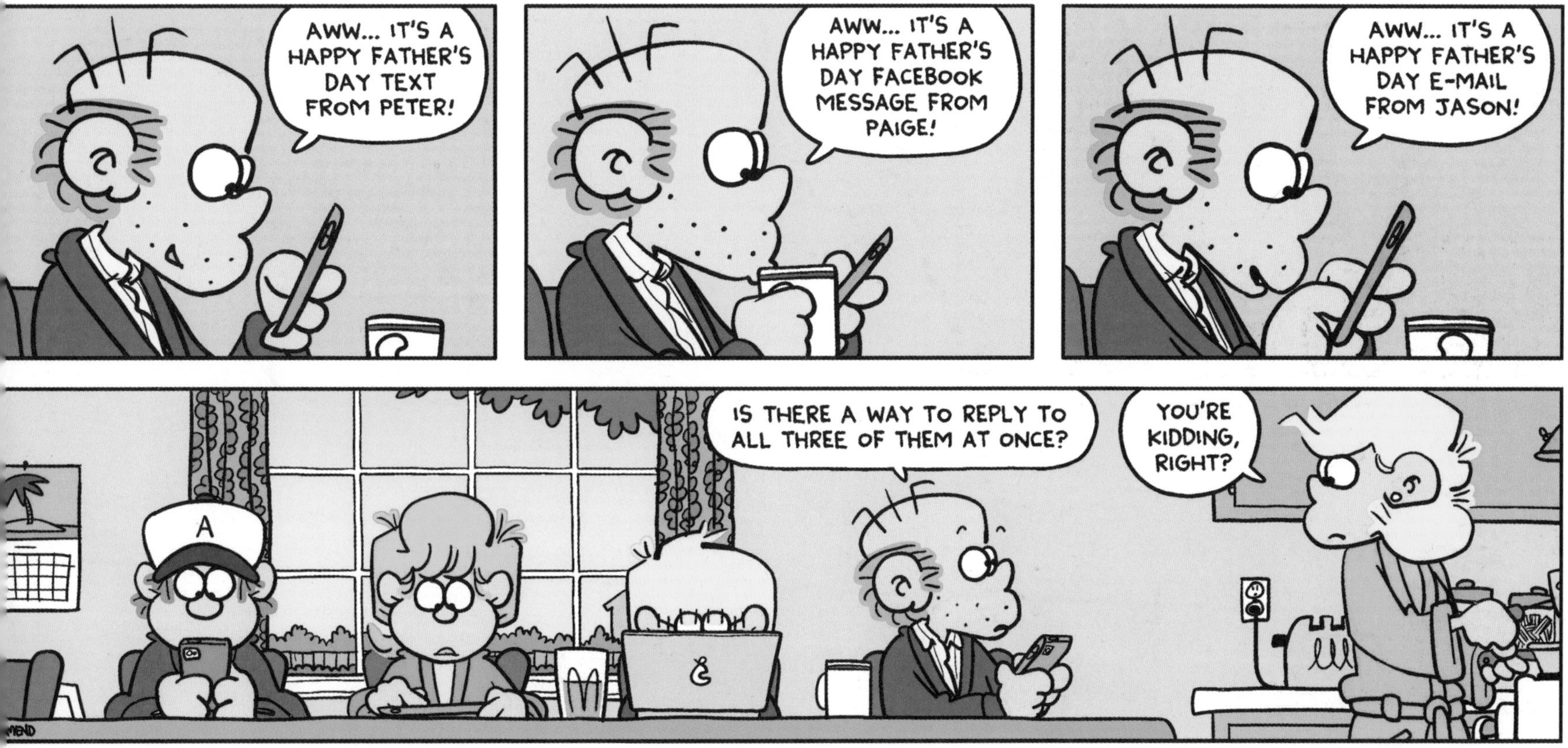
AWW... IT'S A HAPPY FATHER'S DAY TEXT FROM PETER!
AWW... IT'S A HAPPY FATHER'S DAY FACEBOOK MESSAGE FROM PAIGE!
AWW... IT'S A HAPPY FATHER'S DAY E-MAIL FROM JASON!
A
IS THERE A WAY TO REPLY TO ALL THREE OF THEM AT ONCE?
YOU'RE KIDDING, RIGHT?

Slippyball

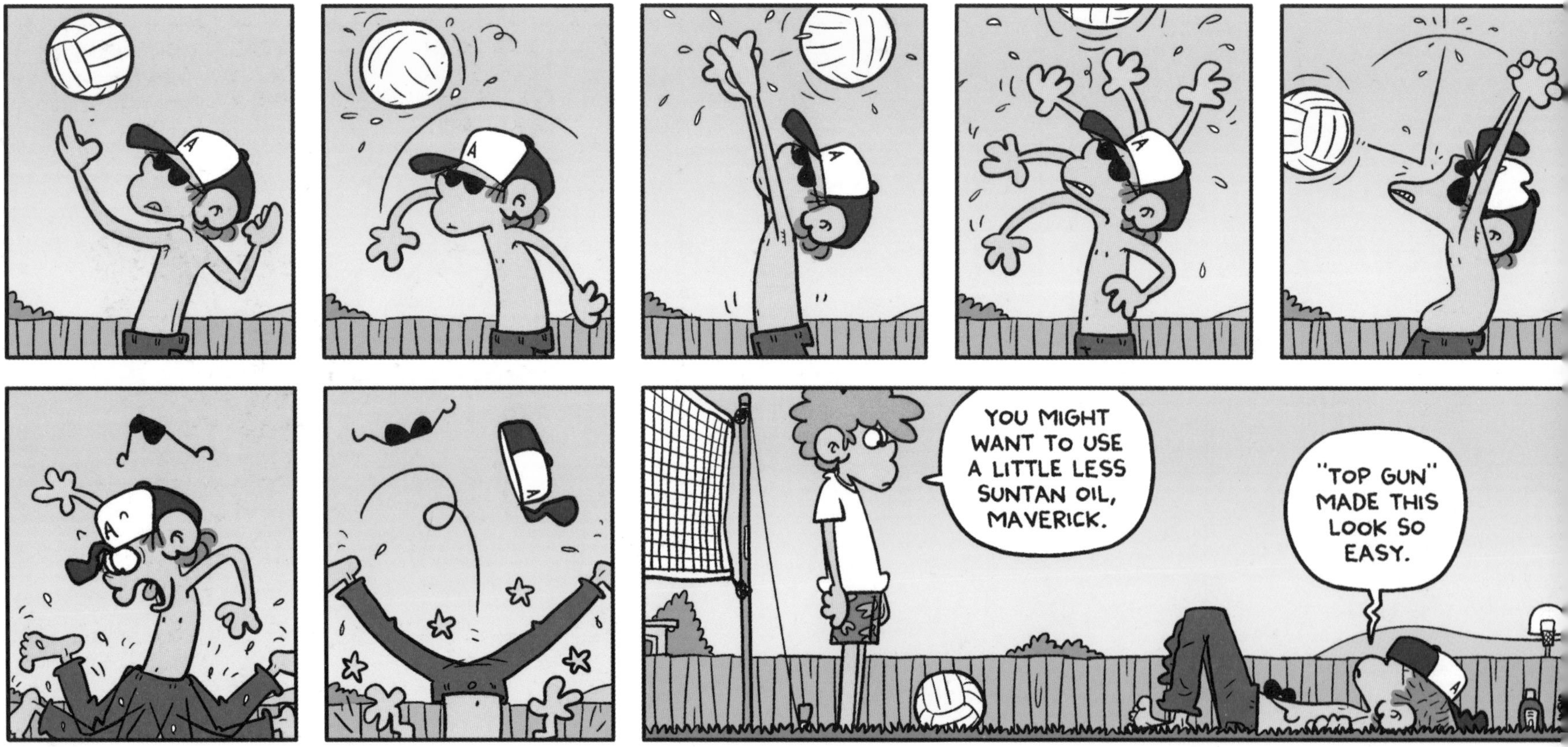
YOU MIGHT WANT TO USE A LITTLE LESS SUNTAN OIL, MAVERICK.
"TOP GUN" MADE THIS LOOK SO EASY.

Skywrithing

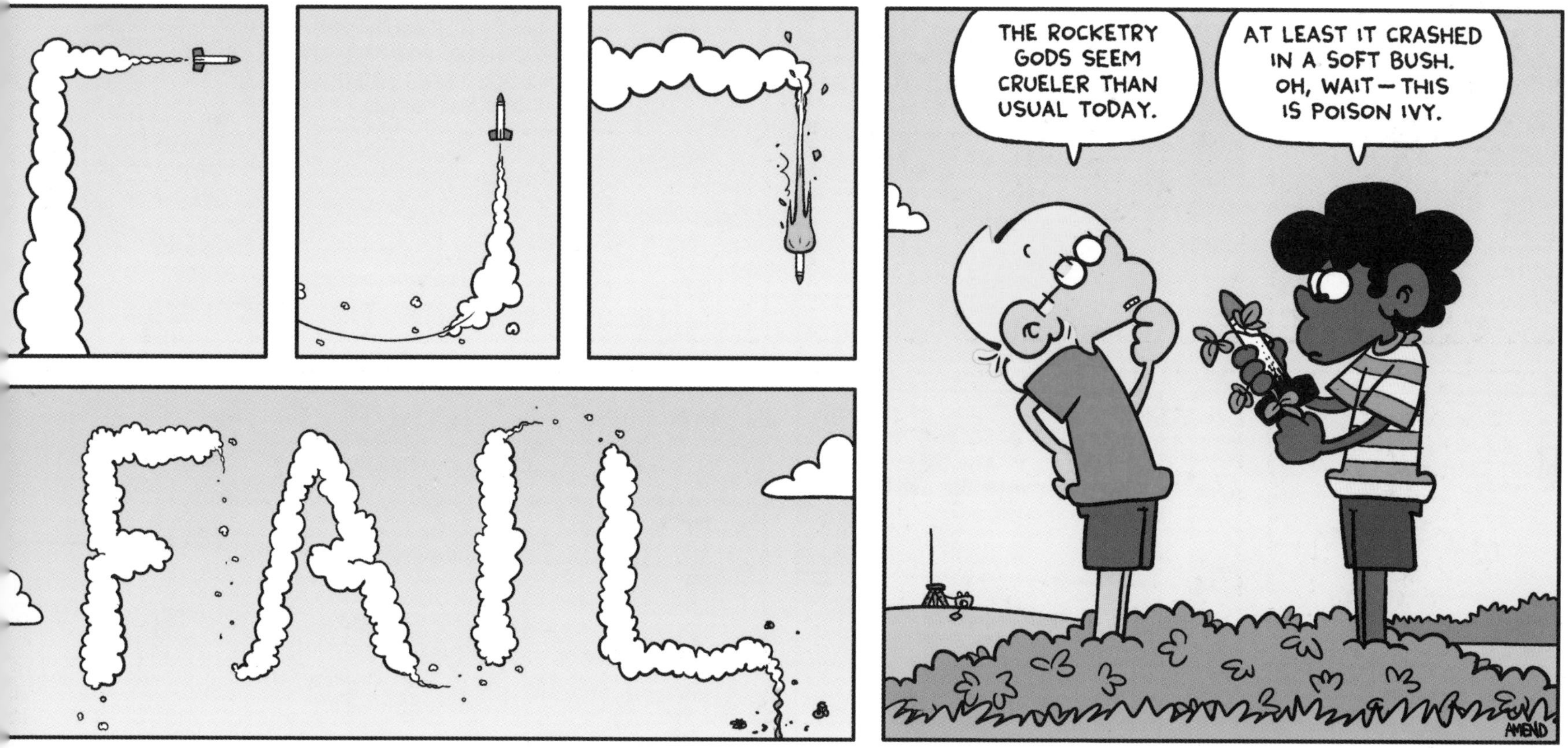
FAIL
THE ROCKETRY GODS SEEM CRUELER THAN USUAL TODAY.
AT LEAST IT CRASHED IN A SOFT BUSH. OH, WAIT—THIS IS POISON IVY.
AMEND

Wicked Bad

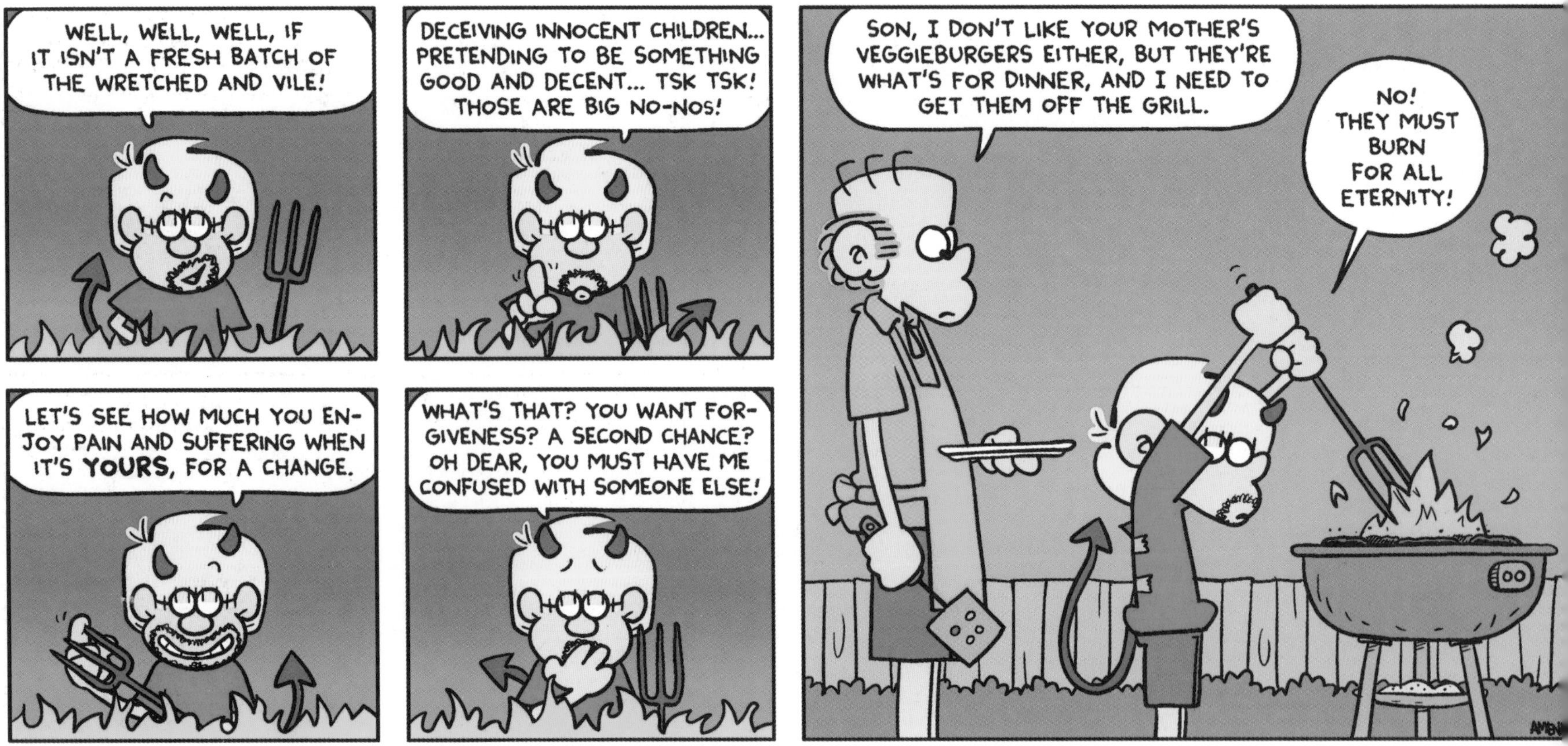
WELL, WELL, WELL, IF IT ISN'T A FRESH BATCH OF THE WRETCHED AND VILE!
DECEIVING INNOCENT CHILDREN... PRETENDING TO BE SOMETHING GOOD AND DECENT... TSK TSK! THOSE ARE BIG NO-NOS!
LET'S SEE HOW MUCH YOU ENJOY PAIN AND SUFFERING WHEN IT'S **YOURS**, FOR A CHANGE.
WHAT'S THAT? YOU WANT FORGIVENESS? A SECOND CHANCE? OH DEAR, YOU MUST HAVE ME CONFUSED WITH SOMEONE ELSE!
SON, I DON'T LIKE YOUR MOTHER'S VEGGIEBURGERS EITHER, BUT THEY'RE WHAT'S FOR DINNER, AND I NEED TO GET THEM OFF THE GRILL.
NO! THEY MUST BURN FOR ALL ETERNITY!

Server Issues

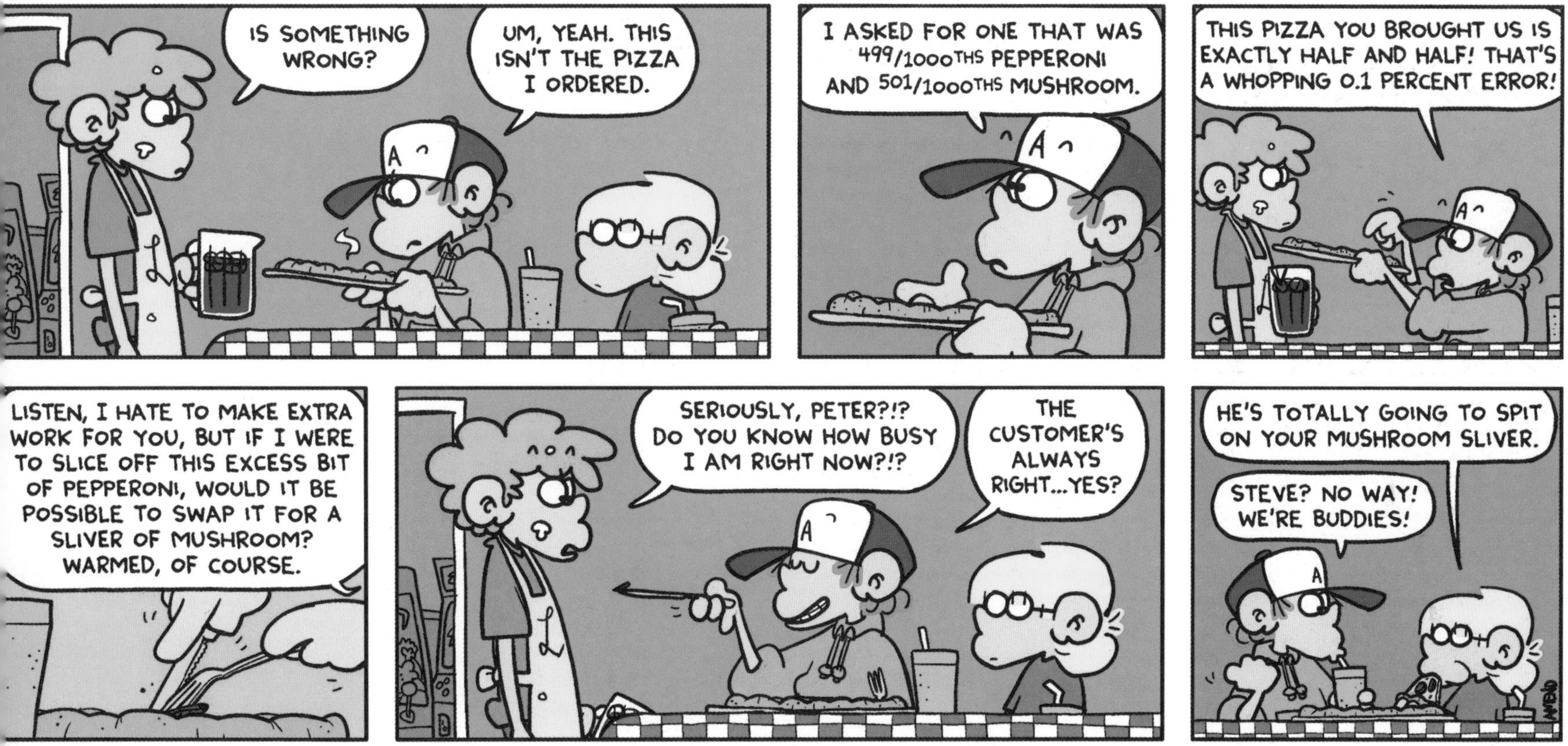
IS SOMETHING WRONG?
UM, YEAH. THIS ISN'T THE PIZZA I ORDERED.
I ASKED FOR ONE THAT WAS 499/1000THS PEPPERONI AND 501/1000THS MUSHROOM.
THIS PIZZA YOU BROUGHT US IS EXACTLY HALF AND HALF! THAT'S A WHOPPING 0.1 PERCENT ERROR!
LISTEN, I HATE TO MAKE EXTRA WORK FOR YOU, BUT IF I WERE TO SLICE OFF THIS EXCESS BIT OF PEPPERONI, WOULD IT BE POSSIBLE TO SWAP IT FOR A SLIVER OF MUSHROOM? WARMED, OF COURSE.
SERIOUSLY, PETER?!? DO YOU KNOW HOW BUSY I AM RIGHT NOW?!?
THE CUSTOMER'S ALWAYS RIGHT...YES?
HE'S TOTALLY GOING TO SPIT ON YOUR MUSHROOM SLIVER.
STEVE? NO WAY! WE'RE BUDDIES!

Trekno Babble

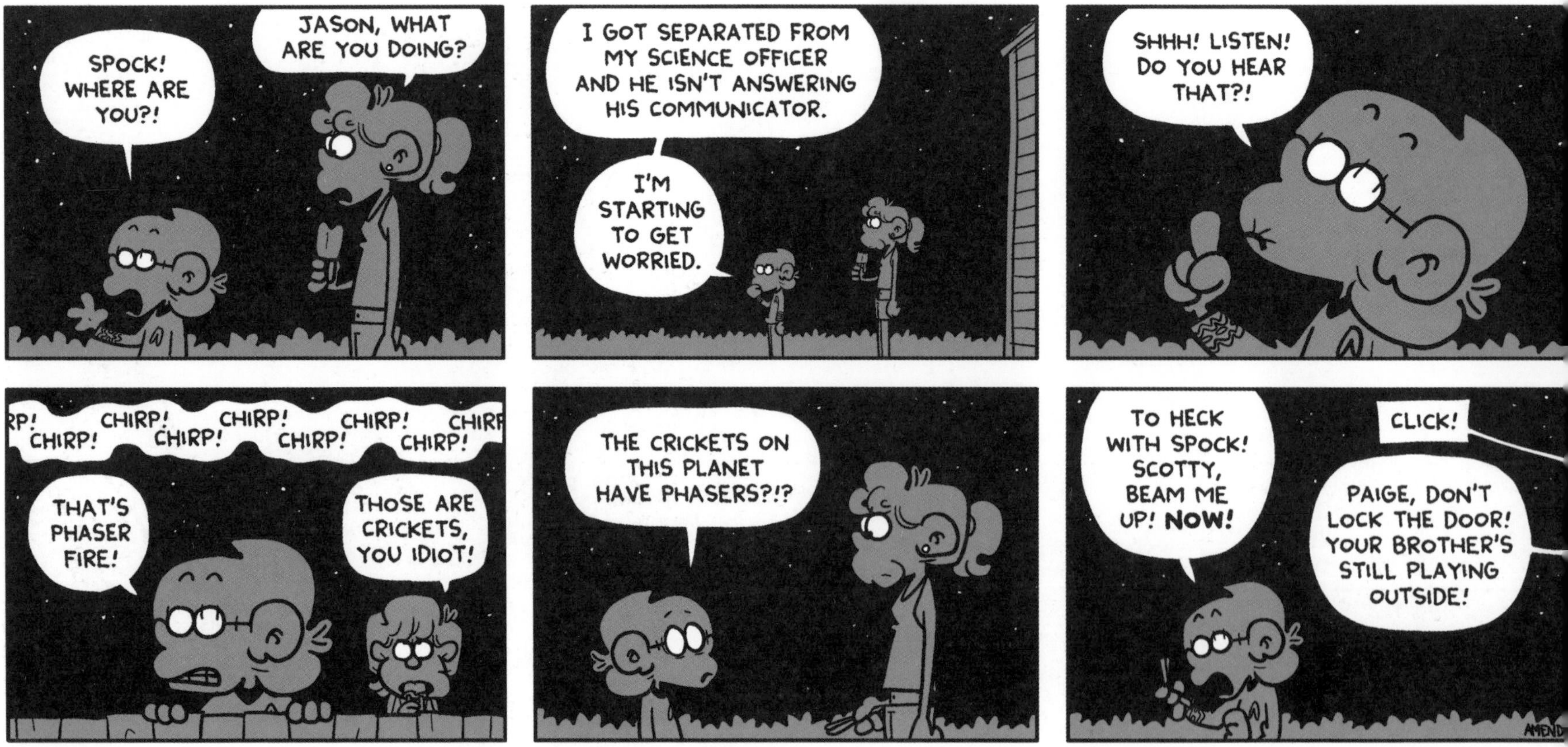

SPOCK! WHERE ARE YOU?!
JASON, WHAT ARE YOU DOING?
I GOT SEPARATED FROM MY SCIENCE OFFICER AND HE ISN'T ANSWERING HIS COMMUNICATOR.
I'M STARTING TO GET WORRIED.
SHHH! LISTEN! DO YOU HEAR THAT?!
RP! CHIRP! CHIRP! CHIRP! CHIRP! CHIRP! CHIRP! CHIRP! CHIRP
THAT'S PHASER FIRE!
THOSE ARE CRICKETS, YOU IDIOT!
THE CRICKETS ON THIS PLANET HAVE PHASERS?!?
TO HECK WITH SPOCK! SCOTTY, BEAM ME UP! **NOW!**
CLICK!
PAIGE, DON'T LOCK THE DOOR! YOUR BROTHER'S STILL PLAYING OUTSIDE!

Bruinen Love

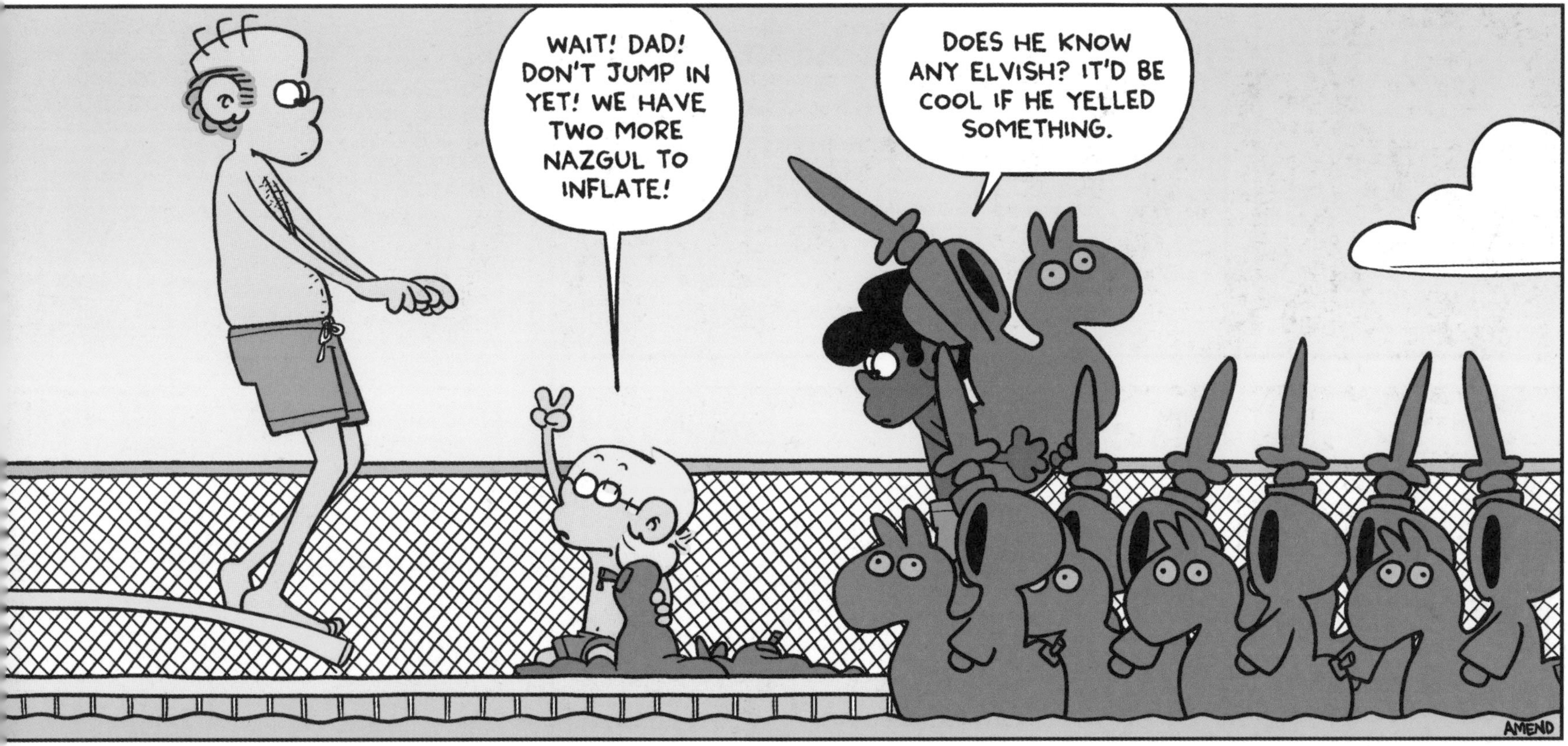
WAIT! DAD! DON'T JUMP IN YET! WE HAVE TWO MORE NAZGUL TO INFLATE!
DOES HE KNOW ANY ELVISH? IT'D BE COOL IF HE YELLED SOMETHING.
AMEND

Glassy

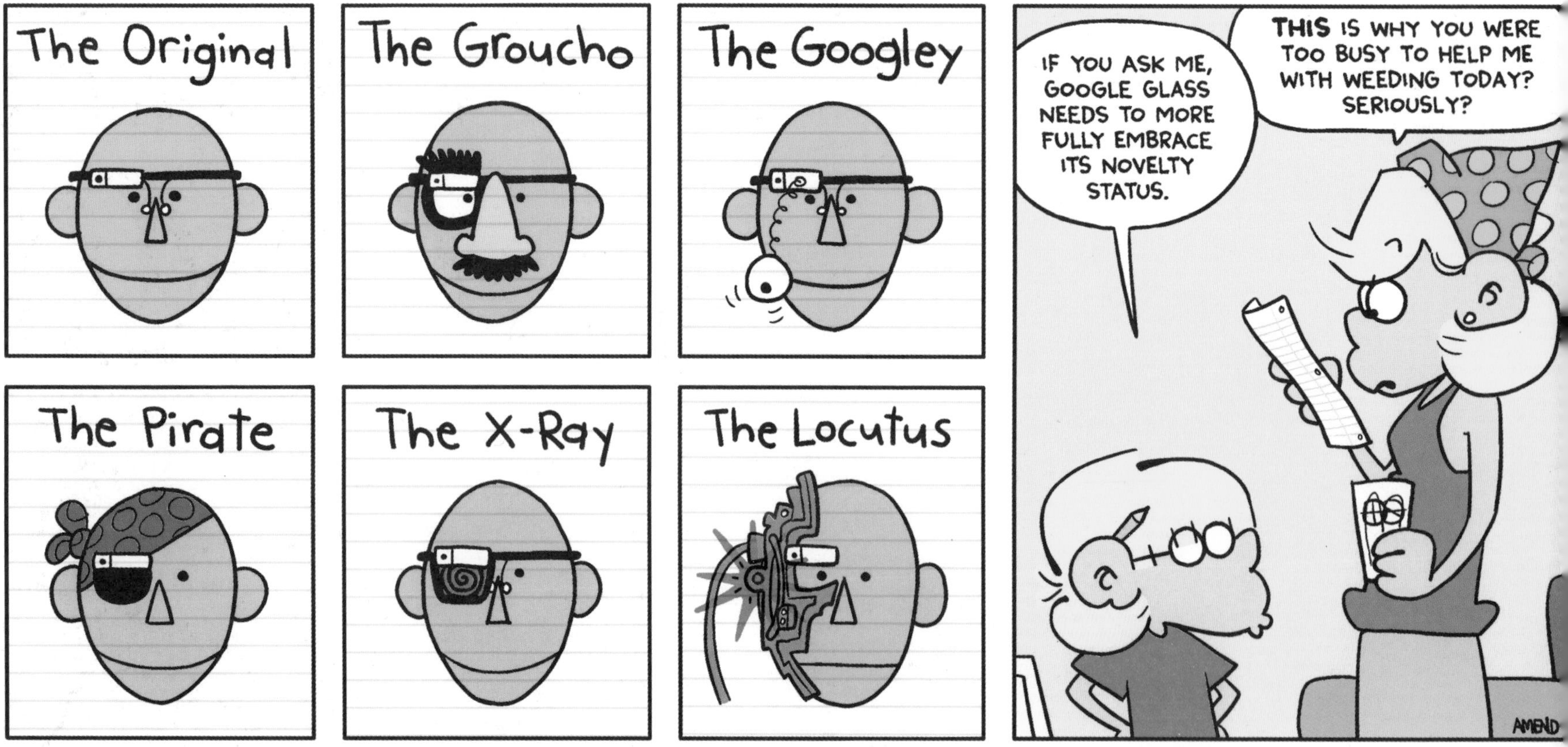

The Original
The Groucho
The Googley
The Pirate
The X-Ray
The Locutus
IF YOU ASK ME, GOOGLE GLASS NEEDS TO MORE FULLY EMBRACE ITS NOVELTY STATUS.
THIS IS WHY YOU WERE TOO BUSY TO HELP ME WITH WEEDING TODAY? SERIOUSLY?
AMEND

Summer Fling

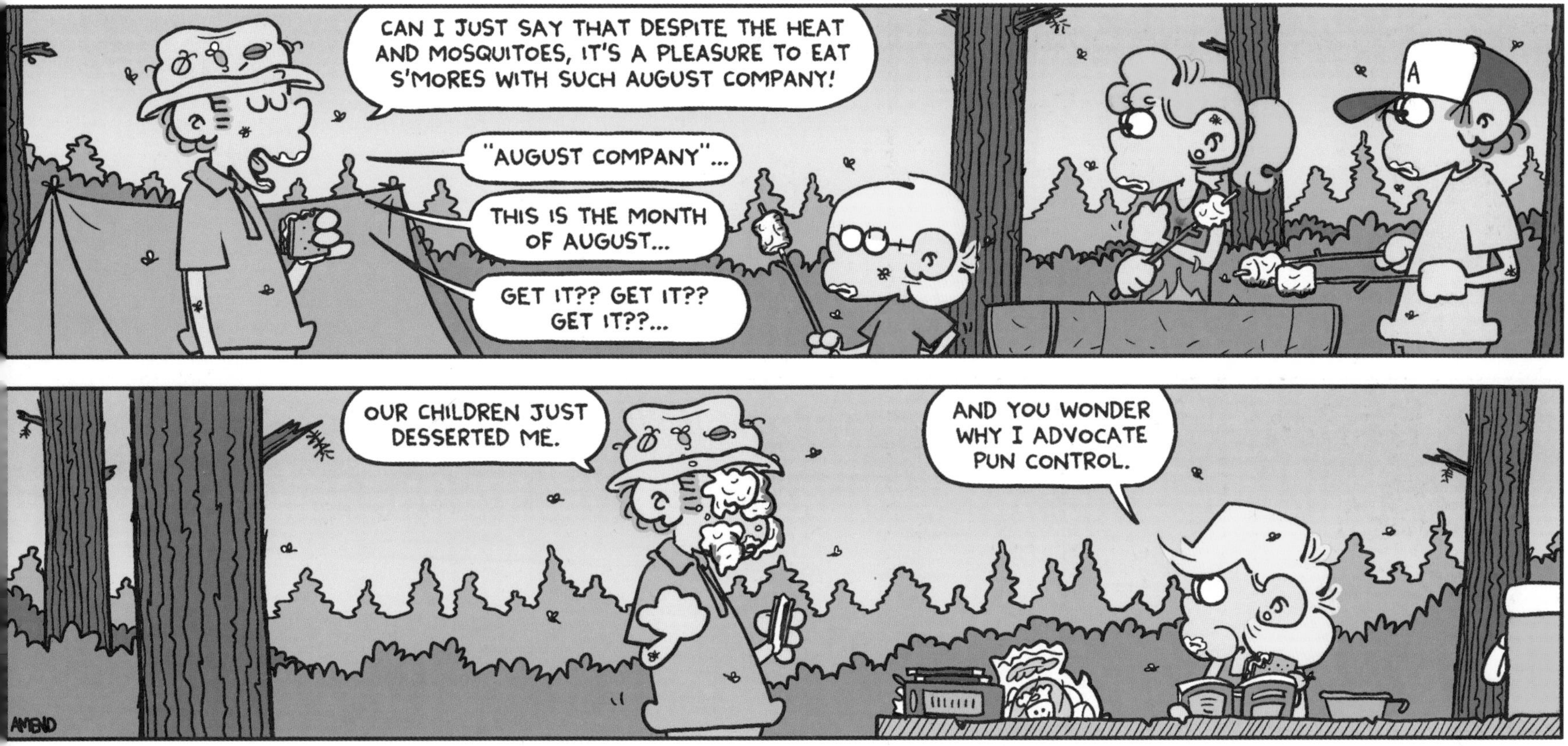
CAN I JUST SAY THAT DESPITE THE HEAT AND MOSQUITOES, IT'S A PLEASURE TO EAT S'MORES WITH SUCH AUGUST COMPANY!
"AUGUST COMPANY"...
THIS IS THE MONTH OF AUGUST...
GET IT?? GET IT?? GET IT??...
OUR CHILDREN JUST DESSERTED ME.
AND YOU WONDER WHY I ADVOCATE PUN CONTROL.
AMEND

Fun with Dad

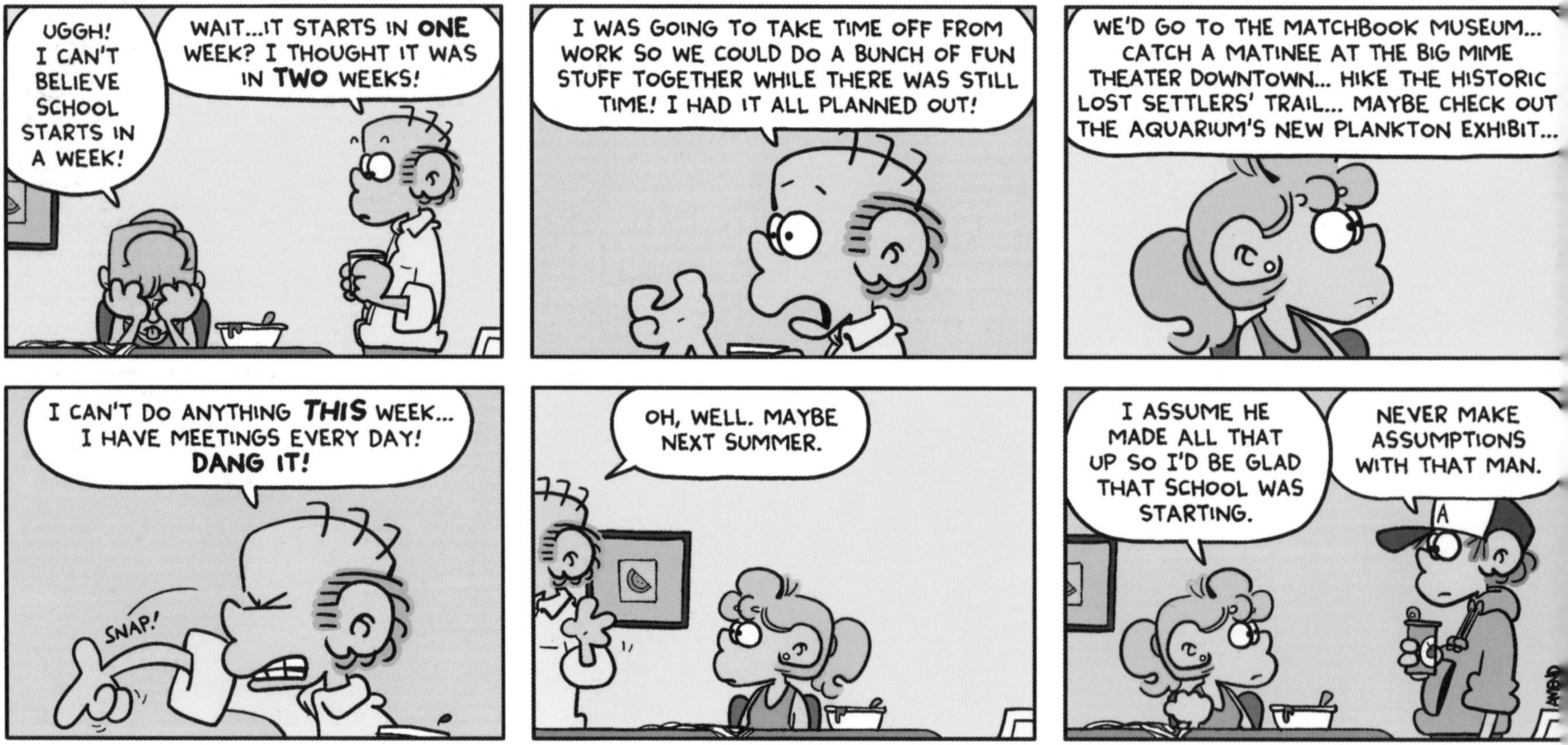

UGGH! I CAN'T BELIEVE SCHOOL STARTS IN A WEEK!
WAIT...IT STARTS IN **ONE** WEEK? I THOUGHT IT WAS IN **TWO** WEEKS!
I WAS GOING TO TAKE TIME OFF FROM WORK SO WE COULD DO A BUNCH OF FUN STUFF TOGETHER WHILE THERE WAS STILL TIME! I HAD IT ALL PLANNED OUT!
WE'D GO TO THE MATCHBOOK MUSEUM... CATCH A MATINEE AT THE BIG MIME THEATER DOWNTOWN... HIKE THE HISTORIC LOST SETTLERS' TRAIL... MAYBE CHECK OUT THE AQUARIUM'S NEW PLANKTON EXHIBIT...
I CAN'T DO ANYTHING **THIS** WEEK... I HAVE MEETINGS EVERY DAY! **DANG IT!**
SNAP!
OH, WELL. MAYBE NEXT SUMMER.
I ASSUME HE MADE ALL THAT UP SO I'D BE GLAD THAT SCHOOL WAS STARTING.
NEVER MAKE ASSUMPTIONS WITH THAT MAN.

Knowledge Most Awesome

Foxtails

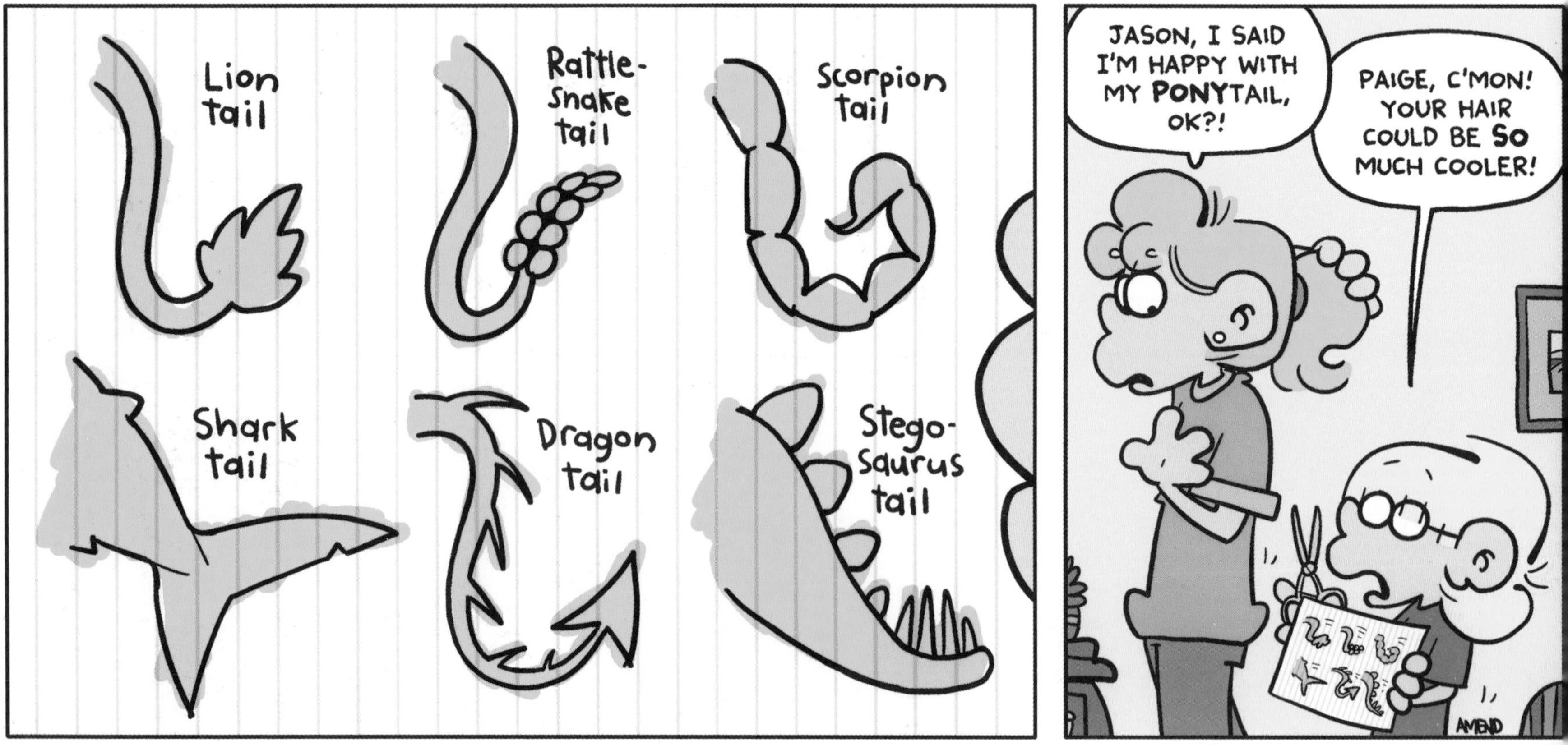

Lion tail
Rattle-snake tail
Scorpion tail
Shark tail
Dragon tail
Stego-saurus tail
JASON, I SAID I'M HAPPY WITH MY **PONY**TAIL, OK?!
PAIGE, C'MON! YOUR HAIR COULD BE **SO** MUCH COOLER!
AMEND

Sorry Jason

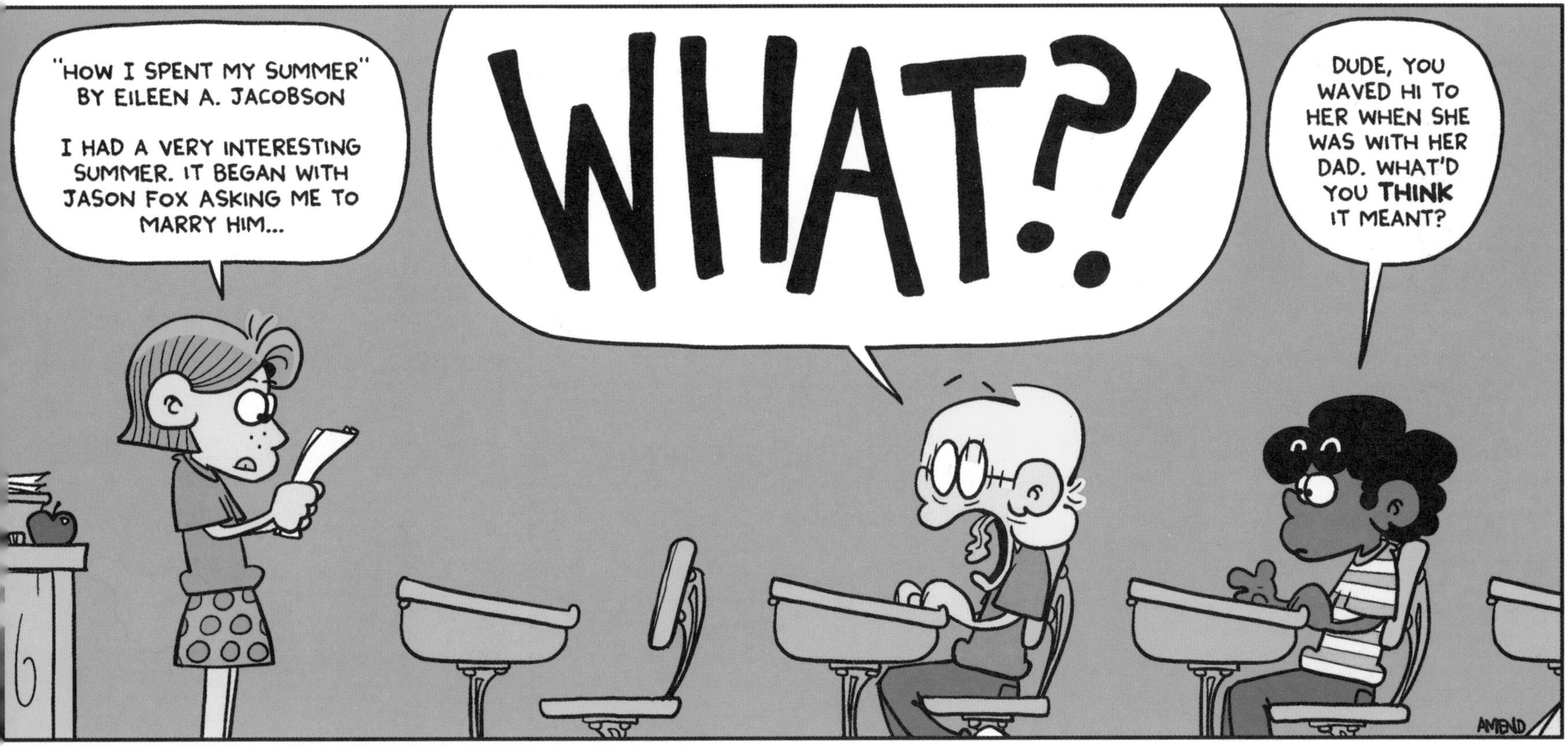
"HOW I SPENT MY SUMMER" BY EILEEN A. JACOBSON I HAD A VERY INTERESTING SUMMER. IT BEGAN WITH JASON FOX ASKING ME TO MARRY HIM...
WHAT?!
DUDE, YOU WAVED HI TO HER WHEN SHE WAS WITH HER DAD. WHAT'D YOU **THINK** IT MEANT?
AMEND

Keeping It Clean

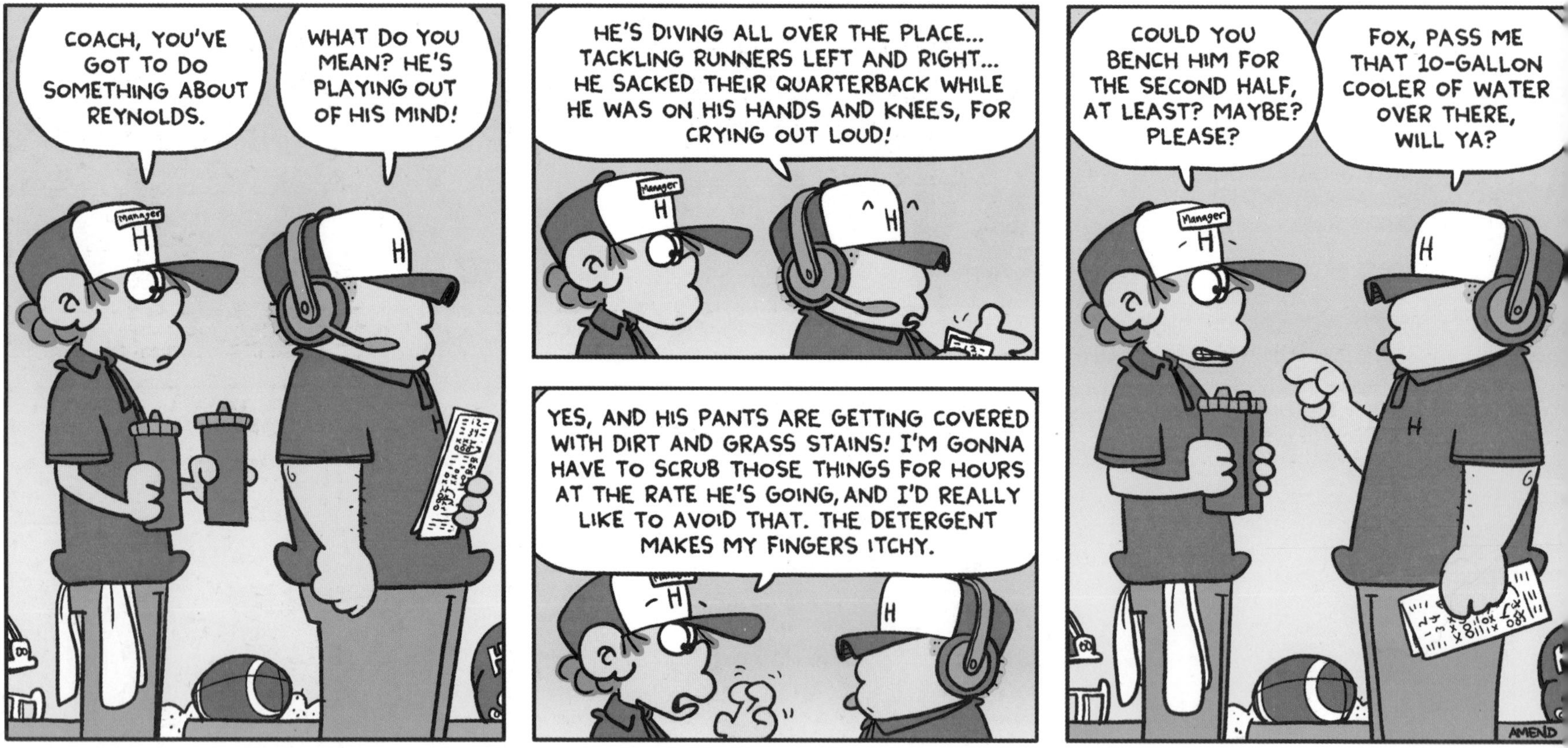
COACH, YOU'VE GOT TO DO SOMETHING ABOUT REYNOLDS.
WHAT DO YOU MEAN? HE'S PLAYING OUT OF HIS MIND!
HE'S DIVING ALL OVER THE PLACE... TACKLING RUNNERS LEFT AND RIGHT... HE SACKED THEIR QUARTERBACK WHILE HE WAS ON HIS HANDS AND KNEES, FOR CRYING OUT LOUD!
YES, AND HIS PANTS ARE GETTING COVERED WITH DIRT AND GRASS STAINS! I'M GONNA HAVE TO SCRUB THOSE THINGS FOR HOURS AT THE RATE HE'S GOING, AND I'D REALLY LIKE TO AVOID THAT. THE DETERGENT MAKES MY FINGERS ITCHY.
COULD YOU BENCH HIM FOR THE SECOND HALF, AT LEAST? MAYBE? PLEASE?
FOX, PASS ME THAT 10-GALLON COOLER OF WATER OVER THERE, WILL YA?
AMEND

iWear

Panel 1:
PAIGE, YOU'RE INTO FASHION. ANY WAY YOU COULD HOOK US UP WITH A CLOTHING MANUFACTURER?

HUH?

Panel 2:
WITH APPLE AND SAMSUNG MAKING BIGGER AND BIGGER PHONES, MARCUS AND I THINK WE'VE FIGURED OUT THE NEXT BIG THING IN PANTS...

Panel 3:
SPANDEX POCKETS!

Panel 4:
GOT A BIG 4.7-INCH PHONE? THIS STRETCHY BACK POCKET WILL ACCOMMODATE IT FINE!

Panel 5:
GOT A BIGGER 5.5-INCH PHONE? THIS STRETCHY BACK POCKET WILL **STILL** ACCOMMODATE IT FINE!

Panel 6:
GOT A 27-INCH MONITOR YOU WANT TO BRING TO A LAN PARTY?

YOU WERE SUPPOSED TO LET ME SAY, "OH, THERE'S ONE MORE THING..."

GUYS...

The Joy of Mathing

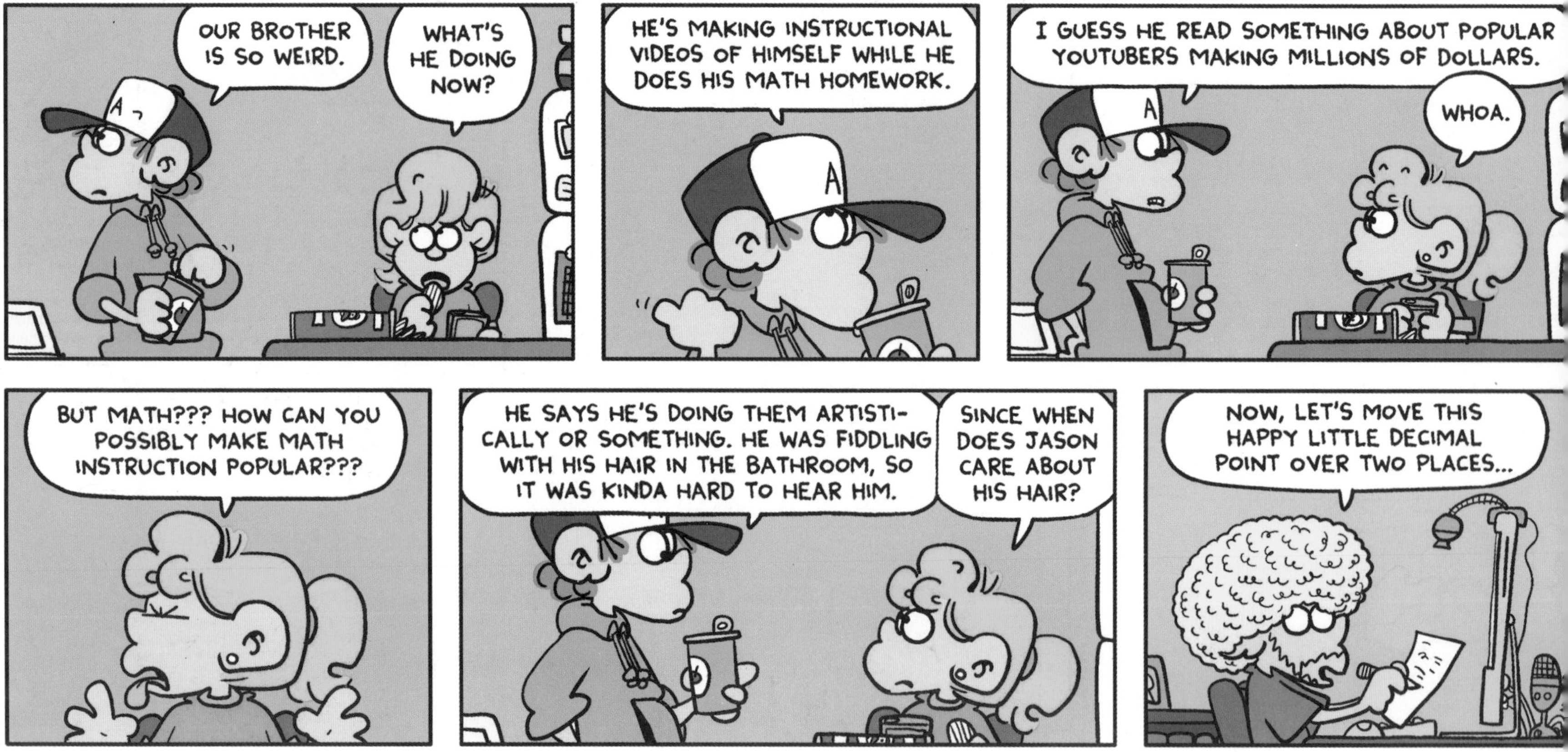
OUR BROTHER IS SO WEIRD.
WHAT'S HE DOING NOW?
HE'S MAKING INSTRUCTIONAL VIDEOS OF HIMSELF WHILE HE DOES HIS MATH HOMEWORK.
I GUESS HE READ SOMETHING ABOUT POPULAR YOUTUBERS MAKING MILLIONS OF DOLLARS.
WHOA.
BUT MATH??? HOW CAN YOU POSSIBLY MAKE MATH INSTRUCTION POPULAR???
HE SAYS HE'S DOING THEM ARTISTI-CALLY OR SOMETHING. HE WAS FIDDLING WITH HIS HAIR IN THE BATHROOM, SO IT WAS KINDA HARD TO HEAR HIM.
SINCE WHEN DOES JASON CARE ABOUT HIS HAIR?
NOW, LET'S MOVE THIS HAPPY LITTLE DECIMAL POINT OVER TWO PLACES...

Raining Cat Pics and Docs

baking.f

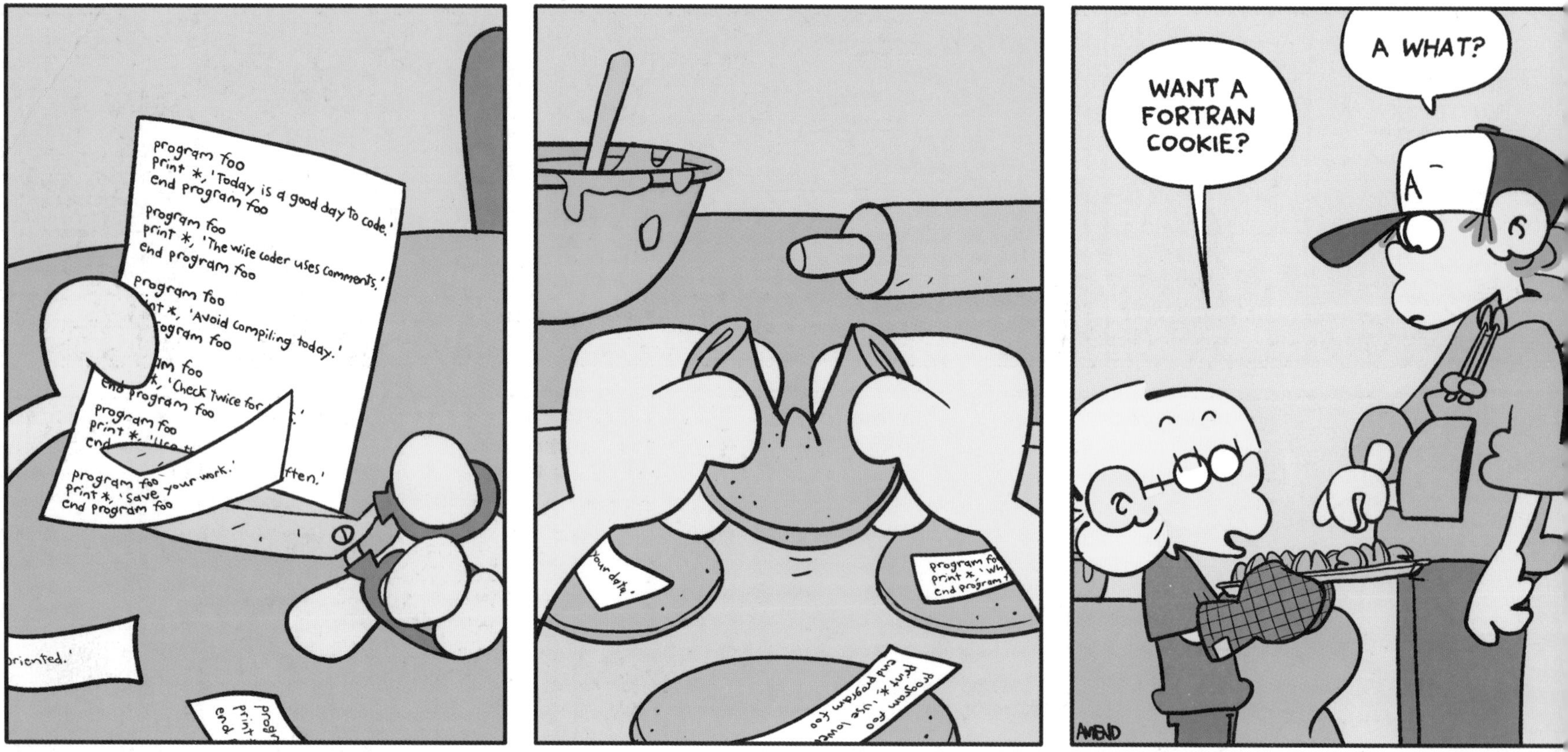
program foo
print *, 'Today is a good day to code.'
end program foo
program foo
print *, 'The wise coder uses comments.'
end program foo
WANT A FORTRAN COOKIE?
A WHAT?
AMEND

Halloween Horrors

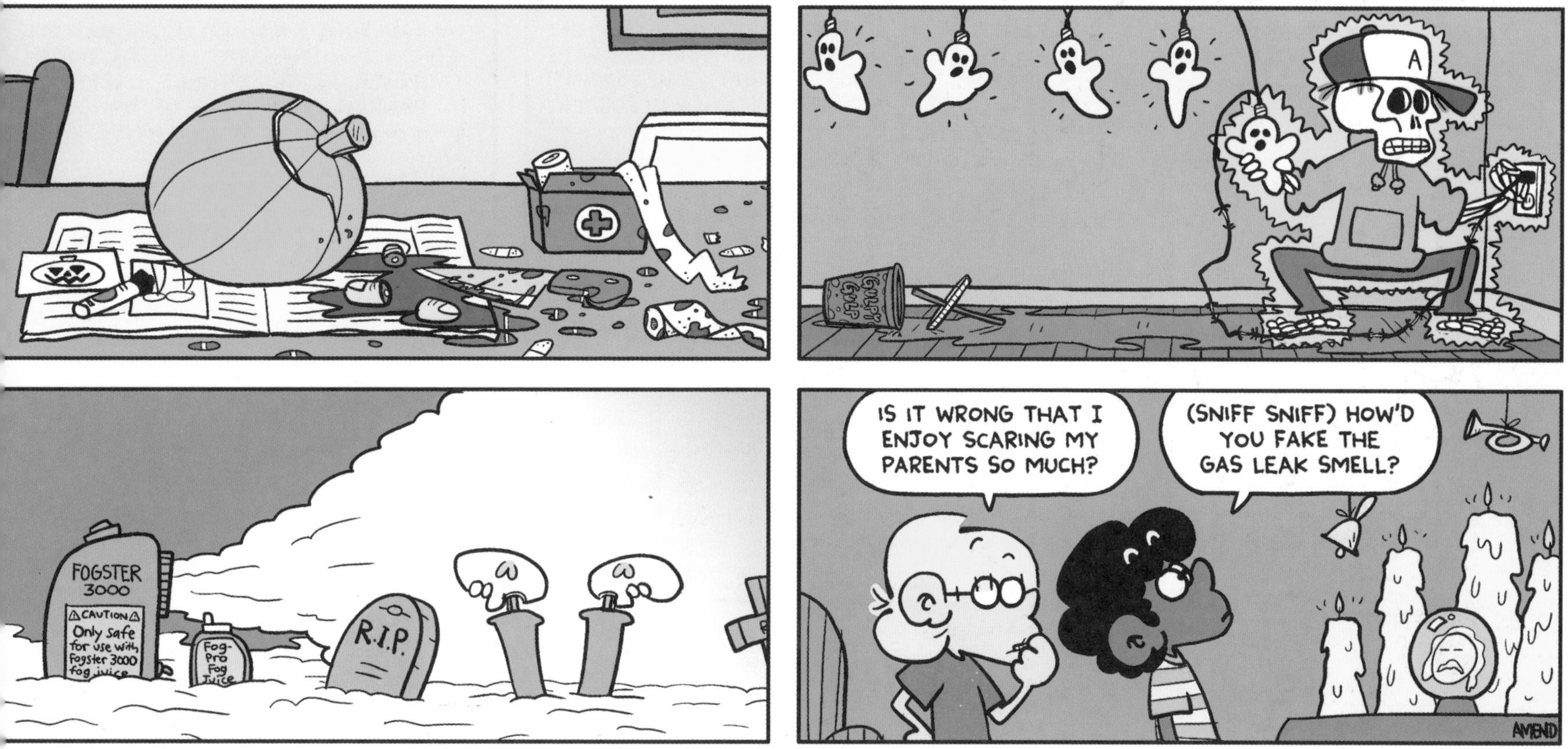

GULP! GULP
FOGSTER 3000
⚠CAUTION⚠
Only safe for use with Fogster 3000 fog juice
Fog-Pro Fog Juice
R.I.P.
IS IT WRONG THAT I ENJOY SCARING MY PARENTS SO MUCH?
(SNIFF SNIFF) HOW'D YOU FAKE THE GAS LEAK SMELL?
AMEND

Route Vegetables

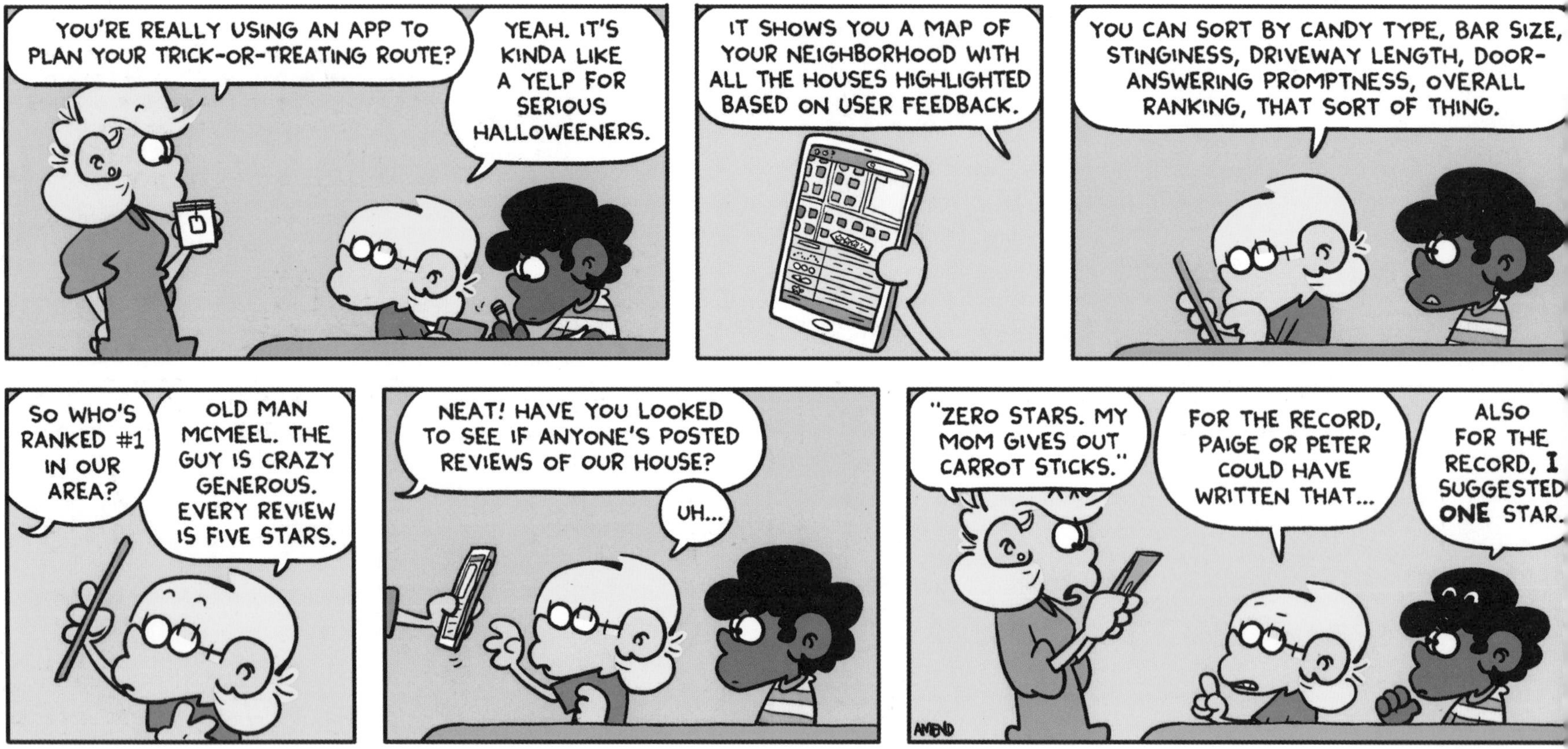

YOU'RE REALLY USING AN APP TO PLAN YOUR TRICK-OR-TREATING ROUTE?
YEAH. IT'S KINDA LIKE A YELP FOR SERIOUS HALLOWEENERS.
IT SHOWS YOU A MAP OF YOUR NEIGHBORHOOD WITH ALL THE HOUSES HIGHLIGHTED BASED ON USER FEEDBACK.
YOU CAN SORT BY CANDY TYPE, BAR SIZE, STINGINESS, DRIVEWAY LENGTH, DOOR-ANSWERING PROMPTNESS, OVERALL RANKING, THAT SORT OF THING.
SO WHO'S RANKED #1 IN OUR AREA?
OLD MAN MCMEEL. THE GUY IS CRAZY GENEROUS. EVERY REVIEW IS FIVE STARS.
NEAT! HAVE YOU LOOKED TO SEE IF ANYONE'S POSTED REVIEWS OF OUR HOUSE?
UH...
"ZERO STARS. MY MOM GIVES OUT CARROT STICKS."
FOR THE RECORD, PAIGE OR PETER COULD HAVE WRITTEN THAT...
ALSO FOR THE RECORD, **I** SUGGESTED **ONE** STAR.
AMEND

Worth a Shot

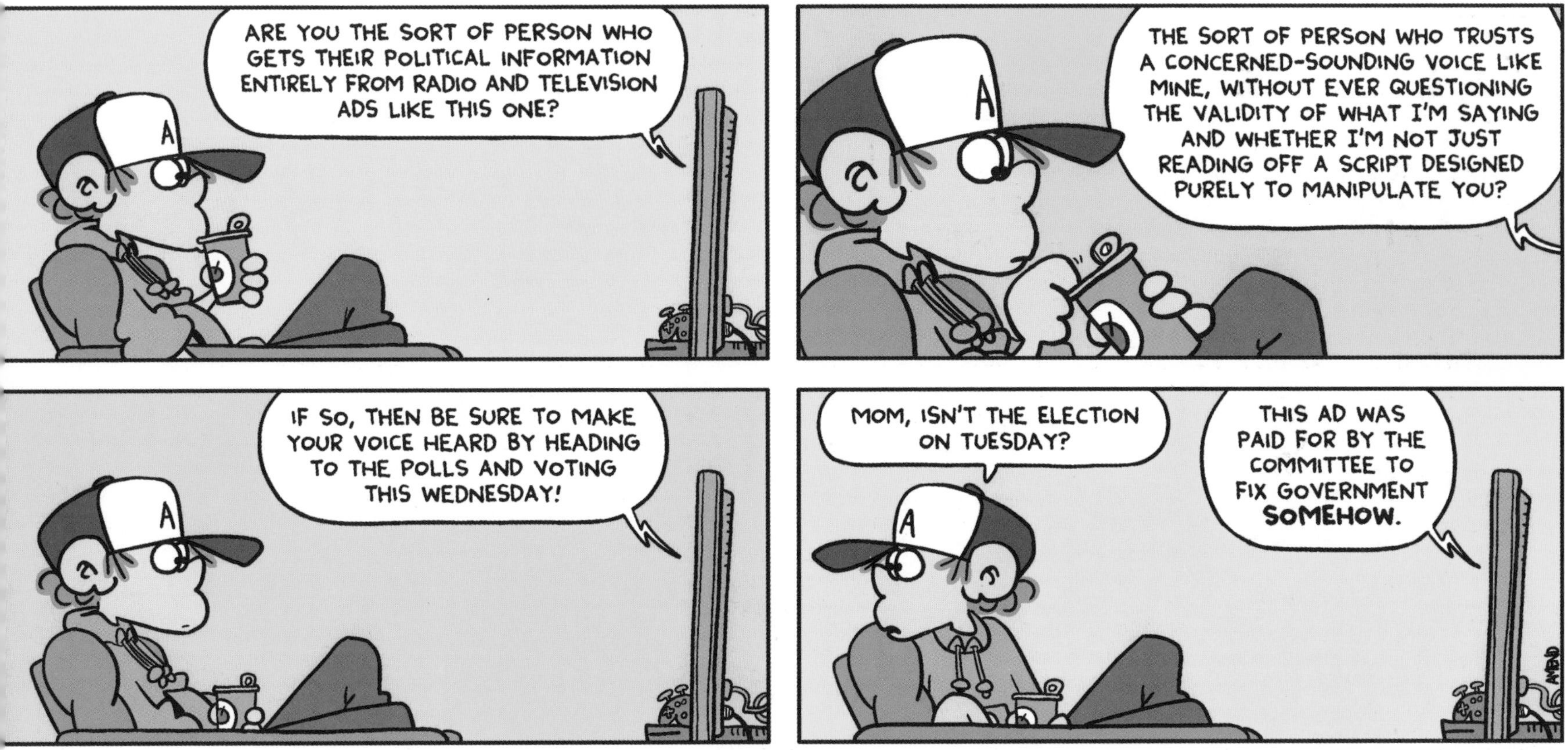
ARE YOU THE SORT OF PERSON WHO GETS THEIR POLITICAL INFORMATION ENTIRELY FROM RADIO AND TELEVISION ADS LIKE THIS ONE?
THE SORT OF PERSON WHO TRUSTS A CONCERNED-SOUNDING VOICE LIKE MINE, WITHOUT EVER QUESTIONING THE VALIDITY OF WHAT I'M SAYING AND WHETHER I'M NOT JUST READING OFF A SCRIPT DESIGNED PURELY TO MANIPULATE YOU?
IF SO, THEN BE SURE TO MAKE YOUR VOICE HEARD BY HEADING TO THE POLLS AND VOTING THIS WEDNESDAY!
MOM, ISN'T THE ELECTION ON TUESDAY?
THIS AD WAS PAID FOR BY THE COMMITTEE TO FIX GOVERNMENT **SOMEHOW**.

Paige Goes Emo

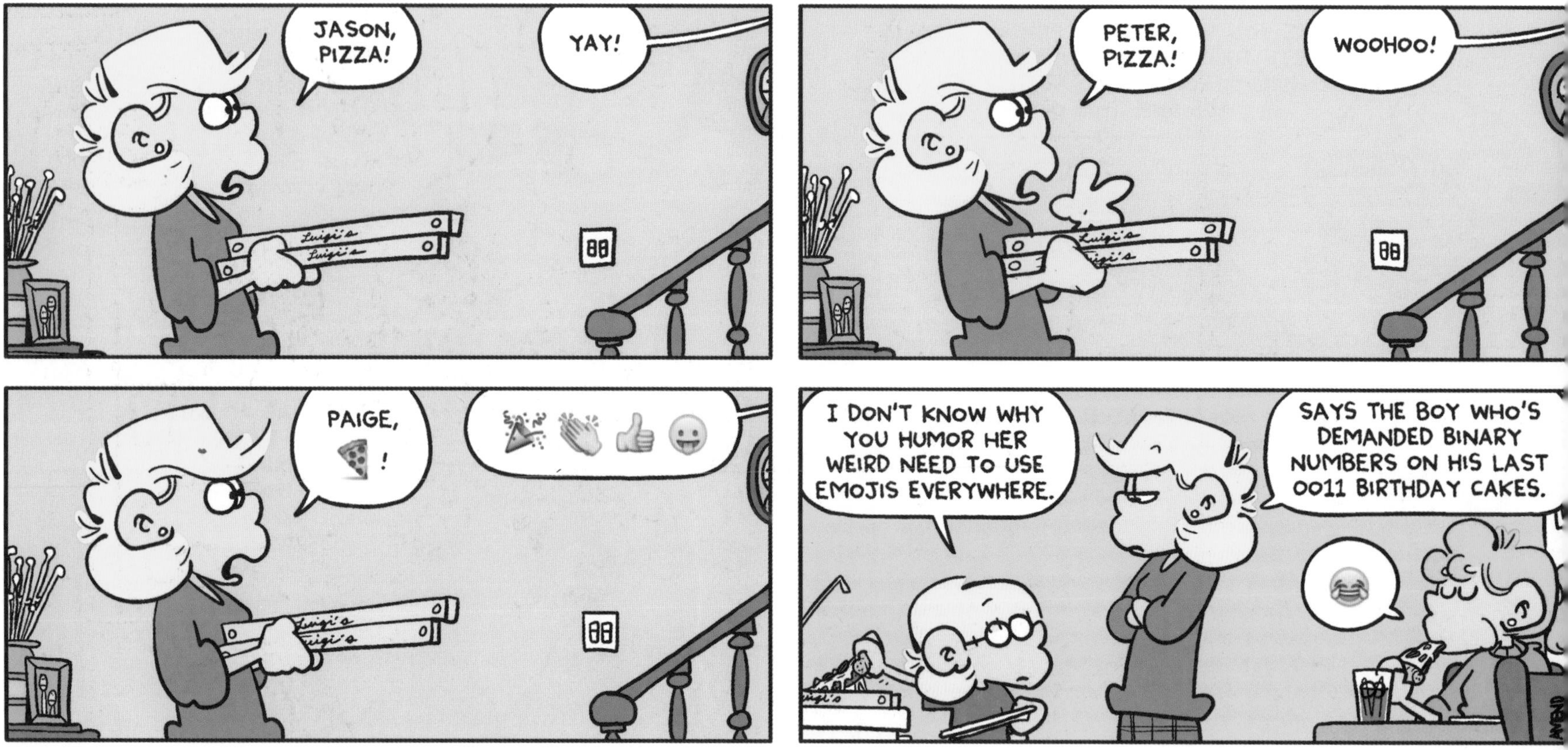
JASON, PIZZA!
YAY!
PETER, PIZZA!
WOOHOO!
PAIGE, 🍕 !
🎉 👏 👍 😛
I DON'T KNOW WHY YOU HUMOR HER WEIRD NEED TO USE EMOJIS EVERYWHERE.
SAYS THE BOY WHO'S DEMANDED BINARY NUMBERS ON HIS LAST 0011 BIRTHDAY CAKES.
😂

Moisturizing

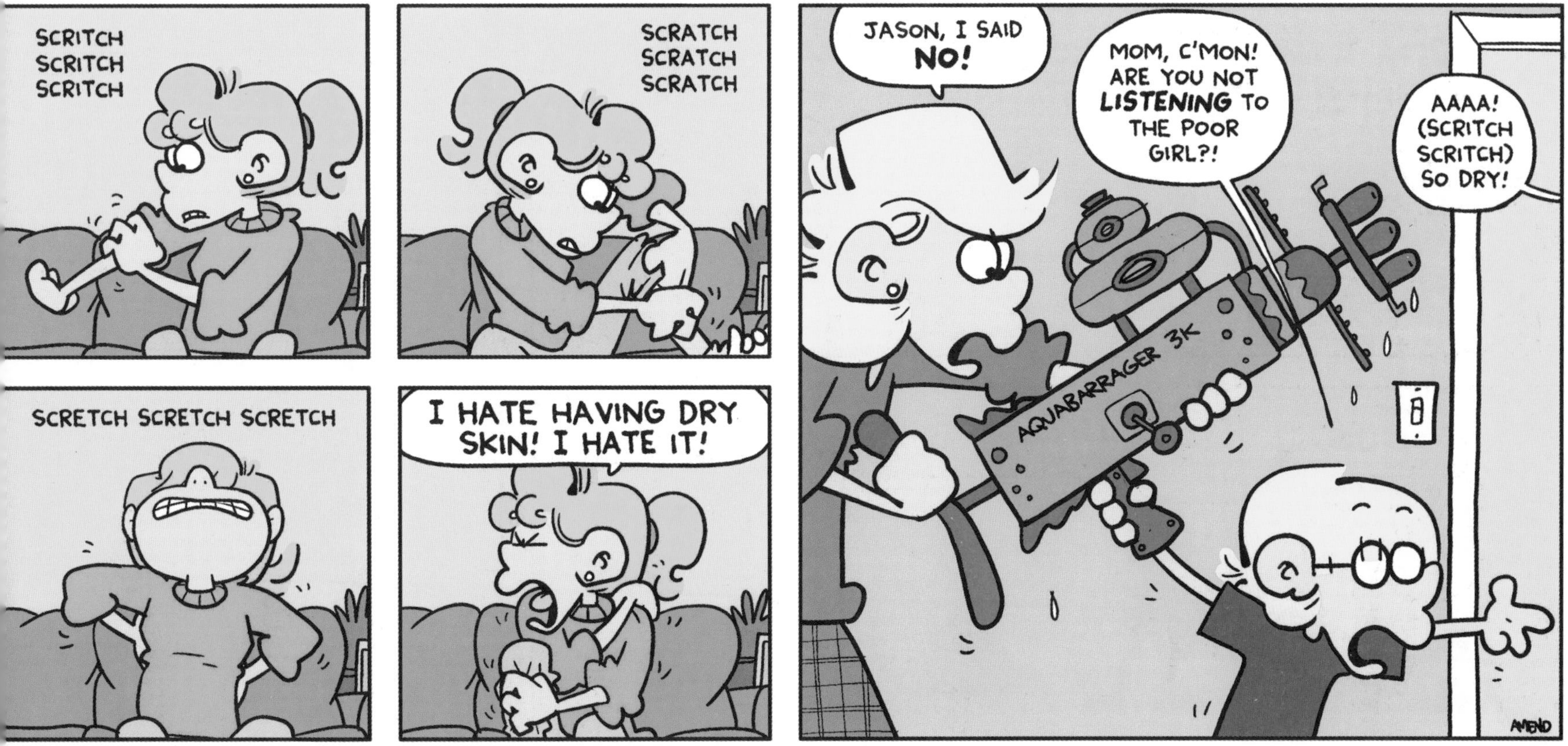
SCRITCH
SCRITCH
SCRITCH
SCRATCH
SCRATCH
SCRATCH
SCRETCH SCRETCH SCRETCH
I HATE HAVING DRY SKIN! I HATE IT!
JASON, I SAID **NO!**
MOM, C'MON! ARE YOU NOT **LISTENING** TO THE POOR GIRL?!
AAAA! (SCRITCH SCRITCH) SO DRY!
AQUABARRAGER 3K
AMEND

Henjutsu

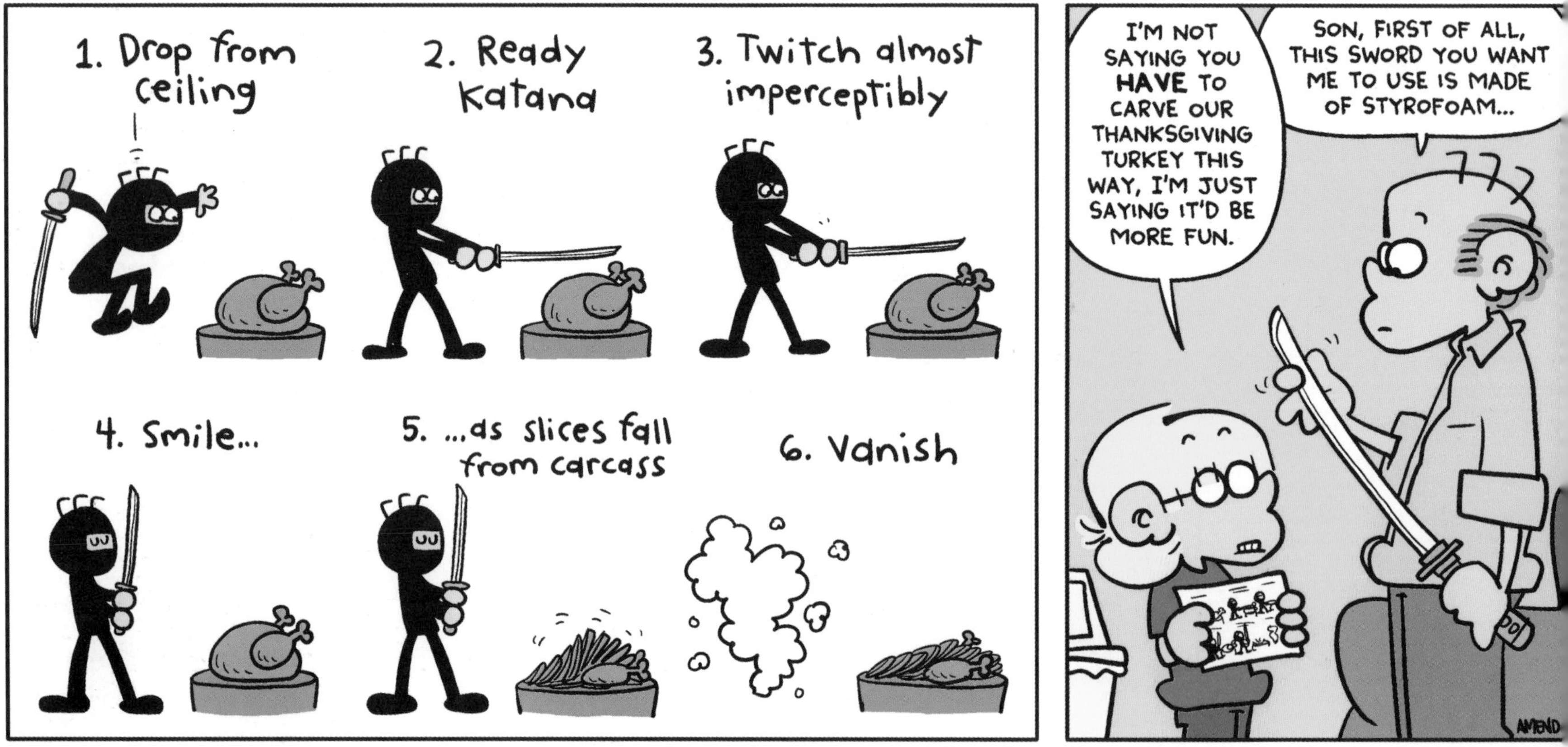
1. Drop from ceiling
2. Ready katana
3. Twitch almost imperceptibly
4. Smile...
5. ...as slices fall from carcass
6. Vanish
I'M NOT SAYING YOU **HAVE** TO CARVE OUR THANKSGIVING TURKEY THIS WAY, I'M JUST SAYING IT'D BE MORE FUN.
SON, FIRST OF ALL, THIS SWORD YOU WANT ME TO USE IS MADE OF STYROFOAM...
AMEND

Food Network

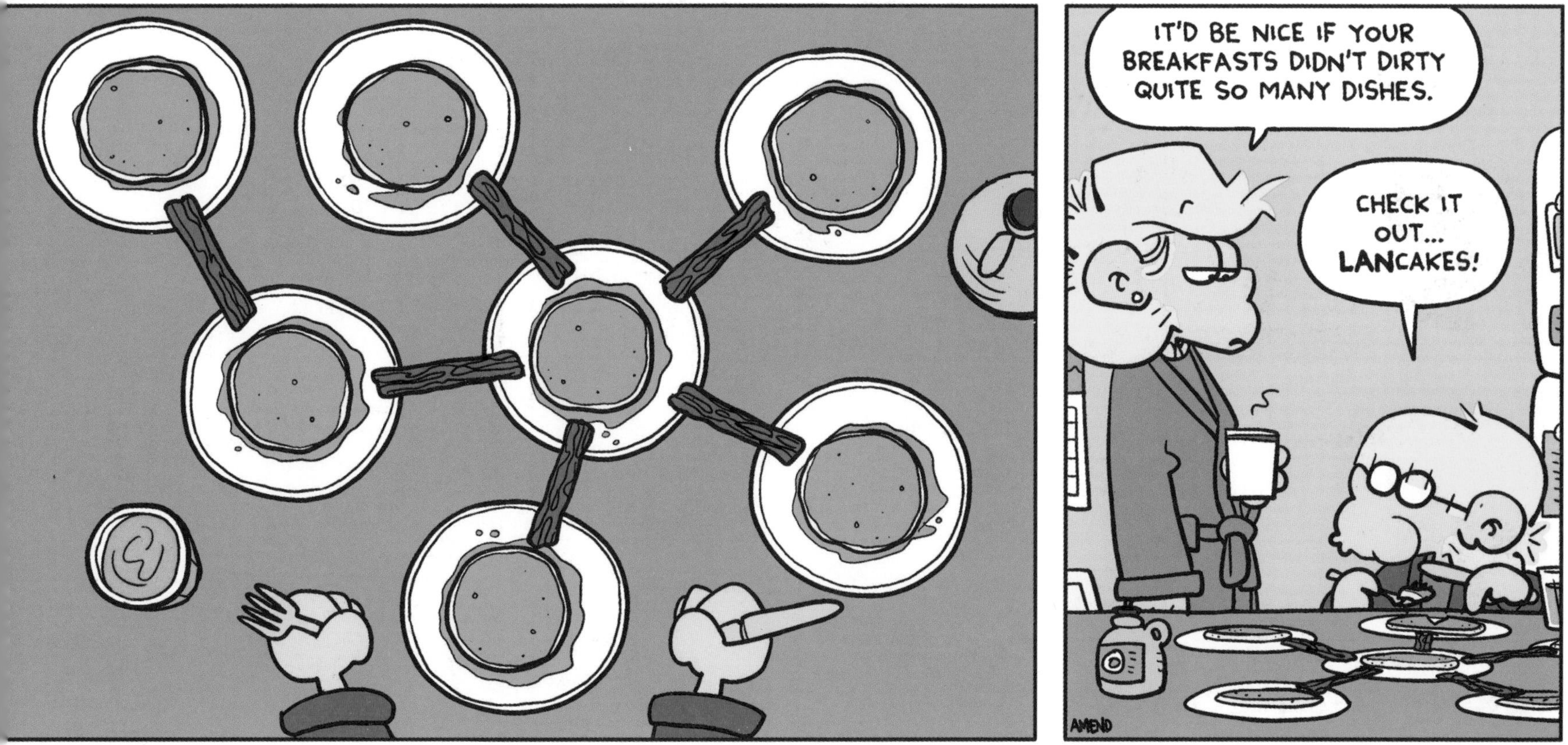
IT'D BE NICE IF YOUR BREAKFASTS DIDN'T DIRTY QUITE SO MANY DISHES.
CHECK IT OUT... LANCAKES!
AMEND

Degrees Illustrated

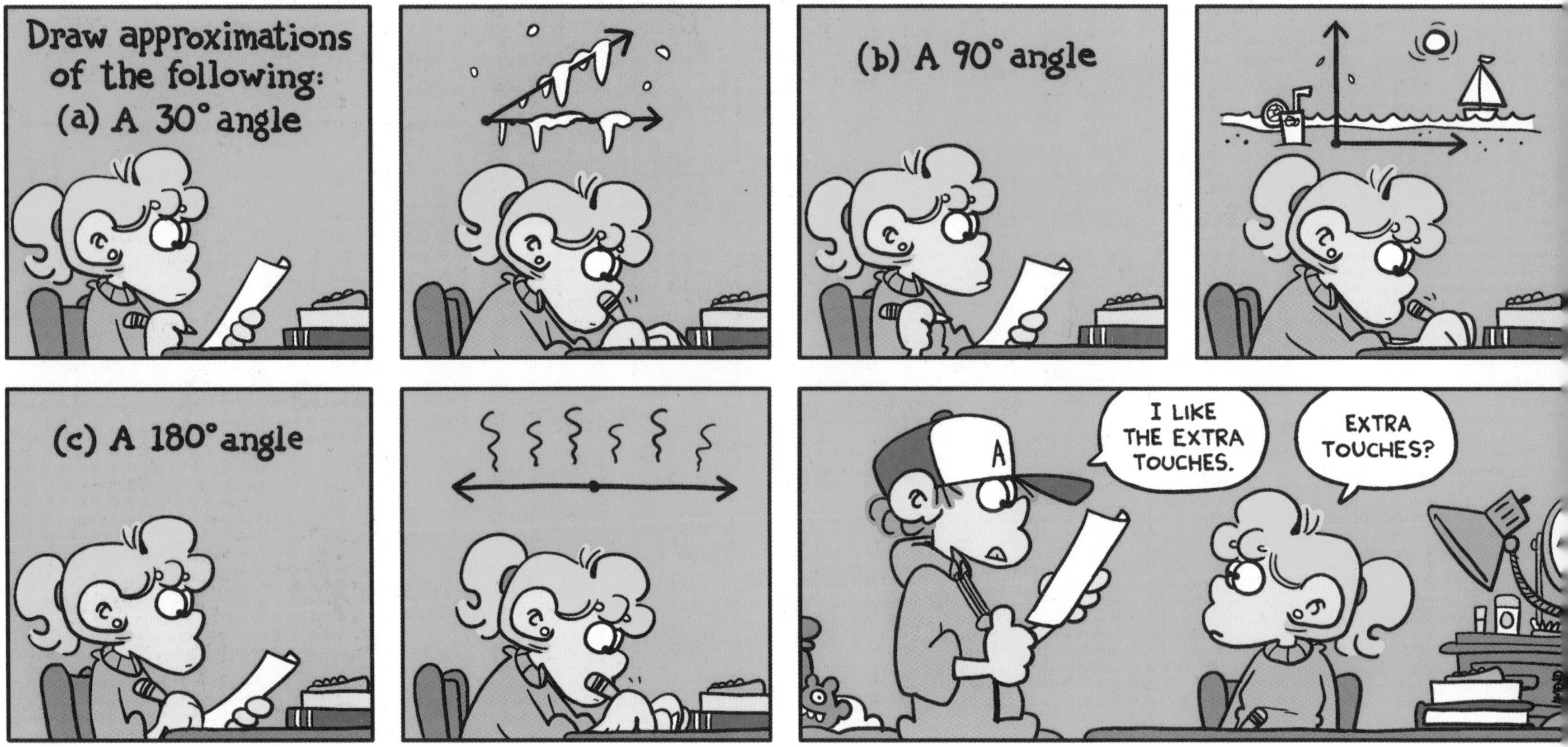

Draw approximations of the following: (a) A 30° angle
(b) A 90° angle
(c) A 180° angle
I LIKE THE EXTRA TOUCHES.
EXTRA TOUCHES?

A Light Suggestion

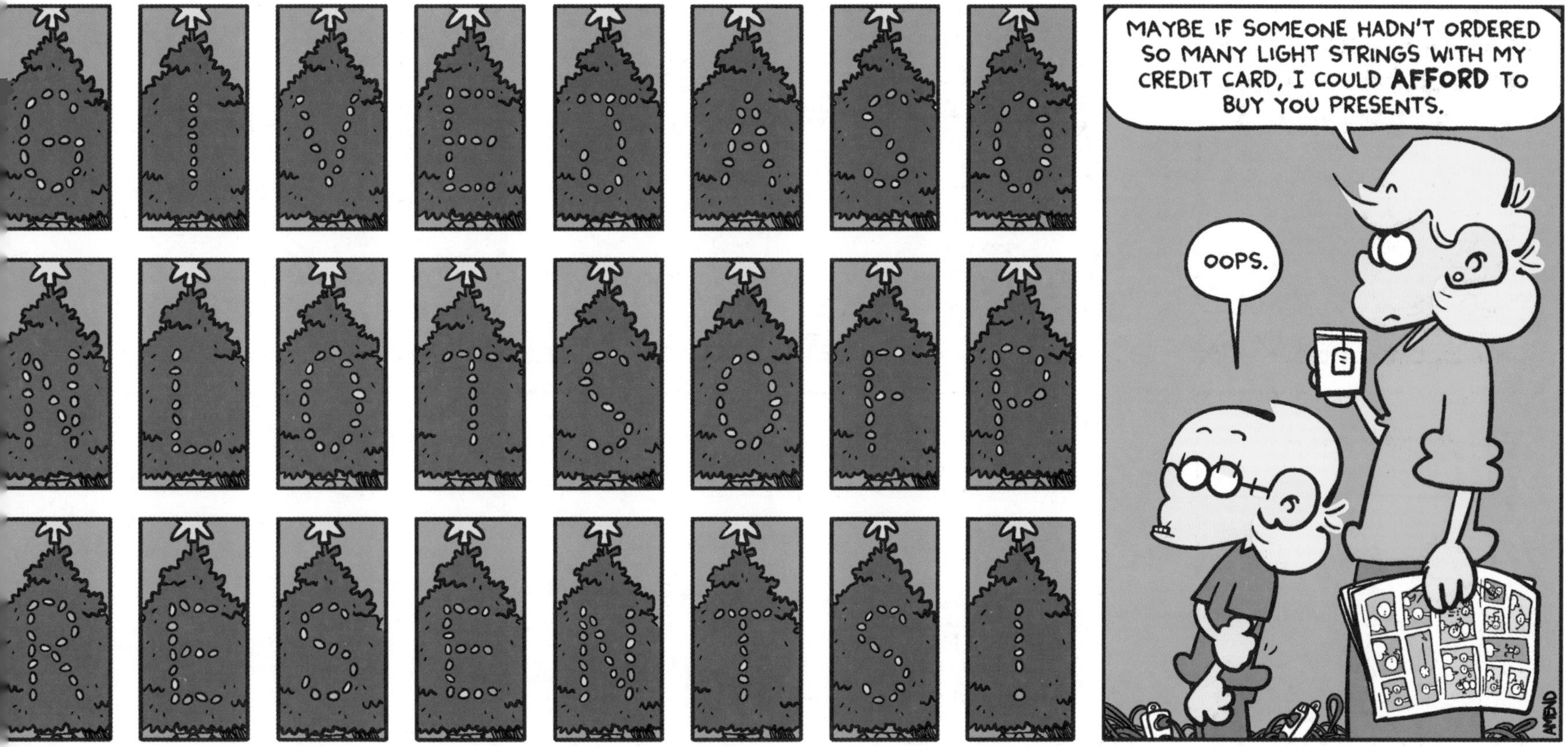
GIVE AS
GOOD AS
MONEY
INCLUDES
ONE
PRESENTS!
MAYBE IF SOMEONE HADN'T ORDERED SO MANY LIGHT STRINGS WITH MY CREDIT CARD, I COULD **AFFORD** TO BUY YOU PRESENTS.
OOPS.
AMEND

Card Games

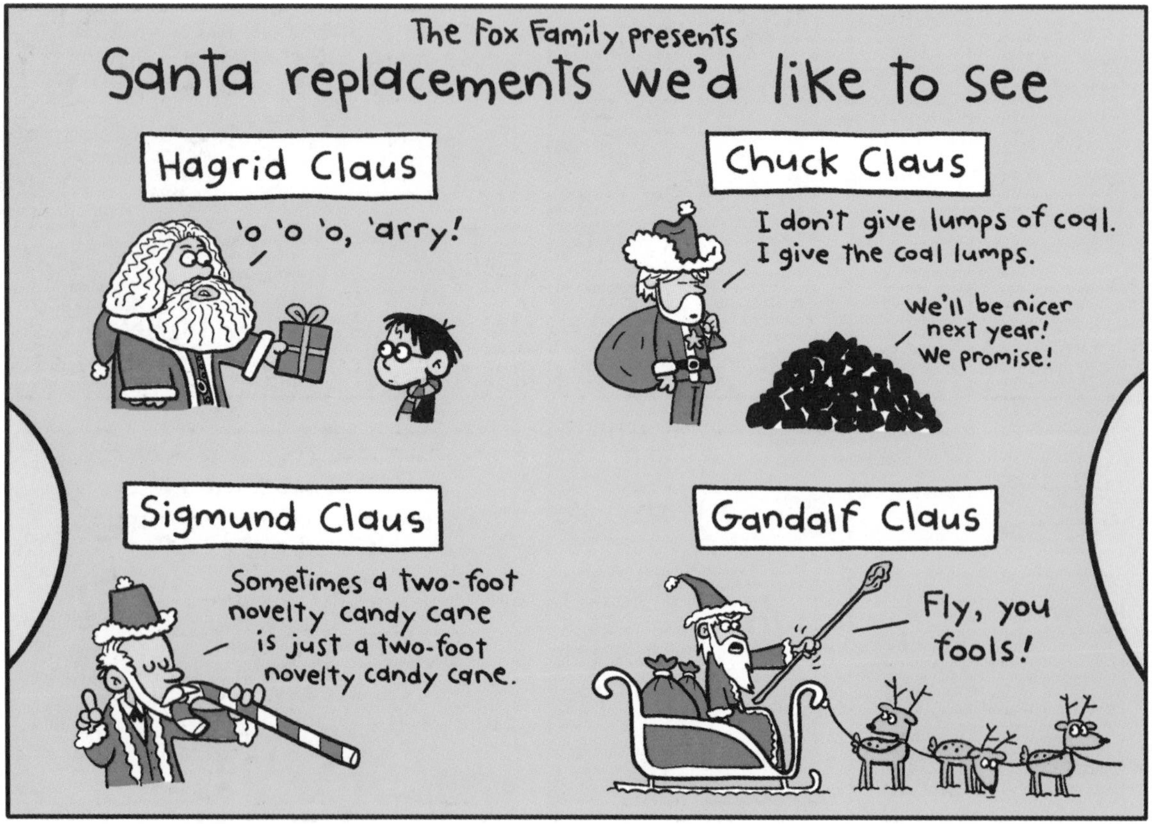
The Fox Family presents
Santa replacements we'd like to see
Hagrid Claus
'o 'o 'o, 'arry!
Chuck Claus
I don't give lumps of coal. I give the coal lumps.
We'll be nicer next year! We promise!
Sigmund Claus
Sometimes a two-foot novelty candy cane is just a two-foot novelty candy cane.
Gandalf Claus
Fly, you fools!

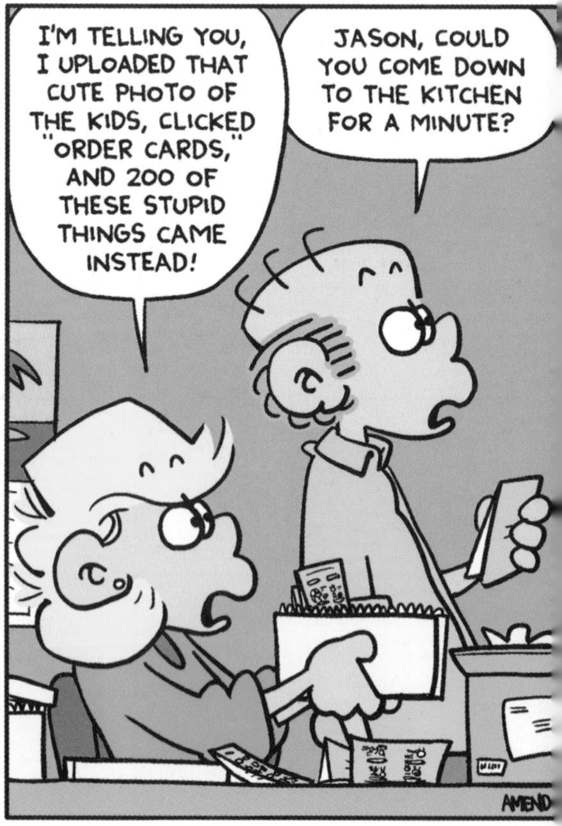
I'M TELLING YOU, I UPLOADED THAT CUTE PHOTO OF THE KIDS, CLICKED "ORDER CARDS," AND 200 OF THESE STUPID THINGS CAME INSTEAD!
JASON, COULD YOU COME DOWN TO THE KITCHEN FOR A MINUTE?
AMEND

Minor Rule Change

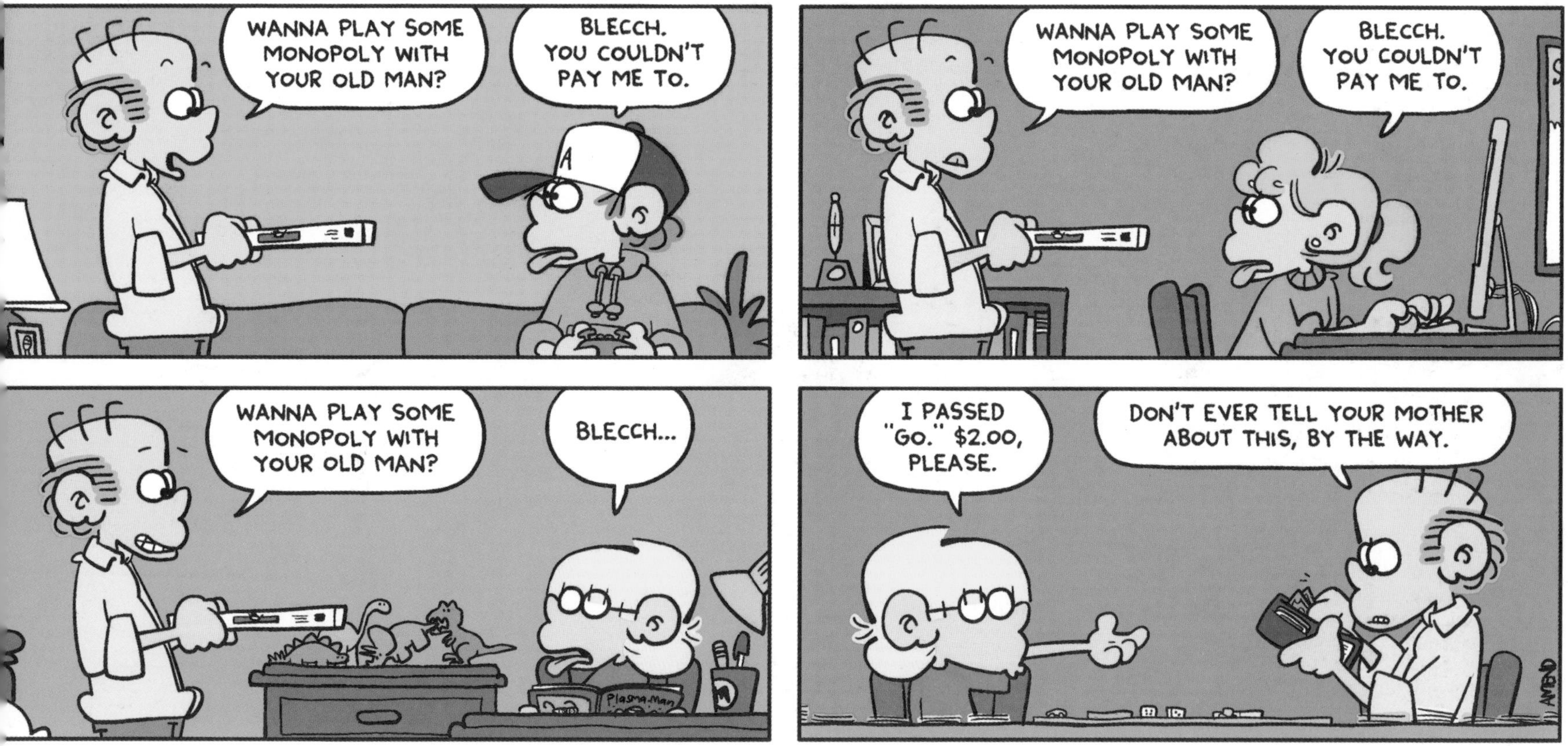
WANNA PLAY SOME MONOPOLY WITH YOUR OLD MAN?
BLECCH. YOU COULDN'T PAY ME TO.
WANNA PLAY SOME MONOPOLY WITH YOUR OLD MAN?
BLECCH. YOU COULDN'T PAY ME TO.
WANNA PLAY SOME MONOPOLY WITH YOUR OLD MAN?
BLECCH...
I PASSED "GO." $2.00, PLEASE.
DON'T EVER TELL YOUR MOTHER ABOUT THIS, BY THE WAY.

FoxTrot is distributed internationally by Universal Uclick.

Some Clever Title © 2016 by Bill Amend. All rights reserved. Printed in China. No part of this book may be used or reproduced in any manner whatsoever without written permission except in the case of reprints in the context of reviews.

Andrews McMeel Publishing
a division of Andrews McMeel Universal
1130 Walnut Street, Kansas City, Missouri 64106

16 17 18 19 20 SDB 10 9 8 7 6 5 4 3 2 1

ISBN: 978-1-4494-7810-0

Library of Congress Control Number: 2015955517

www.andrewsmcmeel.com

www.foxtrot.com

ATTENTION: SCHOOLS AND BUSINESSES

Andrews McMeel books are available at quantity discounts with bulk purchase for educational, business, or sales promotional use. For information, please e-mail the Andrews McMeel Publishing Special Sales Department: specialsales@amuniversal.com.